3/97

LIB/LEND/001
LR/LEND/001

UNIVERSITY OF WOLVERHAMPTON

Harrison Learning Centre
Wolverhampton Campus
University of Wolverhampton
St Peter's Square
Wolverhampton WV1 1RH
Telephone: 0845 408 1631

Telephone Renewals: 01902 321333
**This item may be recalled at any time. Keeping it after it has
been recalled or beyond the date stamped may result in a fine.**
See tariff of fines displayed at the counter.

0 7 MAR 2006

2 8 SEP 2007

WITHDRAWN

G9829

D0544263

THE WILEY SERIES IN CLINICAL PSYCHOLOGY

Series Editor

J. Mark G. Williams   *Department of Psychology, University College of North Wales, Bangor, UK*

Paul Dickens   Quality and Excellence in Human Services

Graham C. L. Davey and Frank Tallis (Editors)   Worrying: Perspectives on Theory, Assessment and Treatment

Chris Barker, Nancy Pistrang and Robert Elliott   Research Methods in Clinical and and Counselling Psychology

Further titles in preparation

A full list of series titles follows the index

CHRIS BARKER
NANCY PISTRANG
*University College
London, UK and*
ROBERT ELLIOTT
*University of Toledo,
USA*

Research Methods in Clinical and Counselling Psychology

UNIVERSITY OF WOLVERHAMPTON
LIBRARY

2093186 CLASS 312

CONTROL
047193612X 616. 89

DATE   SITE
25 FEB 1997 RS BAR

SHs   Psych

JOHN WILEY & SONS
Chichester·New York·Brisbane·Toronto·Singapore

Copyright © 1994 by John Wiley & Sons Ltd,
Baffins Lane, Chichester,
West Sussex PO19 1UD, England

Telephone (+44) 1243 779777

First published in hardback 1994
Published in paperback October 1995

All rights reserved.

No part of this book may be reproduced by any means,
or transmitted, or translated into a machine language
without the written permission of the publisher.

Other Wiley Editorial Offices

John Wiley & Sons, Inc., 605 Third Avenue,
New York, NY 10158-0012, USA

Jacaranda Wiley Ltd, 33 Park Road, Milton
Queensland 4064, Australia

John Wiley & Sons (Canada) Ltd, 22 Worcester Road,
Rexdale, Ontario M9W 1L1, Canada

John Wiley & Sons (SEA) Pte Ltd, 37 Jalan Pemimpin #05-04,
Block B, Union Industrial Building, Singapore 2057

Library of Congress Cataloging-in-Publication Data

Barker, Chris, *1948–*
    Research methods in clinical and counselling psychology / Chris
Barker and Nancy Pistrang and Robert Elliott.
        p.   cm. — (Wiley series in clinical psychology)
    Includes bibliographical references and index.
    ISBN 0-471-93612-X
        1. Clinical psychology—Research—Methodology.   2. Counselling–
–Research—Methodology.   3. Psychotherapy—Research—Methodology.
I. Pistrang, Nancy.   II. Elliott, Robert, *1950–* .   III. Title.
IV. Series.
        [DNLM: 1. Psychology, Clinical.   2. Counseling.   3. Research–
–methods.   4. Psychotherapy.   WM 105 B255a 1994]
    RC467.8.B37   1994
    616.89'0072—dc20
    DNLM/DLC
    for Library of Congress   94–15972
                                                                    CIP

British Library Cataloguing in Publication Data

A catalogue record for this book is available from the British Library

ISBN 0–471–93612–X (cased)
ISBN 0–471–96297–X (paper)

Typeset in 11/13pt Palatino by Dobbie Typesetting Ltd, Tavistock, Devon
Printed and bound in Great Britain by Biddles Ltd, Guildford and King's Lynn

CONTENTS

ABOUT THE AUTHORS

Chris Barker   *Department of Psychology,*
Nancy Pistrang   *University College London,*
Gower Street, London
WC1E 6BT, UK

Robert Elliott   *Department of Psychology,*
University of Toledo,
Toledo, Ohio 43606-3390, USA

All three authors obtained their clinical psychology doctorates from UCLA, where they acquired a taste for psychological research in general and studying interpersonal processes in particular.

Chris Barker and *Nancy Pistrang* are both currently senior lecturers in psychology at University College London and clinical psychologists in Camden and Islington Community Health Services Trust, London.

Robert Elliott is Professor of Psychology and Director of Clinical Training at the University of Toledo, Ohio. He is the co-editor of *Psychotherapy Research*.

SERIES PREFACE

The Wiley Series in Clinical Psychology brings together books which, between them, represent the central themes in applying psychology to clinical practice. Each book combines theory, research and practical application founded on the best available research evidence. To maintain the impetus of careful observation and research as the corner-stone of clinical practice, we need regularly to re-visit the methods on which our research is based. Only then can our research practice develop and new researchers learn how it is done. This book "tells the story" of research. It takes the reader through the process of research from the first attempt to define what questions to ask, to the final stage of analysis, interpretation and dissemination of results. In addition the authors examine the key philosophical, professional and ethical issues which may arise, and give helpful guidelines in each case. The authors are "methodological pluralists". For example, they show how both quantitative and qualitative methods may be combined so that more valid and reliable results can be achieved. As the delivery of health care becomes more concerned with the need to understand and evaluate its methods, research is becoming a more prominent theme in the training and continued professional development of many health professionals. This book will be a major contribution in this endeavour.

J. Mark G. Williams
Series Editor

PREFACE

This book has grown out of our experience in teaching research methods, advising mental health professionals who were struggling to conduct research, and carrying out research projects ourselves. It aims to help readers become both better consumers and better producers of research in clinical and counselling psychology. We hope that, at a minimum, it will encourage and enable practitioners to read research reports critically and to evaluate a study's strengths and weaknesses. We further hope to inspire at least some of our readers to produce research themselves. In addition to teaching the tools of the trade, we will try to convince readers that doing research can be stimulating, challenging and fun.

The book presents a practical description of the research process, using a chronological framework. It takes readers through the sequence of steps involved in executing a project: groundwork, measurement, design, analysis and interpretation. In addition to these technical aspects of research, the book also addresses some essential background issues, such as the underlying philosophy of the various research methods. We also look at sociopolitical issues, since clinical and counselling research is often conducted in working service settings and it is potentially threatening as well as illuminating. For simplicity, the book has been written from the perspective of producers rather than consumers of research, but we intend it to be of equal use to both audiences.

We have tried to be comprehensive in terms of breadth, but not in terms of depth: there are entire books covering material which we encompass in a chapter. We cover the essential areas and guide the interested reader towards more specialised literature as appropriate. Most of the statistical aspects of research methods are omitted, since this is a separate field in itself. We have aimed the book at clinical and counselling psychology students and practitioners; others who might find it useful are students and practitioners in health and community psychology, counselling, psychiatry, psychiatric nursing and social work.

The terms therapy, psychotherapy and counselling will mostly be used interchangeably to refer to face-to-face work with clients. Where a broader sense of the psychologist's role is intended, e.g., to encompass prevention or consultation, we will use the terms clinical work or psychological intervention. All three of us have worked in both clinical and counselling settings and we publish in both clinical and counselling journals. We regard the different labels as more indicative of differences in training and professional allegiance than differences in the work done with clients. However, for even-handedness, we tend to use the phrase clinical and counselling psychologists, except where it is too cumbersome, in which case we say clinician, counsellor or therapist alone for convenience. Whatever the language, we always have in mind anyone engaged in clinical, counselling or psychotherapeutic work.

The book addresses those issues faced by clinical and counselling psychologists who do research that are not covered in the more general social and behavioural science research texts. The advantage of having a clinical or counselling psychology training is that you are likely to conduct research with more practical relevance, to ask less superficial questions and to have a strong sense of the complexities of human experience and behaviour. The interviewing skills acquired in clinical and counselling training are also helpful in doing research, but research and therapeutic interviews have crucial differences; therefore researchers may need to unlearn certain interventions used in therapeutic settings. Being trained in clinical or counselling psychology also makes one aware of the tension between the scientific and the therapeutic stance: in the former case looking for generalities, in the latter uniqueness. Throughout the book, we have tried to place research methods in the clinical and counselling context.

Two central assumptions inform our work. The first is methodological pluralism: that different methods are appropriate to different problems and research questions. Until recently, research methods were largely segmented along the lines of academic disciplines. Sociologists and anthropologists tended to use qualitative methods, such as ethnography or participant observation, whereas psychologists stuck amost exclusively to quantitative methods. Now, however, a significant change is under way, in that psychologists are beginning to regard a variety of research methods, including qualitative ones, as part of their toolkit. For each topic area, such as interviewing or observation, we present the strengths and weaknesses of the various methodological options, quantitative and qualitative. We have tried to be even-handed, to present the arguments and let readers decide for themselves what is best for their particular application. As in our work with clients, we hope to be empowering, to give skills, present options and let our readers make informed choices.

Our second assumption is the importance of the scientist-practitioner model: that clinical and counselling psychologists should be trained to be both competent clinicans and competent researchers (although we hold a broader view of what is scientific than was implicit in the original discussion of the scientist-practitioner model). This model encapsulates the unique contribution psychologists can make to service settings and to the academic development of the field. In practice, many applied psychologists feel that they do not have sufficient research skills, and good intentions to conduct research fail to come to fruition. This book aims to help such practitioners.

The three of us met in the mid-1970s as graduate students on the UCLA clinical psychology PhD program, where we worked together in the Interpersonal Process Research Group. The book bears the hallmark of the excellent eclectic scientist-practitioner training we received at UCLA, but also evidences our struggles against some of the constraints of our professional socialisation. Our own research has continued to be broadly focused on interpersonal processes: such areas as client-therapist interaction, informal helping and couples' communication are what we get excited about. We have inevitably drawn heavily on these areas for our examples, but have tried to make the discussion of general relevance. Our approach to research is strongly influenced by humanistic values: we believe that it is possible to do rigorous psychological research without being reductionist or making a travesty of the phenomenon under study.

We would like to thank the friends and colleagues who helped us by discussing ideas, supplying references and commenting on drafts: John Cape, Lorna Champion, Linda Clare, Neil Devlin, Jerry Goodman (for the slogan "research is fun"), Les Greenberg, Dick Hallam, Maria Koutantji, David Rennie, Laura Rice, Joe Schwartz and Pam Smith. Mark Williams and Connie Hammen provided incisive and helpful reviews of the manuscript. The team at Wiley were consistently supportive: Michael Coombs helped us to get the project off the ground, and Wendy Hudlass, our publishing editor, was a constant source of encouragement and help as the project progressed. Thanks also to our students, who inspired us to develop and clarify our thinking about clinical research and whose encouraging comments on early drafts helped to sustain us. In addition, we are grateful to the research participants with whom we have sought to understand the workings of psychological helping processes. Our interactions with them and the data that they have provided have stimulated and challenged us to broaden our scope as researchers. And finally, many thanks to our children, for constantly reminding us that play is at least as important as work.

CHAPTER 1 Introduction: the research process

"Where do you come from?" said the Red Queen.
"And where are you going? Look up, speak nicely,
and don't twiddle your fingers all the time."
Lewis Carroll, Alice through the Looking Glass, *Chapter 2*

Research tells a story. Ideally, it resembles a detective story, which begins with a mystery and ends with its resolution. Researchers have a problem that they want to investigate; the story will reach its happy ending if they find a solution to that problem.

In practice, however, things are not so simple. (In fact, they are so complicated that we will be reminding you of this again and again throughout the book.) Often a research project doesn't answer the initial question, rather it tells you that you were asking the wrong question in the first place, or that the way that you went about answering it was misconceived. So, next time around, you attempt to answer a better question with a better designed study, and so on. Another way of putting it is that there are stories within stories. Each individual research project tells one story, the series of projects conducted by a researcher or a research team forms a larger story, and the development of the whole research area a yet larger story. And this progression continues up to the level of the history of ideas over the centuries.

How a research area develops over time is illustrated in an article by Hammen (1992), whose title, "Life events and depression: the plot thickens", alludes to the mystery-story aspect of research. The article summarises the author's 20-year-long research programme into depression. She discusses how her original research drew on rather simplistic cognitive models of depression (e.g. that depression is caused by negative appraisals of events). The findings of early studies led her to modify these models (e.g. to take into account that people's appraisals of events may be negative because the events themselves are negative) and thus to ask more complex questions. Her team is currently working with more sophisticated models, which take into account that people may play a role in causing the life events which occur to them.

Another way in which things are not so simple is that not all scholars agree on what constitutes a legitimate story. The situation in psychology is analogous to developments in literature. On the one hand is the traditional story, rather like a Victorian novel, which has a beginning, a middle and an end, and is expected to provide a more or less faithful reflection of reality. On the other hand, in this modern and post-modern age, we encounter narratives which do not follow an orderly chronological sequence or tie up neatly at the end. Furthermore, they may not claim to represent, or may even reject the idea of, reality. A similar shift has occurred in the visual arts, for example in painting's movement from representational to non-representational art.

These developments in the humanities reflect general intellectual developments over the twentieth century which have ramifications across many branches of European and English-speaking culture, both artistic and scientific. Our own field of interest, clinical and counselling psychology, is currently going through a vigorous debate about the nature of research: i.e. which of these narratives we can call research and which are something else. A number of scholars from various corners of the discipline (e.g. Carlson, 1972; Howard, 1991; Kelly, 1990; Mair, 1989; Polkinghorne, 1983; Rogers, 1985; Reason & Rowan, 1981; Sarbin, 1986) have questioned the validity and usefulness of psychology's version of the traditional story, which has been called "received view" or "old paradigm" research: essentially a quantitative, hypothetico-deductive approach, which relies on linear causal models. They call for replacing (or at least supplementing) it with a more qualitative, discovery-oriented, non-linear approach to research.

This debate, as Kimble (1984) points out, is a contemporary manifestation of William James's (1907/1981) distinction between tough-minded and tender-minded ways of thinking, which is itself a translation into psychological terms of the old debate in philosophy over rationalism versus empiricism. However, it is simplistic to view this distinction as a dichotomy, with researchers being either in one camp or the other. It is better viewed as being composed of several bipolar attitude dimensions, e.g. preferences for qualitative versus quantitative methods, exploratory versus confirmatory research questions, and so on (Kimble, 1984).

One consequence of this lack of consensus about acceptable approaches to research is that people who are doing research for the first time may experience considerable anxiety—rather like the existential anxiety that accompanies a loss of meaning (Yalom, 1980). Undertaking a research project without being clear about which standards are to be used to evaluate it is an unsettling experience. Furthermore, there is a political dimension, since people in powerful positions in the academic world—journal editors, grant reviewers and university teachers—often adhere to the more traditional models.

This anxiety is exacerbated because the rules are not always made explicit, which may make new researchers feel like Alice in Wonderland: as if they are in a strange land with mysterious and arbitrary rules that are continually being changed. Researchers are constantly reminded, in various ways, to behave themselves properly according to these scientific rules: to look up, speak nicely and not to twiddle their fingers all the time. This experience can be understandably off-putting for people trying to enter the research wonderland for the first time.

We will reconsider these issues in Chapters 2 and 4, which address the conceptual underpinnings of research. However, it is worth stating at the outset that our own stance is one of methodological pluralism. We do not think that any single approach to research (or indeed that psychological research itself) has all the answers, and believe that researchers need to have at their disposal a range of methods, appropriate to the problems being investigated. We have considerable sympathy with the critics of the received view, but are not convinced that the consequence of accepting their criticisms is the abandonment of traditional quantitative methods. We believe that it is now becoming possible to articulate a synthesis of the old and new paradigm traditions: that there are fundamental principles common to rigorous research within whatever paradigm. Learning to do psychological research is partly a process of learning disciplined enquiry according to these principles.

At the same time, there are rules of good practice specific to each type of research. We will base our methodological pluralism on a principle of appropriate methodologies (by analogy to the catch-phrase "appropriate technology"). By this, we mean that the methods used should flow out of the research questions asked. Different questions lend themselves to different methods. To resume our literary metaphor, like the different literary genres (romance, science fiction, autobiography, etc.) we can think of different research genres, such as survey research, experimentation and discourse analysis.

We will attempt to clarify these rules and principles, so that you will better appreciate other people's research and, we hope, feel less intimidated about the prospect of conducting your own. Also, the more explicit the rules of research are, the more one is able to challenge them.

Research is demanding: it does require clear and rigorous thought, but it is also fascinating and exciting and, we hope, beneficial to the public that psychologists ultimately profess to serve.

The Research Process

The book is structured around a simple chronological framework, which we call the "research process": that is, the sequence of steps that researchers go through during a project. The steps can be grouped into four major stages. Like all such frameworks, ours is idealised, in that the stages are not always distinct and they may interact with each other. However, we find it a useful way of thinking about how research is conducted, both one's own and other people's.

1. *Groundwork* (Chapter 3). This stage involves both scientific issues—choosing the topic, specifying the conceptual model, reviewing the literature, formulating the research questions— and practical issues—resolving organisational, political, financial or ethical problems. Sometimes researchers give the groundwork short shrift, being anxious to get on with the business of running the project itself. However, we will argue that devoting careful thought at this stage repays itself with interest over the rest of the project.

2. *Measurement* (Chapters 4, 5 and 6). Having formulated the study, the next step is to decide how to measure the psychological constructs that are specified in the research questions. We are here using the term measurement in its broadest sense, to encompass qualitative as well as quantitative approaches.

3. *Design* (Chapters 7, 8 and 9). Research design issues concern when and on whom the data will be collected, for example, who will be the participants, will there be an experimental design with a control group, and so on. These issues can usually be considered independently of measurement issues.

The research questions, measurement procedures and design together constitute the research protocol, the blueprint for the study. Having gone through these first three stages, researchers will usually conduct a small pilot study, whose results may cause them to rethink the protocol and possibly to conduct further pilots. Eventually the protocol is finalised; the last stage then consists of implementing it.

4. *Analysis, interpretation and dissemination* (Chapter 11). The data are collected, analysed, interpreted, written up, possibly published and, let us hope, acted upon.

These stages in the research process constitute our framework for the book. However, we will also examine some key philosophical, professional, political and ethical issues that are central to thinking about the whole research enterprise (Chapters 2, 4, 9 and 10). Whilst following these arguments is not necessary for learning purely technical research skills, it is important to understand the wider context in which research is being conducted, as doing so will lead to more focused, coherent and useful research programmes.

The first part of this background material is given in the next chapter, which analyses the meaning of some of the terms we have so far left undefined, such as research itself. We will also discuss why on earth anyone might want to engage in research at all.

CHAPTER 2   Philosophical, professional and personal issues

This chapter examines some important background issues, in order to give you a sense of the context in which research is conducted. They include the philosophical framework (i.e. the set of assumptions about the research process), the professional context (i.e. how research fits in to the clinical and counselling psychology professions) and also the personal context (i.e. each individual researcher's attitudes towards research).

Understanding these issues is helpful both in reading other people's research and in conducting your own. It helps to make sense of other people's research if you understand the framework within which it was conducted. If you are doing research yourself, the more you are aware of your assumptions, the more you are able to make informed choices about which methods to use. This is similar to clinical and counselling work, where clients who have more insight into their motivating forces are generally more able to live freer and more productive lives. However, again as in clinical and counselling work, making decisions can become a burden as you become aware of the multiple possibilities of action instead of making automatic choices.

The chapter has three sections, covering philosophical, professional and personal issues. The other important "P", political, is addressed in all three sections.

PHILOSOPHICAL ISSUES

This section examines what is meant by two key terms: research and science. It is worth starting out with a couple of disclaimers.

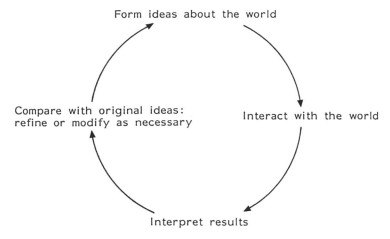

Figure 2.1 The research cycle

Several of the ideas are complex and require philosophical expertise to appraise them properly. We do not possess such expertise, nor do we expect the great majority of our readers to. Furthermore, we are concerned that grappling with difficult issues, such as what is the nature of reality, can be heavy going at this early stage. In philosophy, there are often more questions than answers. We attempt to give an overview of some interesting contemporary issues; it is not necessary to follow them in detail in order to conduct or critique research. However, having a broad grasp of them will help you to understand (perhaps more clearly than the researchers themselves) what a piece of research is attempting to achieve.

Philosophical issues that relate more specifically to psychological measurement (namely discussion of the positivist and phenomenological positions) are covered in Chapter 4.

What is Research?

Conducting research is essentially a circular activity, which in highly simplified form looks something like Figure 2.1

As the figure suggests, this activity is potentially everlasting, and is allied to the human propensity to lead an "examined life". Some writers, e.g. Cook and Campbell (1979), consider that the psychological roots of research have evolutionary significance: that there is survival value in our attempts to understand the world and ourselves.

Note that this model does not attempt to explain where we get our ideas about the world from in the first place. There is a long-standing debate in philosophy and developmental psychology, which we will side-step for the moment, about whether acquiring knowledge of the world is possible without some forestructure of understanding. Our emphasis is on how the educated adult discovers and tests ideas.

Research demands a degree of psychological flexibility, that is an ability to modify one's ideas if they are not supported by the evidence. It may be helpful to view various sorts of disruptions in the circular model as corresponding to various maladaptive psychological styles. For instance, a refusal to interact with the world at all, elaborating theories without ever testing them against the "real world" (i.e. never moving down from the first stage of our circular model), is a solipsistic stance of building dream castles with no basis in reality. It is a stance captured in the phrase "the ivory tower", and was forcefully parodied in Hesse's (1943) novel *The Glass Bead Game*. A second example is that a refusal to modify one's ideas, by dismissing or distorting the evidence (i.e. not carrying out the third and fourth steps in our model), characterises a rigid, dogmatic stance. This can be seen in people who cling to various kinds of orthodoxies and fundamentalist beliefs. Thus we view the enquiring, open-minded research attitude as one aspect of good psychological functioning. It is similar to Jahoda's (1958) concept of "adequate perception of reality" as one criterion for positive mental health.

Thus far, our characterisation of research applies to everyday life as much as to organised science. We all do research informally; it is one way in which we form our mental representation of the world. This is what Reason and Rowan (1981) call "naive enquiry". George Kelly (1955) elaborated the idea of the person as a scientist into an entire theory of personality: that people are continually building and testing their set of "personal constructs". However, cognitive and social scientists have also shown that people display pervasive biases in the way that they process information (Fiske & Taylor, 1991; Mahoney, 1976; Nisbett & Ross, 1980). The fundamental reason for the development of rigorous research methods is to attempt to eliminate or minimise biases in drawing conclusions from evidence (Rogers, 1955).

Finally, we should make it clear at the outset that we do not see research as being the only, or even an especially privileged, route to knowledge. One can learn much of relevance to being a good psychologist in Shakespeare, Tolstoy or George Eliot. Great works of art or literature will often have a ring of truth that will immediately resonate with the reader or viewer. Furthermore, everyday life experiences also help to build a knowledge base. In Morrow-Bradley and Elliott's (1986) survey on sources of psychotherapeutic knowledge, therapists reported that they learned most from experience with their clients, followed by theoretical or practical writings, being a client themselves, supervision, and practical workshops. Research presentations and research reports were ranked first by only 10% of the sample of practising therapists (in contrast to experience with clients, which was ranked first by 48%).

However, the strength of formal research is that it is a systematic way of looking at the world and of describing its regularities, and it provides knowledge that allows us to decide between conflicting claims to truth that may be put forward by rival proponents. For example, about 20 years ago there was a vogue for encounter groups, a form of group therapy which stressed honest confrontation. There was no shortage of psychological theory and personal testimonial as to their benefits. However, it was not until the first systematic study (Lieberman, Yalom & Miles, 1973) that it became apparent that the style of encounter group leadership had an enormous impact on the outcome and also that some participants had such negative outcomes that they could reasonably be classified as "encounter group casualties". Although, like all psychological research, this study had its limitations, it was enormously helpful in persuading professionals to take a measured look at what was then a new phenomenon.

Furthermore, because research is a shared, public activity, it has a crucial role in contributing to the development of theory and professional knowledge. Although interactions with clients, conversations with fellow professionals and personal growth experiences are all useful ways of educating oneself, research, theoretical writings and published case reports are public documents and are a way of advancing the development of the profession as a whole.

We will explore such professional issues more fully in the next section, and then, in the final section, discuss why individual psychologists might want (or might not want) to do research. However, before we can do this, we need to examine the meaning of some of our core terminology in greater depth.

Definition of research

The *Oxford English Dictionary*'s definition of research serves as a good starting point. It is: "A search or investigation directed to the discovery of some fact by careful consideration or study of a subject; a course of critical or scientific enquiry." Five aspects of this definition are worth elaborating.

Firstly, the definition stresses the methodical aspect of research, that research is careful and disciplined. It is a craft that requires considerable dedication and often quite obsessional attention to detail. There is also, however, a chance element to research: not all discoveries are necessarily planned (Merbaum & Lowe, 1982). One classic example of an accidental scientific discovery is Fleming's isolation of penicillin, when he noticed that some mould in a dish stopped the growth of bacteria he was attempting to cultivate. However, to take advantage of a chance discovery, you must have sufficient experience and knowledge to appreciate its significance.

Secondly, the definition emphasises a detached, critical, scientific or scholarly attitude. This attitude is an important feature of the applied psychology discipline. Clinical and counselling psychologists are trained to raise fundamental questions about the basis of their professional practice, e.g. "What's going on?", "How do you know?", "What's the evidence for that assertion?"—a sceptical attitude which may not always endear them to their professional colleagues from other disciplines. It can contribute to the common perception of psychologists as slightly alien from other professionals in a team or service, standing at one step removed.

Thirdly, the definition does not specify the method of research. It includes conceptual research, sometimes pejoratively labelled armchair philosophising. Such research is important in other disciplines, especially the humanities, but also is the method of the so-called "queen of the sciences", mathematics, which proceeds from *a priori* axioms to a set of deductions, in the form of theorems. Psychology is primarily an empirical science, concerned with systematically gathering data, which are then used, in ways we will discuss below, to test its theories. However, there is also an important role for conceptual research to formulate theories and explicate underlying principles. This issue of research method relates back to the centuries-old philosophical debate between rationalists and empiricists over the source of human knowledge (Russell, 1961).

Fourthly, the definition states that research is a process of discovery. This raises the distinction between discovery-oriented research, which sets out to find something new, and confirmatory research, which sets out to evaluate existing theory (see Chapter 3). Philosophers of science use parallel language to distinguish between the context of discovery and the context of justification of a particular finding (Reichenbach, 1938). We include both discovery-oriented and confirmatory approaches under the definition of research.

Finally, the definition says that research is directed towards the discovery of facts. The *Oxford English Dictionary* defines a fact as "something that has really occurred or is the case". However, this definition begs some difficult philosophical questions about how we come to know what is true. *Epistemology* is the area of philosophy devoted to describing how people come to know things or believe things to be true or real. When psychologists talk about validity and reliability, they are talking in epistemological terms. According to Hamlyn (1970), there are four fundamental epistemological positions, or criteria of truth:

1. The *correspondence theory* of truth, the basis of realist philosophies, holds that a belief is true if it matches reality.

2. *Coherence theory*, the basis of rationalist philosophies, holds that something is true if it is internally consistent or logically non-contradictory.

3. The *pragmatist* or *utilitarian criterion* holds that if a belief is useful or produces practical benefits, then it can be said, for practical purposes, to be true.

4. *Consensus criterion*, the basis of sociological theories of knowledge (see below), holds that truth is intersubjective and refers to beliefs which are shared and upheld by a group of people.

None of these theories is completely adequate; all have serious logical flaws. For example, correspondence theory involves an infinite regress, because reality must be measured validly before the degree of correspondence can be assessed (referred to as the criterion problem in measurement). Furthermore, counter-instances of each of the other three criteria can readily be imagined (e.g. an elegant theory which has no bearing on reality; a false belief which nevertheless proves useful; and a false consensus or collective delusion). On the other hand, all four theories have some value, as practical, but fallible guidelines (Anderson, Hughes & Sharrock, 1986), suggesting the importance of a pluralist epistemology. Optimally, one would attempt to realise all four truth criteria in one's research (cf. Elliott, Fischer & Rennie, 1994).

Traditionally, psychologists have adopted a "critical realist" position (Cook & Campbell, 1979). This assumes that there is a real world out there that has regularities, although we can never know it with certainty: all understandings are essentially tentative. The critical realist position emphasises the replicability of research: that other researchers should be able to repeat your work and get the same results, or in more technical language, that knowledge should be "intersubjectively testable" (Cook & Campbell, 1979; Popper, 1959). This means that researchers must be explicit about how they collect their data and draw their conclusions, so that other researchers can evaluate their conclusions or replicate the study themselves.

One alternative to the widely adopted critical realist position is social constructionism, which overlaps considerably with post-modernism and post-structuralism (Gergen, 1985; Guba & Lincoln, 1989; Lyotard, 1984; Neimeyer, 1993). These are all somewhat imprecise terms, but they share a common stance of dispensing with the assumption of an objective reality and instead studying people's interpretations. Post-modernists are impatient with what they call "grand theory". Instead they present a more multifaceted, fractured world view, some taking the extreme point of view that there are no true and false stories, only different stories. We disagree with such radical constructionist or post-modernist views, in that it does not seem likely that all constructions are equally accurate, consistent, replicable or useful. That smoking causes lung cancer or that poverty reduces one's quality of life, although not unassailable propositions, seem to describe important consistencies in the world.

We do, however, agree with two related points that the social constructionists emphasise, which stem from regarding the research setting as a specialised form of social interaction. The first point is that the researcher is not a detached observer: his or her presence will affect the behaviour and experience of the other participants in the setting (this problem of reactivity is discussed in Chapter 6). The second point is the interdependence of the knower and the known. That is to say, in coming to know a thing, both the state of our knowledge and the thing itself may be changed; facts are a joint construction of the things themselves and our knowing process. For example, the process of interviewing a client about her reactions to a recent counselling session may change the way that she feels about the session, her counsellor or herself.

Pure and applied research

There are many ways to classify research, e.g. according to content, setting, population or method. One important distinction is between basic academic research and applied (including evaluation) research. Although often presented as a dichotomy, the two positions are better thought of as two ends of a continuum (Milne, 1987; Patton, 1990).

Basic (or pure) research addresses the generation and testing of theory. What are the underlying processes that help us to understand the regularities in nature? Two examples of pure research are studies testing hypotheses derived from client-centred theory about the nature of change processes in therapy, and studies investigating the role of learned helplessness in the aetiology of depression.

Applied research addresses practical questions, e.g. whether a particular intervention works for a particular client group. Applied research may primarily address the needs of a local service, in which case it is known as evaluation research, or it may have a broader relevance. It is often motivated by pragmatic concerns, such as the need to maintain funding for a particular service. Clinical work can also be seen as a form of applied research, in that the clinician is attempting to analyse which approach works best for each individual client. Although the methods used in pure and applied research overlap considerably, we will address some issues particular to evaluation in Chapter 10.

The distinction between pure and applied research is not always clear. As our two examples above demonstrate, there is always an element of application in clinical research: that is what makes it clinical. Many examples of clinical and counselling research lie in the middle ground. For instance, psychotherapy outcome research addresses questions of both theory and application. Since we see the pure/applied distinction as a continuum rather than a dichotomy, we adhere to a definition of research which encompasses the full spectrum.

What is Science?

We have used the word "science" above without questioning its meaning. Yet there is a lively debate about what science consists of, a debate that goes to the heart of some enduring controversies within clinical and counselling psychology and related fields. It addresses the question of how knowledge is acquired and which methods of research are "scientific" (and therefore respectable). In a much used example, how can we distinguish between legitimate science and voodoo, or astrology? Or is such a distinction bogus? Closer to home, in what sense is psychoanalysis a science? Or, indeed, psychology in general?

The literature on this area is enormous: philosophy of science is an entire academic specialty in itself. Here we briefly review the main ideas. Since much undergraduate psychology education is implicitly based on a traditional view of science, it is important for psychologists to know about the positions presented here and in Chapter 4, to understand the context of the traditional view and to be aware of its alternatives.

Induction

An initial, common-sense way of attempting to characterise science is that it is based on careful observation, from which theories are then formulated. The derivation of theory from observation is known as induction. Astronomy is a good example: the astronomer gazes at the heavens, records what he or she sees, and attempts to derive general principles therefrom. Within psychology, clinical observation also uses induction. For example, the psychoanalyst carefully observes a number of patients within the analytic setting, and then attempts to formulate his or her impressions into a theory.

Unfortunately, there are two insuperable problems with induction as a guiding principle of science (Chalmers, 1982). The first is that it is impossible to have pure observations: what we observe and how we observe it are, implicitly or explicitly, based on theory. This phenomenon is known as the theory dependence of observation. For example, a psychoanalyst, a Skinnerian and a lay person will notice very different things in a videotape of a client–counsellor interaction. The second problem is that there is no logical basis for the principle of induction. Because something has been observed to happen on 10 occasions, it does not necessarily follow that it will happen on the 11th. This means that theories can never be conclusively verified, only temporarily corroborated by scientific evidence. The philosopher Karl Popper, who was a contemporary of Freud and Adler in 1920s Vienna, has put this point of view forcefully. It is worth giving an extended quote, which is of enduring relevance to psychologists:

> I found that those of my friends who were admirers of Marx, Freud, and Adler, were impressed by a number of points common to these theories, and especially by their apparent *explanatory power*. These theories appeared to be able to explain practically everything that happened within the fields to which they referred . . .

> The most characteristic element in this situation seemed to me the incessant stream of confirmations, of observations which "verified" the theories in question; and this point was constantly emphasized by their adherents. . . . The Freudian analysts emphasized that their theories were constantly verified by their "clinical observations". As for Adler, I was much impressed by a personal experience. Once, in 1919, I reported to him a case which to me did not seem particularly Adlerian, but which he found no difficulty in analysing in terms of his theory of inferiority feelings, although he had not even seen the child. Slightly shocked, I asked him how he could be so sure. "Because of my

thousandfold experience", he replied; whereupon I could not help saying: "And with this new case, I suppose, your experience has become thousand-and-one fold."

What I had in mind was that his previous observations may not have been much sounder than this new one; that each in its turn had been interpreted in the light of "previous experience", and at the same time counted as additional confirmation . . . I could not think of any human behaviour which could not be interpreted in terms of either theory. It was precisely this fact—that they always fitted, that they were always confirmed—which in the eyes of their admirers constituted the strongest argument in favour of these theories. It began to dawn on me that this apparent strength was in fact their weakness.

(Professor K. R. Popper, 1963, pp. 34–35; reproduced by permission)

This quotation illustrates several issues: the limits of a verificationist approach, problems of *post hoc* explanation, the theory dependence of observation and also some psychologists' tendency to jump to conclusions without careful data gathering—Adler might have been more convincing if he had actually seen the child in question. (However, we are not suggesting here that induction be abandoned altogether, rather that it be conducted within a rigorous framework; we will return to this in several subsequent chapters.)

Falsification

Having rejected the principle of induction as a secure foundation for science, Popper attempted to turn the problem on its head: he looked at solutions based on deduction rather than induction, on falsification rather than verification. His landmark volume, *The Logic of Scientific Discovery* (1959, first published 1934), sets out to establish a demarcation between science and non-science (or "pseudo-science"). Popper's central criterion is that a science must be able to formulate hypotheses that are capable of refutation or, in his preferred terminology, falsification. For example, Newtonian physics generates the proposition that a ball thrown up in the air will come down to land again. If tennis balls started shooting out into space, the theory would have a lot of explaining to do. In a more technical example, Newtonian physics also generates the proposition that light travels in a straight line. Although this proposition seems almost self-evident, it was ultimately falsified in a spectacular way

Popper also urges researchers to put their thoughts into clear and precise language. As an example, Rogers' (1957) seminal paper on the necessary and sufficient conditions of therapeutic personality change is written with admirable clarity and makes bold hypotheses about the central mechanisms of therapeutic change.

Kuhn also encourages the taking of intellectual risks, although from a different standpoint. By clearly delineating the constrictions of "normal science", he urges researchers to question the assumptions of the paradigm that they are implicitly or explicitly working within, and to ask whether that paradigm is worth challenging. His work also suggests that scientists look ahead to the next paradigm revolution and ask whether their work will have any enduring value.

The methodological pluralist stance that informs this book owes something to the spirit that animates Feyerabend's writing. We agree with his stress on the value of diversity and the dangers of scientific conformity. We do, however, strongly disagree with his rejection of the canons of scientific method. As we hope to show, it is possible to articulate criteria to evaluate work conducted within the various different scientific traditions in clinical and counselling psychology. For the remainder of this book we will be adopting a broad working definition of science, as a body of knowledge founded upon systematic conceptual and empirical research.

Social and Political Issues

As Kuhn (1970) illustrates, science is not conducted in a cultural and political vacuum. It is done by scientists working within a particular scientific, professional and cultural community at a specific moment in history. Sociologists of knowledge (e.g. Berger & Luckmann, 1966) and social constructionists (e.g. Gergen, 1985) look at how social factors influence the development of thought. For example, what is seen as "real" may vary from culture to culture.

Sociological and historical methods can be applied to examine science itself, to look at how socioeconomic and political forces shape the kind of science that is practised within a given culture (Chalmers, 1990; Schwartz, 1992): how one set of ideas gains prominence over another. These analyses are often carried out

by Eddington's expedition to observe a solar eclipse in Africa, in order to test a deduction from Einstein's theory of relativity that light will bend in the presence of a gravitational field.

In psychology, such unequivocal falsifications of theoretically derived predictions are less common. One area where they can be found is in neuropsychological case studies of patients with acquired brain damage. The presence of certain patterns of dysfunction in a single case can be used to refute theories of mental structure (Shallice, 1988).

As an example of a non-falsifiable theory, consider this statement, by the painter Mondrian: "The positive and the negative break up oneness, they are the cause of all unhappiness. The union of the positive and negative is happiness" (quoted by Wilson, 1990, p. 144). This certainly appears to be some sort of psychological theory, but it is not clear to what extent it could generate falsifiable propositions, and thus what could be done to test its validity. According to Popper, a statement that cannot be falsified is unscientific (although it is not necessarily meaningless). Religion and poetry may have meaning, but they are not falsifiable.

For Popper, good science is characterised by a series of bold conjectures, which will be ultimately falsified. This approach is encapsulated in the title of one his books, *Conjectures and Refutations* (1963). A good theory is one that makes a large number of falsifiable propositions. A bad theory, or an unscientific one, is one that is incapable of falsification. However, all theories must be considered to be tentative; it is impossible to know the world exactly. Every theory in its time will be falsified and replaced by another (as Newtonian mechanics was supplanted by Einstein's theory of relativity).

The falsifiability criterion places those fields which rely on *post hoc* explanatory methods outside the boundaries of science. In particular, it rules out psychoanalysis and Marxism, fashionable theories in Popper's Vienna of the 1920s, which he explicitly says were his main targets (Popper, 1963). On the other hand, behavioural approaches, with their philosophy of "prediction and control" (Skinner, 1953), would be included.

This version of falsificationism has a number of problems. The main one is that no theory ever completely accounts for all the known data. Inconsistencies always exist, but the theory may well be retained in spite of them, as they could be explained in other ways than the falsification of the theory, e.g. measurement error or unexplained extra variables. Refutation is never cut and dried: there is always scope to deny that it has occurred. One example is in the extended debate in the psychotherapy outcome literature over the effectiveness of psychodynamically oriented therapy. Comparative outcome studies have now demonstrated beyond reasonable doubt that psychodynamically oriented therapy, as well as other forms of therapy, have, on average, beneficial effects (Stiles, Shapiro & Elliott, 1986). However, some critics fought a long rearguard action against this conclusion, which was possible to do if the evidence was appraised in a partisan way (Shapiro & Shapiro, 1977).

Paradigms and scientific revolutions

It therefore becomes a central problem to explain how one theory is replaced by another. Since there are always unexplained or contradictory observations within a scientific field, what determines when one theory is rejected and replaced by another? This issue is the point of departure for the work of Thomas Kuhn, one of the central figures of twentieth-century philosophy of science. In *The Structure of Scientific Revolutions* (1970), he applies the tools of historical analysis to address these questions.

Kuhn proposed the concept of a "paradigm", that is, the central body of ideas within which a body of scientists are working at any given time. The paradigm determines which phenomena scientists consider important and the methods that they use to make their observations. Scientists working within a paradigm are said to be doing "normal science": they are elaborating theories rather than attempting to refute them. Eventually, the accumulated deficiencies of a paradigm lead to its overthrow and replacement by another paradigm, in what Kuhn labels a "scientific revolution". For example, the replacement of Aristotelian cosmology (that the earth was at the centre of the universe) by Copernican theory (that the earth moved around the sun) was a scientific revolution.

The concept of a paradigm is central to Kuhn's work. It fits well with the physical sciences, but there is much debate about how

well it can be applied in the social sciences (Lambie, 1991). What is the guiding paradigm of psychology, or are there multiple paradigms—or is it still in a pre-paradigmatic state? Arguably, cognitive behaviourism and Freudian psychoanalysis may be considered as concurrent paradigms, although this is perhaps ducking awkward questions of which theory better accounts for the available evidence (Lambie, 1991).

Kuhn's views and their relationship to those of Popper were hotly debated when they first appeared (Lakatos & Musgrave, 1970). Lakatos accused Kuhn of propounding a "mob psychology" of scientific revolutions (Lakatos, 1970, p. 178).

The problem in Kuhn's work is that it proposes no criteria for considering one theory as better than another, and thus no sense in which scientific understanding could be said to be progressing. Feyerabend's (1975) anarchistic view takes this to an extreme. Under a slogan of "anything goes", Feyerabend appears to be claiming that different theories are "incommensurable" and that there are therefore no rational grounds for preferring one to another. For example, psychoanalysis and experimental psychology may be incommensurable since they have different criteria for which evidence is acceptable: psychoanalysis derives its evidence from the consulting room, experimental psychology from the laboratory (Fonagy, 1982). So the anarchistic view would accord astrology, voodoo and Babylonian astronomy the same scientific status as quantum mechanics or relativity (Chalmers, 1982). The viewpoint is pithily summed up by the composer and poet Moondog (1991):

> "What I say of science here, I say without condition
> That science is the latest and the greatest superstition."
> (Louis Hardin, Managarm; reproduced by permission)

It seems as though the views of Popper and of Kuhn are "incommensurable": they are using different concepts to discuss somewhat different phenomena. Popper takes a logical approach, Kuhn a historical one. While trying to avoid the danger of falling into a relativist, "anything goes" position ourselves, we would contend that much of value can be taken from both sets of writings.

From Popper, researchers can take the central admonition of making bold theories that lead to clear and risky predictions, and being ready to give these theories up in the face of contradictory evidence.

within a Marxist framework, which examines the influence of class interests on scientific thought (Albury & Schwartz, 1982). For example, genetic explanations of individual differences in IQ scores fit in well with racist and fascist ideologies, and some of the impetus behind the development of IQ tests undoubtedly came from such a background (Rose, Kamin & Lewontin, 1984).

Also, the prevailing methodology of science may be a response to the political climate. Irvine, Miles and Evans (1979) analyse the development of statistical methods, arguing, for example, that the stress on quantification arose as a response to the needs of nineteenth-century capitalism. For example, in the UK, partly as a result of Conservative reforms that introduced "market forces" into the rationing of healthcare, health professionals in the British National Health Service are required to produce quantitative "performance indicators", such as number of patients seen, lengths of waiting times, etc. The almost exclusive emphasis on quantification seems driven by its possibility of conversion to finances, and omits more important, but less tangible, measures of the quality of care that cannot be costed as simply.

Rigid rules for what is and is not science sometimes serve political purposes (e.g. fighting for limited funds from government or universities) and may have the unfortunate consequence of squelching healthy diversity and progress on studying complex clinical phenomena (Feyerabend, 1975). Psychology now seems more secure as a discipline and so psychologists do not feel they have to cling as much to the cloak of scientific respectability.

One other important source of sociopolitical influence on scientific activity stems from the fact that research is conducted within an organised professional context. The official pronouncements of the clinical and counselling psychology professions have stressed the value of conducting research and have also sought to prescribe what type of research is regarded as legitimate. The various ways in which this is expressed are examined below.

PROFESSIONAL ISSUES

It now seems almost uniformly accepted that research should be part of clinical and counselling psychologists' training and practice.

How did this idea arise? We will examine the issues in the context of clinical psychology, since that is where the arguments have been most strongly articulated, although parallel developments have occurred within counselling psychology (American Psychological Association, 1952; Howard, 1992).

Since its inception, psychology has been a university-based discipline. It originally emerged out of philosophy in the nineteenth century, and was later aligned with the natural sciences in order to give it increased respectability in the academic world. The profession of clinical psychology started life in the first decades of the twentieth century when it was concerned with "mental testing" as an aid to selection and diagnosis; it was only after World War II that its role expanded to include treatment (Korchin, 1976). However, during its transition from university to clinic, the profession sought to retain its academic roots, in that the distinctive role of the psychologist was seen to lie in his or her academic, scientific or scholarly viewpoint. As we have mentioned above, this academic viewpoint may lead to tensions with other colleagues in multidisciplinary clinical teams.

This role has received somewhat different emphases in the USA and the UK. In the USA it is known as the "scientist–practitioner" (or Boulder) model, in the UK the "applied scientist" model.

The Scientist–Practitioner Model

The post-war expansion of US clinical psychology, especially in the Veterans Administration Hospitals, led to an upgrading of training from the Masters to the Doctoral level, and to an examination of what such training should consist of (Barlow, Hayes & Nelson, 1984). The consensus view at the time was expressed in a conference at Boulder, Colorado in 1949, and became known, naturally enough, as the "Boulder model". At that time, the field was in its infancy, its knowledge base was tiny, and there was a great need to place the clinical psychology profession on a firm scientific footing, to know whether its procedures worked. The conference concluded that clinical psychologists should be able to function both as scientists and practitioners, capable of conducting research as well as practising. A quotation from an article written slightly earlier than the Boulder conference gives the flavour:

> Participants [in doctoral training programmes] should receive training in three functions: diagnosis, research, and therapy, with the special contributions of the psychologist as research worker emphasised throughout. (American Psychological Association, 1947, p. 549).

Thus the scientist–practitioner is a twin-track model, emphasising research and practice as separate, parallel activities.

Applied Scientist Model

In the UK, the applied scientist model took a different emphasis, less on research and clinical work as separate activities, more on the application of scientific method to clinical work. Monte Shapiro, one of the founders of British clinical psychology, set out the three aspects of the applied scientist role (Shapiro, 1967, 1985):

1. Applying the findings of general psychology to the area of mental health.
2. Only using methods of assessment that had been scientifically validated.
3. Doing clinical work within the framework of the scientific method, by forming hypotheses about the nature and determinants of the client's problems and collecting data to test these hypotheses.

Thus, in Shapiro's applied scientist model, research and practice are not dichotomised but integrated. This approach is also manifested in the behavioural tradition of single-case experimental designs (Barlow, Hayes & Nelson, 1984).

In sum, the applied scientist is principally a clinician; the scientist–practitioner is both a clinician and a researcher.

Current Developments

With the benefit of hindsight, the scientist–practitioner and the applied scientist models appear as ideals that have not been universally adopted or that may not even be universally desirable (Barlow, Hayes & Nelson, 1984; Peterson, 1991; Shapiro, 1985). Many psychologists have called for a reassessment of the role of research in training. There seems to be some recognition that a broader definition of research needs to be adopted, one that can be more easily integrated with practice (Hoshmand & Polkinghorne, 1992; Peterson, 1991). In the USA this has led to the establishment of "professional schools" of clinical psychology, which award the degree of PsyD (Doctor of Psychology) rather than the PhD, and have a more practice-oriented research dissertation.

At the time of writing, the clinical psychology profession in the UK is currently in the process of upgrading its post-graduate qualification from a Masters to a Doctoral level. This upgrading involves a strengthening of the research component of the training, although it does not require research as extensive as for a PhD, which is becoming primarily a qualification for those who aspire to an academic or research career. It is still too early to appraise the effects of this change on the profession's view of research, but it does seem that the greater stress on teaching research skills will result in more of a scientist–practitioner emphasis.

PERSONAL ISSUES

Having considered philosophical and professional issues, we will make a transition to the individual level. What motivates the individual clinical or counselling psychologist to engage in research—or not to, as the case may be?

Why do Clinical and Counselling Psychologists do Research?

We have already mentioned the strengths of research as a systematic way of developing knowledge and theory. There are also a variety of personal reasons why clinical and counselling psychologists may wish to engage in research (Milne, 1987). Some of the more common ones are described below.

Curiosity. Research exists to answer questions: it must add something to knowledge at the end, otherwise there is no point in doing it. For many researchers, this is an end in itself: they want to help make sense of the world and see research as a way of doing so.

Personal pleasure. Some psychologists do research purely for the intrinsic satisfaction. They may enjoy the challenge of research, feel a need to maintain their intellectual sharpness (especially in the middle or later stages of their career), value the contact it brings with other colleagues or simply see research as a break from everyday routine. There is also the satisfaction of seeing one's work in print and of feeling one is shaping the development of one's profession.

Professional and social change. Ideally, research should not just lead to an accumulation of knowledge, but also to some change in professional practice, or social or legal reforms. Compare Marx's epitaph: "Philosophers have interpreted the world, the point, however, is to change it." For example, many clinicians and counsellors desire to know which interventions work and which do not, and to change their practice, or that of their profession, accordingly. Research findings thus provide what Milne (1987) calls clinical feedback, which enables practitioners to monitor their work by learning what they are doing well and what they are doing badly.

Competition between professions. Similarly, some people may be drawn to research as a way of advancing their professional field. Research is a way of legitimising existing professional practices and of developing new ones. A large part of applied psychology's claim to professional status is that its procedures were legitimised by research. In the currently fashionable marketing jargon, one of psychology's "unique selling points" is that its practitioners possess research expertise.

Individual career needs. The career structure of one's profession may dictate that in order to advance up the hierarchy one must conduct research. There is often a research requirement for students wanting to obtain a professional qualification and a track record of research may be required for appointment to senior positions in the profession.

Institutional demands. In service settings, there is often pressure from management to conduct applied research. For example, the recent reforms of the British National Health Service call for practitioners to measure client satisfaction and to assess community healthcare needs.

Research as avoidance. There may also be negative reasons for conducting research, such as using research to retreat from the stresses of personal contact with clients. Parry & Gowler (1983) look at how psychologists' involvement in research may be a strategy for coping with occupational stress.

Why don't clinical and counselling psychologists do research?

It has often been observed that clinical psychologists do not do research, nor even consume it (Barlow, Hayes & Nelson, 1984; Morrow-Bradley & Elliott, 1986; O'Sullivan & Dryden, 1990). A much cited statistic is that the modal number of publications among practising clinical psychologists is zero. This statistic may give a misleading impression, as psychologists are often involved in research that does not reach the publication stage (Milne, Britton & Wilkinson, 1990). However, there are many reasons voiced by psychologists of all levels of experience to explain why they do not do or use research (Barlow, Hayes & Nelson, 1984; Morrow-Bradley & Elliott, 1986):

Irrelevance. Research is seen as not saying anything useful about practice. It is seen as being overly concerned with rigour at the expense of relevance (i.e. journals are filled with rigorous but irrelevant studies). The main source of learning is felt to be clinical practice, rather than research studies.

Emphasis on generalities. There is a tension between the scientific stance, which looks for generalities and lawfulness, and the clinical stance, which stresses human individuality. Most research has been done within the nomothetic tradition, which emphasises pooling people to look for commonalities, rather than the idiographic tradition, which emphasises individual uniqueness (Allport, 1962).

Mistaken paradigm. The positivist paradigm (see Chapter 4), under which much research is conducted, is seen as being reductive and simplistic. This paradigm may be linked with macropolitical structures, e.g. the feminist critique of the patriarchal nature of psychological research, or the socialist critique of its reinforcing individualism at the expense of collectivism.

Intrusiveness. Research is seen as a blunt instrument that crushes the phenomenon under study. Much as zoologists kill a butterfly to study it, so, for example, the intrusion of research procedures into a therapeutic relationship is felt to damage that relationship. Therapists often fear that the act of tape-recording a session might severely distort the psychological atmosphere, for instance by making the client apprehensive about confidentiality.

Time demands. Research is time consuming and often has a low priority compared to service demands. Also, it is often not supported or valued by managers or colleagues.

Technical expertise. Research is seen as requiring considerable technical expertise, with journal editors and other gatekeepers setting prohibitively high standards that discourage those beginning research.

Ethics. Research in general is felt subtly to dehumanise the participants (by turning them into "subjects"), and there are ethical problems with some psychological studies, e.g. those using deception.

Being scrutinised. Research participants can feel scrutinised, which may arouse great anxiety. This may make the conduct of the research project very difficult, particularly in evaluation studies, where the continuation of a service may depend on the findings.

Disturbing conclusions. Research may come up with findings that you do not like. It can lead to a painful re-examination of your cherished ideas if they do not match up to the facts. It may challenge your assumptions and ways of working, which can be an uncomfortable process.

The last two reasons have to do with the threatening aspects of research. Sometimes, these feelings of threat may find their expression in the form of some of the other reasons listed.

Summary

Different individuals will give different weight to each of the positive and negative considerations described above. Some concentrate entirely on being a practising clinician or counsellor and never conduct research once their training is completed. Others concentrate on an academic career and do little if any practice. Many, however, take a middle road, combining the two activities in their professional work, although perhaps only consuming research and not conducting it. We hope to show, in the remainder of this book, that doing research need not be formidable and that it is possible to conduct research even if you work primarily in a service setting.

FURTHER READING

Alan Chalmers, in his two books *What is This Thing Called Science?* (1982) and *Science and its Fabrication* (1990), explains complex philosophy of science issues with admirable clarity. However, he draws most of his examples from the natural sciences. Polkinghorne's (1983) *Methodology for the Human Sciences* gives a thorough review of the range of philosophy of science positions, including alternatives to the traditional views, as applied to the social sciences.

Since Popper and Kuhn are so often referred to, it is worth reading them both in the original. The obvious choice from Kuhn's work is *The Structure of Scientific Revolutions* (1970). For Popper the choice is wider. Perhaps the most accessible is *Conjectures and Refutations* (1963), especially the chapter of the same title.

Research in the context of professional issues is surveyed in Barlow, Hayes & Nelson (1984) and Korchin (1976) from an American perspective, and by Pilgrim and Treacher (1992) from a British one, and Mahoney (1976) provides a lively and thought-provoking discussion of the fallibility of the scientific enterprise.

CHAPTER 3   Doing the groundwork

In sharp contrast to the previous chapter, this one focuses on practical rather than theoretical issues. It covers the first stage of the research process, which we label the groundwork stage. The researcher's primary task at this stage is to formulate a set of research questions or hypotheses; the secondary task is to tackle organisational or political issues, in order to prepare the ground for data collection. Researchers may also be applying for ethics committee approval and for funding at this stage.

In practice, as we noted in Chapter 1, the groundwork stage overlaps with the other two planning stages: selecting the measures and specifying the design. We are separating them for didactic reasons, but assume that readers who are actually planning a project are working concurrently on measurement and design. For example, we cover funding issues here, but if you are applying for funding the grant-giving committee will want a full plan of your research, including details of measurement and design.

Planning the study is usually quite anxiety provoking, both because you are grappling with difficult intellectual and organisational problems and also because researchers often feel that they are not being productive if they are not collecting or analysing data. You may be tempted to get the planning over and done with as soon as possible. This is usually a mistake. We have been involved with many studies, including some of our own, which have suffered because of inadequate planning. A poorly planned study can cause hours of frustration at the analysis and interpretation stage and, at an extreme, may produce worthless results because of design faults or poorly thought-out research questions. Furthermore, such studies can be confusing to read, as the research questions and the research methods are often not fully consistent. Time put in at the early stages often repays itself with interest later on, so it is worth trying to contain your anxiety and taking care over the planning.

This chapter has two sections. The first considers how the research questions are formulated and justified by the literature, and specified in a research proposal. The second looks at the politics of research in clinical settings and other organisations, in particular how research in such settings can easily come to grief. Ethical issues, which often need to be addressed at this stage, are covered in Chapter 9 in the context of issues about the research participants.

FORMULATING THE RESEARCH QUESTIONS

The first step in undertaking a piece of research is obviously to select a topic to investigate. By topic we mean a broad area of interest, such as "depression in children", "marital communication", or "something in the area of counselling process". This is all that is needed at the beginning of the project. As the planning progresses the topic will become more and more focused, until you eventually arrive at some specific research questions.

It is valuable to start keeping a personal research journal from the time you begin to formulate your research questions. In it you can record your thoughts, observations, actions, feelings and reactions to the research process. It provides a forum to try out ideas and draft sections of the write-up. Gathering together a complete set of research memos (Strauss & Corbin, 1990) can also be very valuable later on in writing up your project.

Choosing the Topic

Ideally, the topic will arise naturally out of an intrinsic interest in the area, perhaps stimulated by clinical work, reading or issues that have arisen in your personal life. (However, it is usually unwise to research a topic that is too close to you personally, as it makes it hard to attain the necessary critical detachment. If you are in the middle of a divorce, avoid doing research on marital satisfaction.) All things being equal, it is better to choose a topic that excites or interests you, as you may have to live with it for a long time and the personal interest helps to keep you going. In the case of PhD research, your choice of topic may influence the direction of your subsequent career.

If the research is being done for extrinsic reasons (the prime example being when it is undertaken to fulfil a requirement for a degree), the problem arises of what to do when inspiration fails to strike. In this case, several possibilities are open. The first is to talk to a colleague or potential supervisor, ideally someone whose work you admire, to see if they can suggest a topic. The second is to go to the library and browse through some current books and journals until something takes your fancy. The third is to choose a topic on practical grounds. Is there some research going on in your institution that you could slot into? Is someone conducting a large project that you could take a part of? The disadvantages of working on a large project are that you may have less sense of ownership and achievement, as the study will not be directly yours, but there are the compensating advantages of being able to work with a team and often having some assistance with data collection and analysis.

The Research Questions

Having chosen your general topic area, the next step is to narrow it down into specific research questions or hypotheses. It is important to get this step right because, as we shall argue repeatedly, the methods of the research will flow naturally from the questions that are asked. Similarly, when you read a research article, the first thing to see is precisely what questions the study is trying to answer. Some papers will clearly state their questions or hypotheses, usually at the end of the Introduction, others will leave the reader to infer them from the general drift of the paper. It makes it much easier for the reader to understand and evaluate the study if its questions are clearly spelled out.

The first step is to formulate a few initial questions which encapsulate what you wish to find out from the study. It is a good idea to ask yourself what the most important thing is that you intend the project to tell you. Keeping this in mind helps you to make choices later on if the study starts to become overcomplicated.

The number and complexity of the research questions will depend on the time scale and the available resources. Practitioners doing service-oriented research on their own, or students carrying out a Masters-level project will need to ask circumscribed questions. Research teams undertaking multiyear projects can set themselves much more ambitious targets.

Always bear in mind that research must be able to teach you something: it must be potentially dangerous, in that it could disconfirm cherished ideas. There is no point in doing a project if it simply confirms what you knew before you started it. It is worth trying to "game out" the study (Horowitz, 1982): in other words, ask yourself what its possible outcomes are, what you would learn from each of them, and which ones would cause you to change your mind about the phenomena you are studying. Good studies yield useful information whatever their outcome, even if they fail to confirm initial predictions.

It is not usually possible to formulate a clear and useful research question at the beginning of the study. You need to formulate an initial question and then refine it by reading the literature, consulting with colleagues, deciding what is feasible in your intended research setting, analysing what is practicable in terms of measurement and research design, and conducting pilot studies. This process of cycling back and forth between formulating and learning often takes several months. In their final form, the research questions should be clear and concise, so that there is no ambiguity about what the study is aiming to achieve (Hand, 1994).

It is important to begin by formulating the research questions in advance of developing your procedures. It often happens that new researchers rush into thinking about what measures they will use before thinking clearly about what they really want to find out. This inevitably muddles their thinking and limits the range of questions they consider. For example, we have often seen researchers use measures simply because they are easily available and well known (locus of control springs to mind as an example). The essence of planning good research is appropriate methods— making the research procedures fit the questions rather than the other way around. In other words, the study should generally be question driven rather than method driven.

Types of question

There are a number of different types of research question. We present a simplified taxonomy below, derived from Horowitz (1982) and Elliott (in press). Each type of question is associated with a different genre of research. For example, questions about definition lend themselves to discovery-oriented qualitative research, while questions about frequency lead to descriptive quantitative methods. Since we have not yet discussed these specific procedures, we cannot pursue this notion of appropriate methods here; we will return to it in subsequent chapters.

Some of the main types of research question are as follows.

Definition. What is the nature of X? What defines or constitutes it, makes it what it is and not something else? What aspects or variations does X have? For example, "What is the nature of the experience of being misunderstood in therapy?", "What kinds of misunderstandings are there?" Definitional questions address the basic, defining nature of something, typically some personal experience (e.g. guilt or shyness). They may also entail defining aspects or variations within something, such as types of depressive experience. The goal is to develop a clearer understanding of what something is.

Description. What features, aspects, patterns or histories of X occur? For example, "What kinds of experiences do clients have in counselling sessions?", "What kinds of interactions occur in families with aggressive children?", "What are the origins and consequences of client–counsellor physical contact?" Descriptive questions focus on the existence, appearance or histories of events; they seek to document that a phenomenon exists and to provide examples of it, or to provide an account or narrative of its origin and unfolding development.

Amount/frequency/intensity. How much of X exists? (How frequent, to what degree or intensity?) How frequent or intense are the different aspects of X? For example, "How common is borderline personality disorder?", "Which response modes are most frequently used by cognitive therapists?" These questions overlap with the previous category, as they also attempt to describe a phenomenon, but the focus is on amount rather than features.

Covariation. Do X and Y vary together? Is the relationship between X and Y in some way affected by Z? For example, "Is degree of social support associated with speed of recovery from depression?", "Is occupational satisfaction among psychologists related to their salary level?"

Comparison. Does X have more of A than Y? (This includes, does it work better?) For example, "Is childhood sexual abuse more common in bulimic than in non-bulimic individuals?", "Is cognitive therapy more effective than medication in reducing relapse in chronically depressed clients?", "When clients present immediate here-and-now internal conflicts, is the Gestalt two-chair technique more effective than psychodynamic interpretation?"

Measurement. How well (reliably, validly and usefully) can X be measured by means of measure M? For example, "Can subtypes of marital conflict be measured reliably and distinguished from one another?", "How consistent are clients' ratings of therapeutic alliance over the course of therapy?"

Thus the first step is to develop a set of research questions for which you would like to find answers. After this, you can consider which type each question is and the appropriate method that goes along with it. As you progress through the groundwork phase of your research, you are likely to revise your questions substantially.

Discovery-oriented or confirmatory research questions

A research question may be expressed in question form, as in the above examples. Or it may be formulated as a statement, that is, a hypothesis to be tested: for example, "ethnic or linguistic matches between therapists and clients result in less premature termination . . . and better client outcomes than do mismatches" (Sue *et al.*, 1991, p. 534). A hypothesis is essentially a tentative prediction of a relationship between two or more variables.

The advantages of the hypothesis form are that it gives an immediate clarity and focus to the investigation and enables you to know immediately whether or not the findings of the study support its predictions. It is part of the hypothetico-deductive view of science, which emphasises the use of theory and previous research to generate testable hypotheses (as in Popper's view of the scientific method, see Chapter 2). Using hypotheses also has the merit of increasing precision and fitting in more closely with the theory of statistical inference (Howell, 1992).

On the other hand, stating the research questions in question form allows an exploratory, discovery-oriented approach (e.g. Elliott, 1984; Mahrer, 1988), in contrast to the confirmatory approach of the hypothetico-deductive model. There may not be sufficient theory or previous research to be able to make meaningful hypotheses, or you may not want to constrain your investigation early on. What is important is to be clear about what you are trying to investigate. Exploratory, discovery-oriented research questions are typically either definitional or descriptive. The research questions which guide discovery-oriented research should be clearly delineated, in order to narrow the research topic to a workable size and to provide a central focus for data collection and analysis. The question "What is the nature of clients' experiences in therapy?" would be too broad (at least for a student research study; but see Rennie, 1990); a narrower question such as "What is the nature of clients' experiences of withholding their negative reactions from therapists?" would be more workable (Rennie, 1993). If you take the attitude, "I want to study x, so I'll just collect some data and see what's interesting," you are likely to end up with an incoherent mishmash of findings.

Discovery-oriented research questions are typically most appropriate under the following circumstances:

- When a research area is relatively new or little is known about it, making it difficult or premature to ask questions about covariation or comparison.

- When a research area is disordered, that is, confusing, contradictory, or not moving forward. This may be due to premature quantification prior to adequate open-ended definitional or descriptive work.

- When the topic is a highly complex event, process or human experience, requiring careful definition or description.

The role of theory

As we noted in Chapter 2, research is always conducted within an explicit or implicit theoretical framework. Therefore, it is almost always useful to work at developing that framework and making it more explicit. For one thing, conducting your research within an explicit theoretical framework will guide the formulation of research questions. As Kurt Lewin said, "There is nothing so practical as a good theory" (quoted in Marrow, 1969). Thus it is an excellent idea to devote time early in the research process to locating an existing theoretical model or to formulating your own model. You can do this by trying to map out the likely relationships between the variables you are studying. For example, if you are studying the relationship between counsellor empathy and client outcome, you might think about what some of the intervening processes might be, as well as variables which might affect both empathy and outcome. Counsellor empathy might facilitate client self-exploration which might lead to better outcome, or client pretreatment self-awareness might facilitate both counsellor empathy and client outcome (see Chapter 7). From a different theoretical perspective, counsellor empathy might act as a reinforcer for client disclosure of feelings or statements of positive self-esteem. The theoretical model could then guide the selection of specific correlational or comparative research questions, suitable for quantitative investigation.

Even in discovery-oriented research, it is good practice for the researcher to try to be as explicit as possible about his or her implicit theories or "preunderstandings" (Packer & Addison, 1989), in the form of expectations, hunches or possible biases. The difference is that in discovery-oriented research these implicit theories are set aside (referred to as "bracketing", see Chapter 4) rather than explicitly tested. After a discovery-oriented study has been completed, the researcher may find it useful to compare the actual results to these original expectations, in order to determine what has been learned.

Literature review

Once the topic area has been chosen, the process of reviewing the literature starts, proceeding in parallel and in interaction with the process of formulating the research questions. The literature review is carried out for several reasons:

1. To assess how well developed the literature is, what kinds of gaps there are in it and whether there has been sufficient preliminary descriptive research to define the phenomena of interest.

2. To see how far the existing literature answers your research question(s). What can your proposed study add to the existing literature? Is there a need for another study? Has the study been done before? However, study duplication is rarely a great problem, because no two people ever seem to design a study in the same way and because it is always easy to devise variations on something that has already been done.

3. To help you formulate your research question(s) in the light of theory or previous research, and possibly to give you a theoretical or conceptual framework to work within.

4. To help with measurement and design issues. To see what measures and approaches have been used in previous studies, and what are the strengths and weaknesses of previous designs.

In established research areas, there may be an enormous amount of literature, which can seem daunting to get to grips with. Several information sources can help to speed up the process of reviewing psychological literature.

- Library catalogues are usually computerised and assist the location of books on specific topics or by specified authors. Also, the low-tech method of just browsing along library shelves, especially those holding new acquisitions, can often yield a useful collection of books to help start your search.

- *Psychological Abstracts* is an American Psychological Association journal which lists articles from a wide range of journals by author, title and keywords. It is available in a microcomputer compact disc (CD-ROM) version, *PsychLit*, which is worth becoming familiar with as it allows researchers to conduct their own individualised literature searches. It is enormously helpful and, once you get the hang of it, enjoyable to browse through.

- *Index Medicus*, for medical journals, is similar to *Psychological Abstracts*. It is also available on CD-ROM, with the same computer interface as *PsychLit*, but it is a much larger database because the volume of medical literature is much greater.

- *Science Citation Index* and *Social Science Citation Index* work like abstracts in reverse. You look up a key article and the index lists all subsequent articles that have cited that key article. (These indexes have not yet been computerised.)

- Current journals of interest in your area. It is worthwhile browsing through the last few years' issues of the three or four most important journals covering your topic area.

- *PsychScan* is an American Psychological Association publication which lists the abstracts of journals covering specific specialties. For example, there are *PsychScans* in clinical psychology, psychoanalysis, etc.

- *Current Contents* is a journal which lists the contents pages of other journals.

- *Clinical Psychology Review* is an American Psychological Association journal which publishes review articles on major areas of research that are relevant to clinical practice.

- Handbooks. Current editions of handbooks in your area, e.g. Bergin and Garfield (1994) for psychotherapy research and Snyder and Forsyth (1991) for social–clinical issues, provide comprehensive reviews of focused topic areas.

- The *Annual Review of Psychology* has authoritative reviews of contemporary developments across the whole of psychology (and there are also annual reviews in related disciplines, e.g. public health and sociology).

Remember as well that librarians are there to be helpful. Their job is not just to collect fines on overdue books; they are trained information locators. They will help you to find sources of reference or to use ones with which you have difficulty. Contrary to the stereotype, many librarians welcome human contact in their job!

The Proposal

As your ideas start to become clearer, it is worth setting them down on paper. This will help you explain to other people what you are planning to do (if you can bear exposing your less than perfect ideas to anyone else) and it will also help you to develop your thoughts yourself, as it is much easier to rethink something that is down on paper rather than just in your head.

At the very least, prepare a one-page outline of your proposed research questions, the theoretical model, and your measures and design, which you can use to obtain some initial feedback. You can then expand it into a longer proposal which you can use to recruit research supervisors (in the USA, doctoral committee members) and get early consultations.

Often, for example with PhD research and grant applications, a formal research proposal is required. This is usually not wasted effort, as the proposal will form the core of the Introduction and Method sections of your final report. It is best approached by successive approximations. The first step is to draft a rough outline, to get something down on paper, no matter how sketchy. Proposals evolve through multiple drafts—six or seven is common—as you continue to read, talk and think about the project.

The structure of the proposal is similar to the Introduction and Method sections of a journal article. It should state what the research topic is and why it is important, briefly review what has already been done and what psychological theory can be brought to bear on the problem, and summarise the intended study and its research questions or hypotheses. The Method section describes in detail the proposed design and measurement aspects of the study. A typical proposal has the following structure:

Introduction

    Statement of the research topic and its importance
    Focused literature review (covering previous research and
      psychological theory)
    Rationale for and overview of the proposed study
    Research questions or hypotheses

---

continues

continued

Method

    Participants
    Design
    Measures
    Ethical considerations
    Data analysis procedures
    Expected results and implications (optional)
    Timetable (optional, see below)

You may want to give an estimated timetable for the project in your proposal. Even if you do not include one, it is usually helpful at this stage to map one out for your own consumption. List each of the major tasks that comprise the project and try to estimate how long each one will take and what other tasks need to be completed before it can be done. However, one rule of thumb, especially in PhD research, is to double any time estimate: expect everything to take twice as long as you think it will (Hodgson & Rollnick, 1989). In our experience, the most common causes of problems in student projects are a slow initial start and unexpected delays later on, often out of your control (e.g. ethics committees, access to participants and data collection problems).

For example, Table 3.1 gives our recommended timetable for a one-year student project.

Consultations

It is a good idea to get a variety of opinions on your proposal from people of different backgrounds, for example colleagues who know the research area, potential research supervisors, psychologists outside your area, non-psychologists, clients or ex-clients from the population that you are studying. No research is carried out in isolation: it is always helpful to get input from lay people and from colleagues in the scientific community. Even if many of their suggestions cannot be implemented, you will often find that something of value emerges each time you present your ideas to someone else.

Table 3.1 Timetable for a one-year student project

June	Start reading the background literature in your general area of interest.
July/August	Decide on the topic and formulate preliminary research questions. Find a supervisor.
September	Draft a one- or two-page proposal. Discuss the project in the setting in which you will carry it out.
October	Apply to your local ethics committee for approval.
November	Finalise the research plan and prepare for data collection.
December	Write the first draft of the introduction and method sections.
January	Begin data collection.
February	Redraft the introduction and method sections.
March	Finish data collection. Begin data analysis.
April/May	Complete the data analysis. Write the first draft of the results and discussion sections.
June	Complete the write-up. Give the final draft to your supervisor for comments. Arrange for duplication and binding (if it needs to be booked in advance).
July	Make final corrections. Duplicate, bind and submit the polished version.

You may also want to write to some key researchers in the field, to ask for measures, reprints or details of current work. Also consider attending a conference, as this is an excellent way to meet people with similar interests to exchange notes and learn about work that has not yet reached the journals.

Piloting

Pilot studies are small-scale try-outs of various aspects of your intended protocol. The first pilots may be done with colleagues or friends role-playing participants. This will help you to get the administrative procedures roughly right and reveal any gross errors in measurement or design. Subsequent pilots can be with people closer to the target population that you intend to study.

The importance of piloting cannot be stressed enough. Just as the Boeing 747 was not built straight from the drawing-board, it is rarely possible to design a study in your armchair and then translate it straight into action. You always need to test out procedures, measures and design. Some things that look good on paper just do not work in practice—they are not understandable to clients or they do not yield useful information. It is also worthwhile performing a few crucial analyses on the pilot data to try out coding and analysis and to see whether the data can actually be used to answer the research questions. A few hours here can save you weeks or months of anguish later on.

Funding

It is possible to obtain funds for clinical or counselling psychology research, if you plan your application in advance. The major expense in most psychological research projects is research assistant time. (Grants will rarely support the principal investigator, on the assumption that he or she is earning a salary from the sponsoring institution.) A secondary expense will be equipment (e.g. for computing or tape-recording) and supplies (e.g. printing, photo-copying and postage), although the equipment component will usually be small, in contrast to biomedical research where it may be a major part of the budget.

The format for proposals varies from agency to agency; it is important to obtain applicants' guidelines from potential agencies before starting work on the proposal. However, proposals will follow the broad outline we have discussed above, with a final section on the proposed costs and timetable of the research (Brooks, 1989; Bruce, 1991; Strain & Kerr, 1984). The goal of the proposal is to convince the awarding body that you have a well thought-out plan for necessary and innovative research. The opinions of non-specialist colleagues can help to predict how the agency might react to your proposal.

Grant-giving bodies often employ a multistage screening process. Administrative staff will first read your proposal to check that it falls within the ambit of the funding body and that its estimated costs are reasonable. Then it will be sent out to professional reviewers, who will be familiar with the area of research that you are proposing. They will give it an overall rating and supply a detailed report. These will be considered by a meeting of the grant-giving committee, who will be professionals in the field, although probably not specialists in your area. They will be looking to support proposals that demonstrate scientific excellence and have a realistic estimate of costs and timetable.

Specific sources of funds are too numerous and rapidly changing to list here. They can be classified into central and local government agencies, charities, businesses, university and health service bodies. Many universities, especially in the USA, have officials that can help you identify funding sources for your research. Competition is great, and even if your project is turned down, it does not mean that it was not worth while. It is worth asking to see the referees' reports, if they are available, to identify any weaknesses in your proposal before revising and resubmitting it elsewhere.

THE POLITICS OF RESEARCH IN APPLIED SETTINGS

Researchers often underestimate the organisational difficulties of conducting research in field, as opposed to laboratory, settings. Obtaining access, especially to highly bureaucratic settings such as hospitals, schools and mental health agencies, may take months. It is vital to start doing your groundwork early on, in order to establish whether it is viable to do the study in your proposed setting. You need to develop a relationship with the gatekeepers and managers, as well as with the clients, patients, staff, etc. Although some people will be supportive of your research, others will oppose it, not always openly.

Access

Negotiating access often requires considerable flexibility, political savvy and interpersonal skills. Many researchers simply avoid the whole process by creating their own settings, which they can control more thoroughly (Cook & Campbell, 1979). However, if you want to study settings outside the laboratory or research clinic, access problems are hard to avoid.

The first step is to identify and approach the gatekeepers of the setting (Taylor & Bogdan, 1984), that is, those who control access and help protect it from disruptive outside interests. Gatekeepers vary in their apparent social and political power, from receptionists who screen out unwanted enquiries to managers, senior doctors, head teachers or school principals. An initial working knowledge of the role structure and formality of the setting greatly facilitates the access process and may prevent disasters or wasted effort. Cowen and Gesten (1980) recommend starting at the top of the setting and working your way down (otherwise leaders are likely to be insulted or suspicious and refuse permission on general principles). They also note that newer programmes tend to be less formal and more flexible. It is generally useful to have a prior association with the setting or the support of someone who is trusted (Cook & Campbell, 1979; Taylor & Bogdan, 1984).

If you have not done so already, it is important to begin your research journal at this point and, in addition, qualitative researchers may start keeping detailed field notes (see Chapter 6). The access process often yields essential information about how the setting functions and how it protects itself, which is worth describing in its own right.

The next step is to present your request to conduct research in the setting. Be clear about what you are proposing to do. It often helps to avoid misinterpretation if you put things in writing, stating the general aim of the research and how the data will be collected. This is an adaptation of the one-page proposal that we suggested above, in everyday, jargon-free language; you might do it as a kind of press release, such as would be given out to a local newspaper. A draft informed consent form is often needed. It is advisable to make your own presentations to the administration or staff, rather than giving in to the temptation to let someone else do it for you, as they will often forget or do a poor job of it (Cowen & Gesten, 1980). Presentations to staff meetings should also be supplemented with personal meetings, especially with resistant individuals, in their own setting rather than yours and on their schedule.

In addition, there is often a formal screening process, such as a human subjects review or research ethics committee. We will address ethical issues in Chapter 9, but it is worth anticipating two points here. First, obtaining ethical approval can take several months as committees may meet infrequently, which may be difficult if you are a student trying to complete your research within a tight timetable. Secondly, ethical committees may raise objections about your research, which you will need to take into account before you proceed with the study.

Responding to Doubts

You often have to work to gain people's goodwill and to get them on your side. They may not be convinced by your research topic— people in applied settings often have little understanding of psychological research—but at least they should trust you. A senior doctor once said to one of us, "I'm allergic to anything beginning with psych!", but he was still willing to cooperate with our project because he trusted us.

People might oppose your project for rational, practical reasons, as even the best run projects inevitably cause disruption and some services are constantly being asked for permission to conduct studies. They might also oppose it in order to protect patients, who may be in danger of being over-researched, even with adequate informed consent procedures. For example, this is currently an issue in the HIV/AIDS services. There are also instances of researchers who exploit the people in the setting by, for example, failing to keep them informed or not acknowledging their contribution when the research is published.

In addition to these rational, practical concerns, research in service settings often arouses feelings of threat and suspicion (Hardy, in press; Weiss, 1972). It can be seen as intrusive, critical and a challenge to the established way of doing things. Be sensitive to such opposition: if you do not listen to and attempt to meet people's fears at the groundwork stage, the likelihood is that the study will be undermined later on. Often these fears may be expressed indirectly: medical and nursing staff may appear overly protective of "their" patients, forms may be mysteriously lost, and so on.

Furthermore, your research may become embroiled in the internal politics of the setting. It is important to be aware of existing organisational tensions, as your study may be used as part of a power struggle: different factions may gain from seeing it carried out or from blocking it (Hardy, in press).

Your clinical and consulting skills are often valuable in both understanding and responding sensitively to the doubts of other people about the research. In responding to their often complex feelings it is important to be open about what you intend to do and why. Goodman (1972) describes how he put the client-centred principles of disclosure, empathy and acceptance into action in a large community psychology project which evaluated the effects of companionship therapy for emotionally troubled boys:

> A careless procedural mistake or two, showing cause for mistrust and generating serious community complaint, could close down the project. We therefore sought to reduce risks by establishing some global operating principles that would simultaneously protect our participants and our research goals.

> Eventually, the principles took the form of a general approach, or a "clinical attitude" toward the community, consistent with the client-centred theory of effective therapist–client relationships. That is, we would try to empathize with any complaints about us, accept community apprehension and protective activities, and disclose our own needs and plans—including the global intervention strategy . . . Sometimes we also disclosed the motives for our disclosures (meta-disclosure). Implementing this approach took extra time initially, but it brought trust and proved efficient in the long run. (Goodman, 1972, p. 2)

The central issue is what the members of the setting get out of being involved in your research. From their point of view, research has a high nuisance factor. You need to minimise such nuisances and help them to realise any possible gains, e.g. potential helpful feedback on procedures, the opportunity for patients to talk about their concerns, the increased status of being part of an academic setting, and so on. In Hardy's (in press) terms, you need to align the goals of the research with the goals of the setting. Where possible, it can be useful to include a staff member as part of the research team and to ask the staff to contribute to the design of the research (Cowen & Gesten, 1980). However, some clinicians will not want any involvement, while others will want to be kept closely informed. It is wise to provide information to all important staff members: circulate updates, show drafts of papers, etc.

Through these contacts, the researcher, gatekeepers and prospective participants engage in a process of negotiation, in which the research contract is developed (Taylor & Bogdan, 1984). This agreement, which can be formal or informal, makes clear what the researcher is asking for, as well as spelling out the researcher's obligations in regard to confidentiality, feedback and avoiding disruption.

Authorship

If you are intending to publish the study, it is worth considering authorship issues from the outset. In applied settings such issues can be complicated, because several people may be involved in different ways in the research. Senior staff sometimes ask to have their name on a paper simply because the research is being done in their unit. Unless they have made a significant contribution to the research this is inappropriate and, for psychologists, unethical (American Psychological Association, 1992). Appreciation for permission to work in a setting should be mentioned in the acknowledgements section of the research paper. (We will discuss publication issues further in Chapter 11.)

FURTHER READING

Hodgson and Rollnick's (1989) amusing chapter entitled "More fun, less stress: how to survive in research" is well worth reading, especially their tongue-in-cheek laws of research (sample: "A research project will change twice in the middle"). Rudestam and Newton's (1992) book *Surviving your dissertation* is especially useful for students and has some good material on planning and writing.

Several specialist texts have material on the politics of working in field settings: e.g. from the point of view of evaluation research (Weiss, 1972), participant observation (Taylor & Bogdan, 1984) and randomised experiments (Cook & Campbell, 1979).

CHAPTER 4   Foundations of measurement

We have now reached the second of the four stages of the research process, measurement, which consists of deciding how to study each of the psychological concepts contained in the research questions. The previous groundwork stage should have culminated in the formulation of a set of research questions. For example, the questions might be about the role of social support in emotional adjustment to stressful life events. The measurement stage of the project would then consist of specifying how each of these constructs is to be assessed; in other words, how to assess social support, how to capture emotional adjustment and what constitutes a stressful life event. There are two separate but interdependent issues to be considered: how each construct is defined and how it is measured.

The boundary between the groundwork and measurement stages (and also the design stage, which we cover in Chapter 7) is not, of course, as watertight as we are implying. For instance, measurement considerations may shape the formulation of the research questions. If an investigator knows there is no available way to measure something, it would be difficult (perhaps impossible) to study it. For example, it would be fascinating to study the content of dreams as they are happening during sleep, but there is presently no conceivable method of doing this, so research about real-time dream images cannot be conducted, we can only rely on people's recall of dreams after they wake up. Furthermore, some types of measurement may be beyond the time constraints or the financial resources of the researcher. For example, in research on the process of family therapy, transcribing interviews and training raters to code them is time consuming and expensive, and therefore it may be inappropriate for a project with little or no funding.

However, it does not greatly distort the basic principles to treat groundwork, measurement and design as three separate, sequential stages. For the rest of this chapter, we will assume that the research questions have been decided on and that we are solely concerned with translating them into measurement procedures.

Separating the groundwork and measurement stages is also helpful in beginning to think about the study. Novice researchers often worry prematurely about measurement. As we argued in Chapter 3, it is better to think first about what to study and only secondarily about how. Ideas about measurement will often flow from clearly formulated research questions: measurement will be less problematic if you have thought through the questions you are asking.

As in the previous groundwork stage, there are several important conceptual issues, some of which are controversial. We are including this material to give essential background information and in order to help you think more broadly about the framework within which research is conducted. The present chapter covers this conceptual material; the next two deal with practical issues in selecting or constructing measures. The first section of this chapter defines some key terms and looks at the general process of measurement. The second and fourth sections examine the respective conceptual foundations of the quantitative and qualitative approaches; they sandwich the third section on psychometric theory. The final section summarises the advantages and disadvantages of quantitative and qualitative approaches and discusses how they might be integrated.

TERMINOLOGY

Domains of Variables

Variables studied in clinical and counselling psychology research can be grouped into five general domains:

1. *Cognitive*: thoughts, attitudes, beliefs, expectations, attributions, memory, reasoning, etc.

2. *Affective*: feelings, emotions, moods, bodily sensations, etc.

3. *Behavioural*: actions, performance, skill, speech, etc.

4. *Biological*: physiological and anatomical, e.g. heart rate, blood pressure, immunological activity, etc.

5. *Social*: acute and chronic stressors, social supports, social activities, work, etc.

These variables form the content of psychological research: the research questions will have been framed in terms of several of them. However, each must be clearly defined and translated into one or more practical measurement methods.

Operationalisation

We will use the term "measurement" in a general sense to refer to the process of translating psychological concepts into concrete observations. This can often be done in several different ways, for example:

- *Phobia*: observed avoidance; self-report of fear; physiological measures of sympathetic nervous system arousal.

- *Pain*: self-report of intensity; behavioural tolerance of painful stimuli; clinician's judgement.

- *Death anxiety*: semi-structured qualitative interview; standardised questionnaires.

The abstract idea (phobia, pain, death anxiety) is known as a "construct" or "variable"; the way of observing it is known as a "measure" of that construct. Although this language is associated with quantitative methods, it can usefully be applied to qualitative methods as well, although in this case researchers may speak of a "phenomenon" rather than of a construct. This section of the chapter is intended to cover both quantitative and qualitative approaches; subsequent sections address the issues involved in adopting each of them.

The technical term for the process of going from a construct to its associated measurement operation is "operationalisation".

Operationalisation

Construct ——————————⟶ Measure

Operationalisation is not a simple process. As the above three examples show, there are often several different ways to operationalise a given variable. Which one(s) to use depends on the research questions, the theoretical framework and the resources available for the study.

In order to facilitate the process of operationalisation, the construct may be given an operational definition, i.e. it may be defined so that it can be easily measured. Thus empathy may be initially conceptualised as "Entering the private perceptual world of the other and becoming thoroughly at home in it" (Rogers, 1975), but for psychotherapy process research it may be operationally defined as how accurately the counsellor responds to the client's expressed feelings, which then leads to its being measured using expert ratings of audiotaped interactions.

It is not always possible, or desirable, to give an operational definition to every construct. Earlier generations of researchers were taught the doctrine of operationism (Stevens, 1935), which implies that a concept is identical to its measurement operations: IQ is what IQ tests measure. However, it is clear that, in the clinical and counselling context, we cannot adequately capture many important constructs by our current measures. Social skills may be operationalised by such behaviours as good eye contact, smiling, etc., but performing only these behaviours does not produce socially skilled interactions; rather the reverse, it tends to produce people who act like robots (or breakfast TV presenters). In line with the critical realist position, we are arguing that most psychological constructs are only partially captured by their associated measures. We will take these issues up again in the following two sections when we discuss positivism and construct validity.

The operational definition of a construct clearly depends on how it is conceptualised theoretically. For example, two ways of operationalising social support—by counting the number of people in a person's social network or by assessing the quality of relationships within that network—have different implications for what is meant by the social support construct itself: whether good social support means lots of supportive relationships available or just a few good ones. This issue is known as the "theory dependence of observation" (see also Chapter 2). Any way of measuring an entity presupposes a view of what that entity consists of: it is impossible to have pure observations. Similarly, qualitative scholars highlight the influence of the researcher's preconceptions on the measurement process: the concept of the hermeneutic circle (e.g. Packer & Addison, 1989) encapsulates the mutual feedback between our current ideas and our understanding of the data.

A final complication is that the act of measurement often changes the person or situation being measured, a phenomenon known as "reactivity of measurement". For example, people may behave differently if they know that they are being observed, and asking a client to monitor the day-to-day frequency of her anxious thoughts may in itself affect the frequency of those thoughts. Research participants are often influenced by their perception of what the researcher is trying to find out.

Measurement Sources and Approaches

Sources of measurement can be categorised into self-report and observation (Korchin, 1976): you can either ask people about themselves or look at what they are doing. (Strictly speaking, self-report data should be called verbal-report, as it can be gathered from several perspectives—for example, the person of interest, a significant other, or a therapist or teacher. Similarly, observational data could be gathered from an observer, a psychological test, or a physiological measure.) Data may be collected from either source using either qualitative or quantitative methods (see Table 4.1).

Table 4.1 Examples of measures classified by source and approach

	Self-report	Observation
Quantitative	Attitude questionnaires Symptom checklists	Behavioural observation Psychological tests of ability Physiological measures
Qualitative	Qualitative interviews Diaries, journals	Participant observation Projective tests

The distinction between quantitative and qualitative methods raises a number of fundamental issues: visions of what science is (as discussed in Chapter 2) and what it means to be human. Each method derives from contrasting academic and philosophical traditions.

Quantitative methods are identified with the so-called "hard science" disciplines, principally physics; qualitative methods with the "soft" social sciences, such as sociology and anthropology, and the humanities. In the early decades of the twentieth century, many influential psychologists felt that the road to academic prestige and legitimacy lay with being considered as "hard science", and thus sought to identify psychology with physics and quantitative methods (Polkinghorne, 1983; Lincoln & Guba, 1985; Packer & Addison, 1989). This issue has been a continuing struggle within psychology, with its roots in older philosophical traditions (idealism and realism) and early schools of psychology (e.g. introspectionism and associationism). The structure of the present chapter reflects this debate. It has a thesis, antithesis, synthesis form: we will attempt to set out the underlying issues for each approach, and then suggest in a final section how they might be integrated in practice.

FOUNDATIONS OF QUANTITATIVE METHODS

Quantitative methods, by definition, are those which use numbers. The main advantages of quantitative measurement are as follows:

- Using numbers enables greater precision in measurement. There is a well-developed theory of reliability and validity to assess measurement errors; this enables researchers to know how much confidence to place in their measures.

- There are well-established statistical methods for analysing the data. The data can be easily summarised, which facilitates communication of the findings.

- Quantitative measurements facilitate comparison. They allow researchers to get the reactions of many people to specific stimuli and to compare responses across individuals.

- Quantitative methods fit in well with hypothetico-deductive approaches. Hypothesised relationships between variables can be specified using a mathematical model and the methods of statistical inference can be used to see how well the data fit the predictions.

- Sampling theory can be used to estimate how well the findings generalise beyond the sample in the study to the wider population from which the sample was drawn.

The development of science would have been impossible without quantification. The necessity of the ancient Egyptians to preserve the dimensions of their fields after the flooding of the Nile led to the development of geometry (Dilke, 1987). If the fields could be measured and mapped out, their boundaries could be restored once the waters had subsided. However, it was not until the late Renaissance that quantification and mathematics began to become an integral part of science. In the seventeenth century, Newton's laws of motion employed fairly simple algebra to provide a tool of great power and beauty that enabled scientists to predict the behaviour of falling apples and orbiting planets.

Positivism

The success of quantitative methods in the physical sciences, especially that of Newtonian mechanics, led to an attempt to extend them into other areas of enquiry. The nineteenth-century philosopher Auguste Comte (1830) articulated the doctrine of positivism, which has been much elaborated by succeeding scholars. These elaborations have not always been consistent with each other or with Comte's original formulation (see Bryant, 1985; Bryman, 1988; Polkinghorne, 1983), making it difficult to define precisely what is meant by positivism. However, its three main tenets are usually taken to be:

1. That scientific attention should be restricted to observable facts ("positive" in this sense means dealing with matters of fact); "inferred constructs", such as beliefs or motives, have no place in science. This is a version of empiricism (the belief that all knowledge is derived from sensory experience).

2. That the methods of the physical sciences (e.g. quantification, separation into independent and dependent variables, and formulation of general laws) should also be applied to the social sciences.

3. That science is objective and value free.

A twentieth-century development, associated with the "Vienna circle" group of philosophers such as Carnap and Wittgenstein, was "logical positivism". This sought to analyse which propositions have meaning and which do not, and then to restrict philosophical discourse to those things that can properly be talked about. Wittgenstein's famous dictum captures the flavour: "What can be said at all can be said clearly, and what we cannot talk about we must pass over in silence" (Wittgenstein, 1921/1961, p. 3). The logical positivists' central criterion, that all philosophical statements should be reducible to sensory experience, rules out discussion of metaphysical concepts. They argue that it is pointless arguing about things like the ultimate nature of the universe, since such propositions can never be proved or disproved (Ayer, 1936).

Methodological behaviourism

The positivist doctrine was incorporated into psychology in the form of methodological behaviourism, whose best-known proponents are Watson and Skinner. They sought to restrict psychology to a "science of behaviour", eschewing consideration of any "inner variables", e.g. cognitions and affects. For instance, Watson urged: "Let us limit ourselves to things that can be observed and formulate laws concerning only those things" (Watson, 1931, p. 6). In other words, methodological behaviourists would not say that a rat was hungry, as hunger is an inferred construct; instead, they would say it had been deprived of food for eight hours, or that it was at three-quarters of its initial body weight. Similarly, they would not talk about aggression, but rather specific behaviours, such as kicking, punching or swearing.

This attitude was a reaction to the perceived limitations of the introspectionism that had preceded it. Introspection consisted of the investigator observing the contents of his or her own consciousness and attempting to expound general theories therefrom. The virtue of sticking to observable behaviour is that it is clear what you are talking about and your conclusions can be replicated by other investigators.

Another important manifestation of methodological behaviourism was found in clinical work, in the behavioural assessment movement (e.g. Goldfried & Kent, 1972). This called for clinical assessment to be tied closely to observable behaviour, to remove the inferences that are made when, for example, you decide that a client has a "hysterical personality".

However, the distinction between high-inference and low-inference measures may be less useful than it seems at first, since inference must occur sooner or later in the research process to give psychological meaning to the data. There is a conservation of inference law: the lower the level of inference in the measurement process, the higher the level of inference needed to connect the observed data to interesting variables or phenomena. Conversely, high-inference measures often do much of the researcher's work early on, requiring less inference to make sense of the data obtained. For example, a measure of non-verbal behaviour in family therapy might use a low level of inference, but the researcher may need to make further inferences in order to make sense of the data, such as interpreting certain body postures as indicating detachment from the family. On the other hand, a measure of transference in psychotherapy might require a high level of inference in rating clients' verbal statements, but further inferences may not be needed to interpret the data.

Criticisms of positivism

The positivist, methodological behaviourist stance has been severely criticised both from within and outside psychology (e.g. Bryman, 1988; Guba & Lincoln, 1989; Harré, 1974; Koch, 1964; Polkinghorne, 1983; Rogers, 1985). The central criticism is that, when carried through rigorously, it leads to draconian restrictions on what can be talked about. Psychological constructs that attempt to capture important aspects of experience, e.g. feelings, values and meanings, are ruled out of court. It leads to a sterile and trivial discipline alienated from human experience. Although few researchers today adopt a strict methodological behaviourism, some articles in mainstream psychological journals still seem to lose sight of the people behind the statistics.

The rise of quantitative methods has also been associated with the rise of capitalism. Young (1979) argues that reducing everything to numbers is a manifestation of a balance-sheet mentality. A brilliant fictional indictment of such a mentality was made a century ago in Dickens' novel *Hard Times*, which starkly depicts the loss of humanity that comes from reducing all transactions to quantitative terms. This criticism is still timely, given recent moves towards performance indicators, clinical audit and cost effectiveness embodied in the UK National Health Service reforms and the US tightening of criteria for insurance reimbursement of psychological therapy. Emphasising easily measurable indices of workload often leaves out the more intangible—and arguably more important—aspects of quality.

Conclusions

In our view, the important message to take from the positivists is the value of being explicit about how your constructs are measured. It reminds researchers and theorists to be conscious of measurement issues, to tie their discourse to potential observations and, when speculating about more abstract constructs, to have an awareness of what measurement operations lie behind them. For instance, if you are attempting to study complex constructs—e.g. defence mechanisms—you need to specify what would lead you to conclude that someone is denying or using projective identification. Cronbach and Meehl's (1955) notion of construct validity, which we discuss below, is an attempt to place the use of inferred constructs on a sound methodological basis.

It is worth noting that, although quantification and positivism are often treated as equivalent, the stress on quantification is actually only a small part of the positivist package, and possibly not even a necessary part. For example, qualitative methods can be used purely descriptively, without using inferred constructs. Also, the role of quantification in science may have been overstated by the positivists. Schwartz (1992) points to examples in the physical and biological sciences, e.g. the double helix model of DNA, that use mainly qualitative methods.

Having described the rationale for quantification, we can now look at the underlying theory of measurement, including the important question of how to evaluate particular measures.

PSYCHOMETRIC THEORY

Psychometric theory refers to the theory underlying psychological measurement. In particular, it leads to ways of evaluating the effectiveness of specific measurement instruments. Although developed in the context of quantitative measurement, its ideas can be translated into qualitative methods. They are essential for all would-be researchers to grasp, whatever approach they ultimately plan to adopt.

Definitions

Scales of measurement

Measurements may have the properties of nominal, ordinal or interval scales (Stevens, 1946). Nominal scales consist of a set of mutually exclusive categories with no implicit ordering. In a sense they are not really scales, but labels (Howell, 1992). For example, researchers in a psychiatric day hospital might use a simplified diagnostic system consisting of four categories: 1 = manic depressive psychosis, 2 = schizophrenia, 3 = personality disorder, 4 = other. In this case the numbers are simply labels for the categories: there is no sense in which 2 is greater than 1, etc., and thus the diagnostic system forms a nominal scale. An ordinal scale has the additional property of ordered categories, that is, it measures a variable along some continuum. For example, psychiatric day-hospital patients might be rated on a scale of psychological impairment, consisting of three categories: 1 = unimpaired, 2 = moderately impaired, 3 = highly impaired. On this scale, someone with a score of 3 is defined to be more impaired than someone with a score of 2, and thus it has ordinal properties. However, there is no assumption that the distance between successive ordinal scale points is the same, that is, the distance between 1 and 2 is not necessarily the same as that between 2 and 3. An interval scale is like an ordinal scale with the additional property that the distances between its points are assumed to be equal. For example, the Beck Depression Inventory (Beck, Steer & Garbin, 1988), a self-report measure of depression, is usually treated as an interval scale. This assumes that the increase in severity of depression from a score of 10 to a score of 15 is equivalent to the increase in severity from 20 to 25.

The importance of distinguishing between these types of measurement is that different statistical methods are typically used to analyse data from the different scale types. Nominal and ordinal scales may require non-parametric or distribution-free methods, whereas interval scales can be analysed using standard statistical methods, such as the t-test and the analysis of variance, provided that the data meet the assumption of a normal distribution (Howell, 1992).

Type of measure

Measures can be divided into either nomothetic or idiographic. Nomothetic measures compare individuals with other individuals; most psychological tests fall into this category. The scores on a nomothetic measure can be norm referenced, when they have no absolute meaning in themselves, but are simply indicative of how the individual stands with respect to the rest of the population. For example, the scores on the Wechsler Adult Intelligence Scale (WAIS) are norm referenced: they are constructed in order to have a population mean of 100 and a standard deviation of 15. A criterion-referenced measure, on the other hand, compares individuals against an absolute standard. For example, a typing speed of 40 words per minute denotes a certain degree of skill at the keyboard; scores on the Global Assessment Scale (Endicott *et al.*, 1976) denote a certain degree of psychiatric symptomatology.

The contrasting approach, idiographic measurement, focuses solely on a single individual, without reference to others (Korchin, 1976). No attempt at comparison is made. Some examples of idiographic methods are repertory grids (Winter, 1992), Q-sorts (e.g. Jones *et al.*, 1993), and the Shapiro personal questionnaire (Phillips, 1986; Shapiro, 1961a). Such measures are often used within small-N research designs, and will be discussed further in that context in Chapter 8.

Reliability

How do we go about evaluating specific measures? The two main criteria, reliability and validity, are derived from a set of assumptions known as classical test theory (Nunnally, 1978). We will first describe them within that framework, and then reconceptualise them in terms of a newer approach, generalisability theory.

The original idea in classical test theory was that in measuring something, one is dealing with consistency across repeated measurements. The consistent part of the score, the part that is the same across measurements, is known as the "true score". It is conceived of either as an ideal score or as the mean of an infinitely large set of scores. The observed score is the sum of the true score and error, which is conceived of as a random fluctuation around the true score.

Reliability refers to the degree of reproducibility of the measurement. If you repeat the measurement in various ways, do you get the same results each time? The more consistent the measurement, the greater the reliability and the less error there is to interfere with measuring what one wants to measure. It is analogous to the signal to noise ratio in electronics. To put it the other way around, unreliability is the amount of error in the measurement: mathematically speaking, the proportion of error variance in the total score. For example, if you were measuring couples' marital satisfaction using a questionnaire, you would expect the score to stay roughly stable, at least over short time periods. If people's scores fluctuated widely over a two-week interval, the measure would be unreliable and probably not worth using.

Higher reliability is therefore useful because it helps to reveal effects which would be obscured if too much error were present. At the lowest extreme, if the measurement is totally unreliable, you are simply recording random error, not whatever it is you want to measure. Unreliability attenuates the observed relationship between two variables, making it more difficult to detect: any obtained relationship between two measures of the variables is a joint function of the true underlying relationship of the variables and the weakening effect of the unreliability of the measures (Nunnally, 1978). Thus if you are studying the correlation between social support and depression, and your measures of those two constructs are unreliable, the correlation you obtain may be low even though the underlying relationship between the variables is moderately strong.

Types of reliability

The way of assessing reliability depends on the type of measuring instrument and the type of consistency that you are interested in. The most common methods are:

1. *Test–retest reliability.* The measure is administered on two separate occasions (e.g. a week or a month apart). Its reliability is assessed by the correlation between the two scores thus obtained, sometimes called the stability coefficient. There may be a problem with practice effects, unless these are uniform across individuals (and so affect the overall mean, not the correlation).

2. *Equivalent forms reliability.* This is an extension of test–retest reliability, where instead of re-administering the same measure on the second occasion, you use an alternate (or "equivalent" or "parallel") form. (Some instruments have a Form A and a Form B to facilitate this.) Again, the reliability coefficient is the correlation between the scores on the two administrations.

3. *Split-half reliability.* Many scales are composed of a number of equivalent or parallel items, i.e. items that all aim to tap the same construct. For instance, two parallel items on the Client Satisfaction Questionnaire (CSQ-8: Larsen *et al.*, 1979), a widely used self-report scale assessing clients' satisfaction with psychological and other healthcare services, are "Did you get the kind of service you wanted?" and "Overall, in a general sense, how satisfied are you with the service you received?" Even though these items ask slightly different questions, they are assumed to be tapping the same underlying construct, satisfaction with the service. Split-half reliability is assessed by correlating two halves of the test given on a single occasion (split halves). However, because there are several ways in which this separation into halves can be done—e.g. into the first and second half, or into odd and even items—the following method, internal consistency, is better.

4. *Internal consistency* is again used with a scale composed of several parallel items. It is a way of estimating reliability from the variances and covariances of all the items with each other (the details are given in the next section). It is mathematically equivalent to the mean of all possible split-half reliability coefficients.

5. *Inter-rater reliability* is used to check the reliability of observations, for example in coding therapist empathy in a therapeutic interaction or in estimating children's mental ages from their drawings. The people making the ratings may be referred to as coders, raters or judges; the reliability is the extent to which their ratings agree (see the next section for computational details). There are two separate issues: how good is the rating system as a whole and how good are individual raters—for example, should one be dropped?

Reliability Statistics

A number of different statistics are used to measure reliability. For some reason, confusion continues to surround their selection and use (Tinsley & Weiss, 1975). The first step is to establish which scale of measurement is involved, since this determines the reliability statistic to be used. For practical purposes only nominal and interval scales need be considered: ordinal scales can usually be analysed as if they were interval scales.

Nominal scales

As psychologists frequently need to calculate the reliability of nominal scale data, we will provide details of the calculations using a running example.

The first thing to do with two sets of categorical measurements on a variable (e.g. diagnostic judgements across judges, occasions, instruments or settings) is to display the data in a two-way classification table. Consider the following simplified example (Table 4.2), in which two clinicians categorise 100 patients into three groups: schizophrenia, affective disorder and other.

Table 4.2 Simplified example of a two-way classification table

	Clinician 2			
Clinician 1	Schizo	Affective	Other	Total
Schizophrenia	10	20	0	30
Affective disorder	10	20	10	40
Other	0	10	20	30
Total	20	50	30	100

The obvious thing to do is to calculate the percentage agreement between the clinicians from the total number of observations in the agreement cells of the table (indicated by underlining in the table), divided by the total number of observations. In the example, the agreement is $(10+20+20)/100 = .50$, or 50% agreement.

However, since raters categorising patients at random would still agree by chance part of the time, a way to control for chance agreement is desirable. Cohen's kappa is used to correct for this (Cohen, 1960). The formula is:

$$\varkappa = (p_o - p_c)/(1 - p_c)$$

where p_o is the proportion of agreement observed (i.e. the total of the numbers in the agreement cells of the table divided by the grand total). To calculate p_c, first calculate the proportion of observations in each row and column, by dividing each row and column total by the grand total. Then p_c is calculated by multiplying corresponding row and column proportions by each other and adding the resulting numbers together. In the example, the proportion of agreement expected by chance (p_c) is given by $0.3*0.2+0.4*0.5+0.3*0.3=0.06+0.20+0.09=0.35$. Using the formula for kappa, the correct agreement statistic is not .50, but only .23.

With nominal scale data it is further possible to analyse the reliability of any particular category within the scale. That is, you can determine which categories have good agreement and which do not. This is done by collapsing the scale into two categories: the category of interest and all other categories combined. In the example above, the researchers might be interested in the reliability of the schizophrenia category. They would then form a smaller table which amalgamated the two non-schizophrenia categories and calculate Cohen's kappa for that table.

Ordinal and interval scales

When using ordinal and interval scale measurements, additional choices for assessing reliability also appear. To begin with, if you are using a cut-off point on an interval scale (e.g. the Beck Depression Inventory), you may turn it into a binary nominal scale (e.g. "depressed—nondepressed").

More commonly, however, the researcher calculates the association between the two measurements, using the product–moment correlation coefficient, r. This statistic is robust enough to use in most applications (Nunnally, 1978). If more than two raters are involved, a more complicated statistic known as the intraclass correlation can be used (Ebel, 1951; Tinsley & Weiss, 1975; Winer, 1971).

In this case, control for chance agreements is not achieved by calculating a different statistic, but by comparing the obtained statistic against a set of standard values (see the later section in this chapter on standards for reliability and validity). Tests of statistical significance of the correlation coefficient are usually irrelevant here, since in most instances they are too lenient, as the null hypothesis of no agreement at all should be easily rejected in most cases.

If the measurements are to be averaged or totalled, for example, in forming a scale made of several parallel items, then the final reliability will be higher than the average correlations, because adding together multiple items averages out the errors in each of them. The internal consistency of such a scale is measured by Cronbach's alpha; the SPSS Reliability subprogram (Norusis/SPSS, 1990) is a standard way of doing the computations.

Since the internal consistency of a scale increases with the number of items in the scale, it is easier to obtain higher reliabilities with, say, a 24-item scale than with an 8-item one. Thus you might want to see how much increasing your scale by various amounts would improve its reliability. The reliability of such combined measurements can be calculated using the Spearman-Brown Prophecy Formula (Nunnally, 1978):

$$r_{kk} = k(r_{11})/(1 + (k-1)r_{11})$$

where r_{kk} refers to the reliability of the combined measurements; k is the factor by which you are increasing the scale; and r_{11} is the original reliability coefficient.

Two examples of common uses of this formula may clarify its application. In the first example, suppose that you have an 8-item scale with a reliability of 0.6, and you want to know how reliable a 24-item version made up of similar items would be. In this case r_{11} is equal to 0.6 and k is 3 (because the new scale is three times as long as the original one). Then the new reliability would be $3*(0.6)/(1 + 2*(0.6)) = 0.82$. In the second example, suppose that you wish to combine 20 parallel items with a small average intercorrelation of 0.3. Then the scale thus formed would have an excellent reliability of 0.89 ($= 20*0.3/(1 + 19*(0.3))$).

Dimensionality

The above discussion has assumed that the measure is attempting to assess a single construct. If, instead, you suspect that it may be capturing several different dimensions, e.g. on a psychological symptom checklist like the SCL-90 (Derogatis, 1977), then factor analysis should be used to investigate the internal structure of the measure (Gorsuch, 1974; Harman, 1976; Nunnally, 1978; Tinsley & Tinsley, 1987).

Validity

There is a two-step process in developing and evaluating measures: first you look at reliability, then validity. The classical definition of validity is "whether the measure measures what it is supposed to measure". For example, does a depression scale actually measure depression or something else, such as self-esteem? Reliability is a necessary but not sufficient condition for validity. To be valid, a measure must first be reliable, otherwise it would consist mainly of error. For example, if two expert raters cannot agree on whether transcripts of a therapy session show evidence of client denial, then the validity of the denial category cannot be established. On the other hand, a measure can be highly reliable but still invalid, e.g. head girth as a measure of intelligence. Some ways of capturing validity are:

1. *Content validity*: do the items adequately sample the different aspects of the construct that are specified in its definition? For example, does a scale measuring depression capture the components of lowered mood, sleep disturbance, appetite change, etc.?

2. *Face validity*: do the items look right? For example, depression items should ask about low mood, but not about attitudes to authority. Face validity is usually desirable but not always so, for instance the Minnesota Multiphasic Personality Inventory (MMPI) has a number of "subtle items", which were designed to make the test more difficult to fake (Weiner, 1948). Face validity is partly a public relations concept, to make sure that the scale looks right to potential consumers. However, it is critical in qualitative research, where phenomenological validity or self-revealingness is central (Packer & Addison, 1989; Smith & Heshusius, 1986).

3. *Criterion validity*: how well does the measure correlate with a relevant criterion or indicator? This is a central consideration of validity. It can be divided into concurrent validity, in which the scale is correlated with a current criterion (e.g. a depression scale with clinicians' ratings of depression) and predictive validity, in which it is correlated with a future criterion (e.g. the use of a hopelessness scale to predict suicidal behaviour). Note that seeing whether a scale can separate two criterion groups (e.g. can a depression scale distinguish between depressed and non-depressed patients?) also falls under this heading; it is an example of concurrent validity, although it is often wrongly referred to as discriminant validity, which is a different concept (see below).

4. *Construct validity*. This is a much more complex consideration, which as its name suggests examines the validity of a construct rather than of individual methods of measuring that construct, which is what the previous validity types consider (Cronbach & Meehl, 1955). It asks whether the pattern of relationships between measures of that construct and measures of other constructs is consistent with theoretical expectations (what

Cronbach & Meehl term the "nomological net"). The relevant associations can be displayed in a multitrait–multimethod matrix (Campbell & Fiske, 1959), which sets out the correlations between several ways of measuring a number of different constructs. You can then see the extent to which measures of your construct of interest are positively correlated with measures of related constructs (convergent validity) and uncorrelated or weakly correlated with measures of unrelated constructs (discriminant validity). For example, creativity measures would be expected to correlate only moderately with memory and IQ, more highly with curiosity, and so on. The multitrait–multimethod matrix also reveals the extent of method variance, the tendency of measures of a similar type to correlate together. For example, scores from self-report measures are often moderately intercorrelated, even though they are attempting to assess quite different constructs. This is why it is important to use different measurement methods within a study or research program, and not to be reliant on just one viewpoint or measure.

Generalisability Theory

Generalisability theory, developed by Cronbach *et al.* (1972), replaces classical test theory with a relativist, multifactorial model (see also Shavelson, Webb & Rowley, 1989; Wiggins, 1973). It asks, "To which conditions of observation can a particular observation be generalised?" or "Of which other situations can a measurement be considered to be representative?" It de-emphasises the concept of the true score in favour of the central activity of analysing sources of variations in the scores. The theory deliberately blurs the distinction between reliability and validity, a distinction that is not clear cut even within classical test theory (Campbell & Fiske, 1959).

Generalisability theory assumes that measurement comprises three elements: persons, variables and facets (or conditions) of measurement. Four facets can be distinguished: observers, occasions, instruments and settings. Generalisation across these facets corresponds to several of the traditional psychometric concepts (see Table 4.3).

Table 4.3 How reliability and validity correspond to generalising across measurement facets

Facet to generalise across	Traditional psychometric concept
1. Observers: across raters, judges	Inter-rater reliability
2. Occasions: across time	Test–retest reliability Predictive validity
3. Instruments: across various ways of measuring the same thing (including individual items)	Parallel forms reliability Inter-item, split half reliability Internal consistency Convergent validity
4. Settings: across situations (usually going from more to less controlled situations)	Criterion validity Convergent validity

In other words, we are interested in the confidence with which we can generalise measurements to other observers, occasions, instruments or settings. If you are developing a test or scale, it is a good idea to define these conditions, and to determine generalisability across the desired range. Such an examination is referred to as a generalisability study, and is typically set up as a multifactorial research design (see Chapter 7) which incorporates each relevant facet as a factor. However, even if you do not actually carry out such a study, the conceptual framework of measurement facets is still useful for understanding the factors important to your instruments.

The more conceptual forms of validity, i.e. content, face and construct validity, do not fit neatly into the framework of generalisability theory. They can be treated separately, or could be considered as aspects of a fifth facet, level of abstraction: generalisation from the concrete, specific definition of the variable (its operational definition) to other representations—theoretical, empirical and phenomenological—including what it is theorised not to be as well as its relationships to other variables.

Utility

In addition to reliability and validity, measures also vary in their utility or practical value. Measures which are easy to complete or take little time to administer or score are more convenient than measures which require more skill and time. Another aspect of utility is the incremental value of the information provided; this includes information which has not been obtained from other measures and which can be put to good use in the study (Lambert, 1983). For example, this criterion weighs against using the Rorschach projective test as a measure of pre–post change in therapy, because it is time consuming and difficult to administer and score—except in circumstances where the Rorschach provides critical information which can be gathered in no other way. On the other hand, piling on additional easy-to-administer self-report outcome measures may also violate utility considerations (in addition to imposing an unacceptable burden on the research participants), because such measures are typically highly intercorrelated and thus do not add useful information. For example, Jackson and Elliott (1990) found that their ten diverse outcome measures loaded on a single clinical distress factor.

The measurement criteria of reliability, validity and utility relate to the four epistemological truth criteria discussed in Chapter 2. Criterion validity is an instance of the correspondence criterion of truth, while construct validity and internal reliability are examples of the coherence (internal consistency) criterion. Furthermore, inter-rater reliability is an example of the social consensus criterion, and utility fits the pragmatist criterion. Thus the different principles of quantitative measurement are all part of a "system of inquiry" (Polkinghorne, 1983) into the truth of psychological phenomena.

Standards for Reliability and Validity

Reliability and validity calculations are useful both for off-the-shelf measures and for measures that you are constructing yourself. The usual practice is to report the reliability of new or uncommon measures in the method section of a research paper. Table 4.4 gives some suggested standards for evaluating the reliability of

Table 4.4 Suggested reliability standards

Good	.80
Acceptable	.70
Marginal	.60
Pilot only	.50

measurements. These have no logical basis; they are simply rules of thumb that represent current standards in the research community (although there are variations between different researchers and journals). We have drawn from the recommendations of Kraemer (1981) and Nunnally (1978), in addition to our own experience in scale development and editorial reviewing.

Generally speaking, the higher the reliability the better. However, it is possible to have too much of a good thing. Reliabilities greater than .90 may indicate either overkill (i.e. too many items or raters) or triviality (selection of superficial but readily ratable variables).

These standards apply to basic research, as opposed to decision making. As Nunnally (1978) points out, if a scale is to be used for practical decisions (e.g. in deciding whether to detain a client in a psychiatric hospital because of the risk of suicide) then higher standards for reliability must be applied. Nunnally suggests that .90 is an acceptable value in this case.

Values in validity research (i.e. research which attempts to generalise across settings) are typically substantially lower than in reliability research (i.e. research which attempts to generalise across raters, occasions or with measures). In this case, values of .70 or higher generally mean that one is really tapping reliability instead of validity (i.e. that the two measures are really measuring the same thing instead of two different things which are supposed to be related). Validity values of .50 can be considered good, and .30 acceptable, but these recommendations are much more tentative, as they are considerably dependent on the particular application area.

Considerations of reliability and validity are central to evaluating quantitative measures, but whether they can be extended to qualitative methods is debatable. We will address these issues at the end of the next section, after examining the rationale behind qualitative approaches in general.

FOUNDATIONS OF QUALITATIVE METHODS

Qualitative methods describe and analyse their subject matter using ordinary language as opposed to numbers. One source of confusion is that the word qualitative is sometimes also used to refer to nominal scale data, to distinguish it from ordinal or interval scale data (see the preceding section on psychometric theory). However, we will reserve the term qualitative for data that are collected by open-ended questions or by observations that yield verbal descriptions. Simple yes/no responses or nominal categories will be considered as a form of quantitative data. The quantitative–qualitative distinction boils down to whether the data are collected and analysed in the form of numbers (including binary yes/no "0-1" values) or words.

The main advantages of qualitative methods are:

- They enable the individual to be studied in depth and detail. They allow the researcher to address questions that are not amenable to quantification.

- They avoid the simplifications imposed by quantification, since some things cannot easily be expressed numerically. They enable more complex aspects of experience to be studied and impose fewer restrictions on the data or the underlying theoretical models than quantitative approaches.

- The data are usually vivid and easy to grasp: the reports of qualitative studies are usually more readable than those of quantitative studies (except that some qualitative researchers, especially those with post-modernist leanings, tend to write in an impenetrable jargon of their own).

- They are good for hypothesis generation, and for exploratory, discovery-oriented research. They permit a more flexible approach, allowing the researcher to modify his or her protocol in mid-stream. The data collection is not constrained by pre-existing hypotheses.

- They usually give more freedom to the participant than structured quantitative methods. The participant's expression is less constrained by the data-collection procedures.

Historically, the use of qualitative methods can be traced back to the ancient Greek historians, such as Herodotus, and to the early explorers, such as Marco Polo. In their modern form, qualitative methods were first used in ethnographic fieldwork in anthropology and sociology, by anthropologists such as Boas and Malinowski in the early decades of the twentieth century and by sociologists such as those of the "Chicago school" between the first and second world wars, who tended to focus on people at the fringes of society, such as criminals and youth gangs. A classic example of this latter genre is Whyte's (1943) *Street Corner Society*, which studied an Italian–American youth gang in Boston, Massachusetts. Ethnographic methods were initially used to study the "weird and wonderful" (from a Eurocentric viewpoint), e.g. Pacific Island tribal cultures, and have been brought progressively closer to the investigators' own culture, terminating in such specialties as medical anthropology (Helman, 1990).

Some ethnographic work is located on the rather fuzzy boundary between sociology and journalism. Examples are Blythe's (1979) *The View in Winter*, about the experience of being old, and Terkel's (1972) *Working*, in which a variety of people describe their jobs. The distinction is that journalism simply seeks to report accurately, whereas social science brings a body of theory to bear on the subject matter, or seeks to develop theory from the data, and it articulates its assumptions and procedures in order to enable replication.

In clinical and counselling research, qualitative methods were first used in case histories (see Chapter 8), e.g. Breuer and Freud's (1895) early work within the psychoanalytic tradition and Watson and Rayner's (1920) case of "Little Albert" within the behavioural tradition. There is also a tradition of participant observation methods in mental health research, although more often conducted by sociologists than psychologists. Classic examples of participant observation studies are Goffman's (1961) *Asylums* and Rosenhan's (1973) "On being sane in insane places" study. The two main qualitative data-collection methods currently used in clinical and counselling psychology research are in-depth interviewing (see Chapter 5) and qualitative observation (see Chapter 6).

Phenomenology

The qualitative approach is built on phenomenology, a philosophical movement which developed in the late nineteenth and early twentieth century. Phenomenology is the study of phenomena, which can be defined as "that which appear real to the senses, regardless of whether their underlying existence is proved real or their nature understood" (Morris, 1981). Thus phenomenology is the study of the possible appearances, forms, and structures of human experience.

Modern philosophical phenomenology is descended from the rationalist/idealist tradition of Plato, Kant and Brentano. Husserl was its founder; Heidegger, Sartre and Merleau-Ponty were key figures in its development (Jennings, 1986; Shlien, 1970). Their ideas were introduced into psychology by Rollo May, Amedeo Giorgi and others (e.g. Giorgi, 1975; May, Angel & Ellenberger, 1958).

We can distinguish four central assumptions of phenomenology. Firstly, perception is regarded as the primary psychological activity, since our perceptions give rise to what we do, think and feel. Because of this, perceived meaning is more important than objects, facts or physical events—so-called "objective reality".

Secondly, understanding (in German, *verstehen*) is regarded as being the true end of science (in contrast to prediction, for example). The aim is to produce explanations of the person's experiences and actions in terms of intentions/purposes and meanings, usually in the form of a descriptive narrative or lists of themes or defining features.

Thirdly, a key assumption is that of multiple perspectives (epistemological pluralism). Each person's perspective has its own validity (i.e. it is how they see things); therefore multiple, differing perspectives are equally valid and of interest for study. These multiple perspectives constitute different self-worlds (in German, *Umwelten*); for example, the same aging oak tree is radically different when perceived by the forester, the lost child, the fox, or the wood beetle. These self-worlds are the object of study for the phenomenologist (Pollio, 1982).

Fourthly, individuals' perceptions of their self-worlds are based on their own hidden assumptions, which phenomenologists also try to understand. That is, what we perceive is built on multiple assumptions about ourselves, others and the world. These assumptions are the taken-for-granted, unquestioned context for our actions and perceptions. For example, if an acquaintance greets you with "How are you?", you are not usually expected to give an accurate or detailed answer; in fact, to anyone but a close friend it would seem quite odd to do so. Although we accept these underlying assumptions or presuppositions, we are not generally aware of them and do not question them. In other words, they are believed to be "known to all" and part of what "everybody knows that everybody knows" (Garfinkel, 1967). One key set of underlying assumptions is known as the "natural attitude", which comprises the unquestioning belief that "things are what they appear to be", including the ideas that the world is made up of objects (rather than fields of interconnection), and that all sane persons share the same world. In fact, in everyday life it is considered strange or deviant to talk about many of these presuppositions, so that their very obviousness at the same time hides them or prevents them from being noticed.

Doing Phenomenological Research

Phenomenology involves the practice of what is called the phenomenological method, which consists of two key steps or rules: bracketing and describing.

Bracketing

Bracketing is an attempt to set aside one's biases, assumptions and expectations, as far as possible (Husserl, 1931). However, because the underlying assumptions are hidden, it requires a special act of reflection to be able to identify them. This act of reflection has been described in several different ways. The most common description is "bracketing the natural attitude" (or "bracketing" for short), based on the metaphor of separating something from the main meaning of a sentence by putting parentheses or brackets around it. This step is also referred to as phenomenological reduction, using the image of a process of refining metals by burning off the unwanted impurities (biases, presumptions) in order to "get back to the things themselves". Another description of this fundamental process is *"epoché"*, a technical French term which means holding back, pausing or suspension of belief. *Epoché* is not disbelief, but instead involves a process of stepping back from the phenomenon in order to see it as if from the outside, as if we were the proverbial observer from Mars. In short, bracketing involves a special kind of turning away from the natural attitude in which the researcher does not accept a description as a statement about the world, but simply as a statement about an experience of the world.

In the clinical context, bracketing is one aspect of the therapeutic process of empathy in client-centred and experiential therapy. When a client says that he or she is "trapped" in a situation, the client-centred therapist is not particularly interested in whether this is factually the case; what is important is that the client feels trapped (Rogers, 1975). In contrast, novice therapists generally tend to stay within the natural attitude by trying to talk the client out of such "irrational" beliefs, often questioning the facts of the situation. However, in the client-centred tradition one important component of empathy is letting go of one's own presuppositions in order to be open to the client. A version of bracketing can also be found in gestalt therapy, another phenomenologically oriented therapy: "creative predecision" refers to allowing oneself to be open to the possibilities that may emerge in the situation. This is not indecision, but balance, waiting for the experience to emerge (Perls, Hefferline & Goodman, 1951).

In research, you might attempt to bracket by mentally steeling yourself and promising to give up your biases. However, a more fruitful alternative is to begin with a study of your assumptions, as Husserl did. At the beginning of a study, the researcher can conduct a thought experiment of carrying out the study in imagination and using this to identify initial expectations. This thought experiment might also be repeated at the end of the study in order to identify additional expectations which only became clear as it progressed. These expectations take the place of hypotheses in traditional research, but they are not the same. In phenomenological research, expectations are not given a place of honour at the end of the introduction, but are figuratively locked in a drawer until the study is over.

Describing

There are several principles involved in good phenomenological descriptions (Spinelli, 1989). First, focus on immediate, concrete or specific impressions, as opposed to the abstract or general. This is harder than it sounds, and takes practice. You might ask the informant to pick a particular example or incident and go through it in detail. Second, avoid evaluative terms such as "good/bad", "important/unimportant" and their many synonyms and euphemisms (e.g. "ineffective", "helpful"), except where these are part of the experience itself. Third, try to avoid explaining, particularly early in the research. The task is to discover meaning, not invent it. This means avoiding "why" questions or anything which encourages the informant to speculate on causes or reasons; such questions encourage intellectualisation and hinder the focus on concrete experience.

A simple illustration of both bracketing and describing comes from an exercise Garfinkel (1967), an eminent ethnomethodologist, gave to his students. They were asked to go home and observe their families as if the students were boarders in the household. Thus they had to bracket their familiar interpretations and describe without evaluation. Here is an excerpt from one student's record:

> A short, stout man entered the house, kissed me on the cheek and asked "How was school?" I answered politely. He walked into the kitchen, kissed the younger of the two women, and said hello to the other . . . He read until the two women had finished putting the food on the table. The three sat down. They exchanged idle chatter about the day's events. The older woman said something in a foreign language which made the others laugh.
>
> (Garfinkel, 1967, p. 45)

Applications of Phenomenological Research

The basic approach of phenomenology has given rise to a number of research variations, which we can only list here. They include the approaches described in Table 4.5.

Table 4.5 Applications of phenomenological research

Psychology	Phenomenological psychology (reflective empirical method or "Duquesne" school; e.g. Giorgi, 1975; Wertz, 1983)
	Hermeneutical–interpretive research (e.g. Messer, Sass & Woolfolk, 1988; Packer & Addison, 1989; Terwee, 1990)
	Heuristic research (e.g. Moustakas, 1990)
	Protocol analysis (e.g. Newell, 1977)
	Client-centred research (e.g. Rogers, 1985; Shlien, 1970)
	Discourse analysis (e.g. Potter & Wetherell, 1987)
	Existential phenomenology (e.g. Laing, 1959)
Sociology	Field and participant observation (e.g. Taylor & Bogdan, 1984)
	Life history or biographical research (e.g. Denzin, 1989; Taylor & Bogdan, 1984)
	Ethnomethodology (e.g. Garfinkel, 1967)
	Conversational analysis (e.g. Sacks, Schegloff & Jefferson, 1974)
	Grounded Theory (e.g. Glaser & Strauss, 1967; Strauss & Corbin, 1990)
Anthropology	Ethnography (Fetterman, 1989)
	Structuralism (e.g. Levi-Strauss, 1958/1963)
Linguistics	Transformational linguistics (e.g. Chomsky, 1965)
	Linguistic phenomenology (e.g. Austin, 1970; Searle, 1969)

Probably the key distinction is between phenomenologies which emphasise structure, content or both. Thus the original European or philosophical phenomenologists (e.g. Husserl, Heidegger) sought to identify the underlying structures of experience. These are referred to as "essences", "constituents" or "invariants"; they are the defining elements, without which the phenomenon would not be what it is, but would instead be some different phenomenon.

On the other hand, North American Grounded Theory researchers (e.g. Glaser & Strauss) and humanistic psychologists (e.g. Rogers, Maslow) are descriptive phenomenologists who have emphasised the contents of experiences such as empathy or the awareness of dying, attempting to describe what an experience generally looks like or its main variations (analogous to statistical means and standard deviations).

Finally, phenomenological and hermeneutic psychologists (e.g. Giorgi, Packer & Addison) emphasise both structure and contents of experience. They are more interpretive than the descriptive phenomenologists and attempt to synthesise both philosophical and descriptive traditions.

New Paradigm, Feminist and Deconstructionist Approaches

In addition to the varieties of phenomenology described above, some contemporary approaches which build on phenomenology are worth delineating. They can be classified into critical and deconstructionist approaches (Lather, 1991).

Critical researchers attempt not only to understand but also to emancipate their informants; they try to minimise the distinction between researcher and "subject" in order to create research in which informant and researcher are co-researchers who interact as equals. They argue that the act of measuring another human being establishes an alienated relationship between them: the researcher treats the "subject" like an object. This viewpoint is forcefully articulated in Reason and Rowan's (1981) volume on "new paradigm research". Other critical research approaches include neo-Marxist approaches, as well as participatory action research and Freirian research (Lather, 1991).

A similar argument is made by some feminist researchers (e.g. Belenky et al. 1986; Carlson, 1972; Phoenix, 1990; Riger, 1992; Wilkinson, 1986). They see traditional paradigms, where the researcher is in charge of the relationship, as replicating patriarchal power relationships. Their critique is not only aimed at quantification and experimental manipulation, but also at more traditional forms of qualitative interviewing (Oakley, 1981). They argue that to empower women one must listen directly to what the women are saying and respond personally without hiding behind the facade of the objective researcher. Several authors (e.g. Carlson, 1972; Wilkinson, 1986) draw on P. Bakan's (1966) distinction between "agentic" and "communal" approaches. Agentic research, involving separating, ordering and controlling, is seen as a male activity; communal research, involving sensitivity and personal participation, is seen as female. However, in a feminist critique of this stance, Peplau & Conrad (1989) argue that attempts to identify a distinctive set of feminist methods are mistaken, and that feminist researchers should avail themselves of the full range of research methods.

Finally, deconstructionist researchers engage in self-critique, embracing a post-structural, post-modern and post-paradigmatic view of the research process. They see the major task of research as self-critique or "deconstruction" of the cultural, social or epistemological assumptions of their work and that of others. They embrace radical pluralism, and attempt to give air to multiple voices while eschewing any attempt to integrate or bring together these voices into a single message. In essence, they attempt to mirror fragmented, post-modern, multi-cultural society in their research (Lather, 1991). For example, a deconstructionist researcher might present his or her findings as a kind of research collage.

Ways of Evaluating Qualitative Research

As must be obvious from the above discussion, the traditional criteria of reliability and validity do not easily carry over to qualitative approaches, although the concepts of face and content validity can be used. Several scholars are currently attempting to articulate criteria for evaluating qualitative studies (Elliott, Fischer & Rennie, 1994; Henwood & Pidgeon, 1992; Miles & Huberman, 1984; Potter & Wetherell, 1987; Stiles, 1993). Some possible criteria are:

1. *Openness*. Where relevant, the researchers clearly describe their theoretical orientation or biases.

2. *Replicability*. The researchers describe their data collection method (e.g. the interview schedule used) in enough detail to allow others to replicate their work.

3. *Grounding*. The researchers provide enough examples of their raw data to illustrate the themes or categories obtained and to allow the reader to evaluate their findings. They also stay close to the data; any speculations which exceed the data are clearly labelled as such.

4. *Verification methods*. The researchers use methods for checking the validity of results, for example, analytic auditing (e.g. using multiple researchers or an additional person who checks the results against the data), testimonial validity (checking the results with the original informants or similar others); triangulation (examining the phenomenon from multiple, varied perspectives).

5. *Uncovering*. From the point of the view of the reader, the results are not only believable but seem to capture or make sense of the phenomenon, enabling the reader to understand the phenomenon more fully.

SUMMARY AND CONCLUSIONS

The tradition in psychology has been to use quantitative measures almost exclusively. However, recently there has been a reaction against that, which has risked going to the other extreme and throwing the baby out with the bath water. We consider that both kinds of measurement have their strengths and their limitations.

Numbers provide a special vocabulary for research, one which is abstract and precise. The abstract character of numerical descriptions makes them easier to manipulate and summarise than verbal descriptions, but sometimes strips away the meaning, subtlety or ambiguity of the actual phenomena being studied. Thus numbers may give a false sense of precision.

Another strength of the quantitative approach is the existence of a well-articulated theory of measurement. Although advances are being made in this direction in the qualitative approach (see above), many qualitative studies are vulnerable to the criticism that what is being reported reflects the investigator's opinions or biases, which are difficult to separate out from the data.

How Do You Choose a Measurement Method?

We espouse the notion of "methodological pluralism": that different research methods are appropriate for different types of research question (see Chapter 3). For example, qualitative methods are good for questions of definition and description within a discovery-oriented framework—for instance, when you are trying to learn about a phenomenon that has not been previously researched. Quantitative methods are good for questions of covariation and comparison, e.g. looking for relationships between variables.

If at all possible, it is better to use multiple methods of measuring important variables, an approach known as "triangulation". In other words, it is unwise to rely solely on one perspective, source or approach (Campbell & Fiske, 1959; Cronbach & Meehl, 1955; Patton, 1990), because all of these have their limitations. For example, in psychotherapy outcome research it is important to use both self-report and observational measures and to assess client change from the perspective of the client, the therapist and a significant other.

Clinical and counselling psychology may gradually be entering a more pluralist phase out of pragmatism. The evidence for this is in the number of publications urging broader definitions of measurement (e.g. Elliott, Fischer & Rennie, 1994; Guba & Lincoln, 1989; Henwood & Pidgeon, 1992; Kelly, 1990; Patton, 1990). However, the acid test—whether qualitative studies achieve publication in prestigious journals—still reveals a strong quantitative leaning. There is a residual attitude that qualitative methods are second class: the saying of Rutherford, the eminent physicist, that "qualitative is bad quantitative" (quoted in Stewart, 1989, p. 219) expresses this viewpoint succinctly. However, there are signs that a pluralist attitude may be taking root among the newer generation of researchers. Qualitative methods seem to appeal particularly to graduate students in applied social sciences, because they allow much closer contact with clinical phenomena. In the institutions with which we are familiar, an increasing number of dissertations and theses now employ qualitative methods (perhaps so much so that there is a danger that traditional quantitative skills are no longer being acquired).

Combining Qualitative and Quantitative Methods

It is possible to do research that combines both quantitative and qualitative methods; the two approaches to measurement can often complement each other. The combination can take several forms:

1. Beginning research in a new area with qualitative studies, either pilot research or more elaborate qualitative investigations.

2. Building quantitative studies on earlier qualitative research.

3. Using qualitative data to elucidate or explore quantitative findings, either as an adjunct to a primarily quantitative study or as a follow-up investigation.

4. Using quantitative data to elucidate qualitative findings, i.e. the reverse of (3), often found in sociology articles.

5. Giving both kinds of data equal weight in the same study (e.g. case studies by Elliott, 1984; Parry, Shapiro & Firth, 1986).

6. Using separate qualitative and quantitative studies of the same participants, either to address different questions, or to address the same question from different angles (Patton, 1990).

As we hope to have made clear, choosing the measurement method depends largely on the question you are trying to answer. The next two chapters examine practical issues in selecting and constructing measures, covering the two major approaches to psychological measurement: self-report and observation.

FURTHER READING

For an extensive but accessible treatment of the quantitative versus qualitative issues, see Bryman (1988) and Polkinghorne (1983). Nunnally's (1978) excellent text gives a thorough treatment of psychometric issues. It is worth becoming acquainted with two classic papers in psychometric theory: Cronbach and Meehl (1955) on construct validity and Campbell and Fiske (1959) on convergent and discriminant validity. They are both rather heavy going to read in their entirety, but are worth dipping into in order to get a flavour of the reasoning.

Lincoln and Guba (1985) and Patton (1990) give good treatments of qualitative methods, and Taylor and Bogdan (1984) include some illustrative studies. Since many qualitative approaches have their roots in literary theory, it is also worth reading about them in that context. Eagleton (1983) gives an excellent exposition and critique of, among other things, phenomenology, hermeneutics and post-structuralism as applied to the analysis of literary texts.

CHAPTER 5   Self-report methods

When you want to know something about a person, the most natural way to find out is to ask. Research methods which use the approach of asking the person directly are known as self-report methods, and mainly take the form of interviews, questionnaires and rating scales. They are probably the most commonly used type of measure in the social sciences in general and in clinical and counselling psychology in particular.

For example, suppose that you have set up a new counselling service for adolescents and want to evaluate its effectiveness. You ask the users to rate the severity of their problems before and after counselling, using a standardised instrument. You also devise a semi-structured interview to assess the adolescents' overall satisfaction with the service and any specific criticisms they had of it. (Consumer satisfaction studies like this have become important in the UK, with the increased emphasis on accountability to the consumer: see Chapter 10.)

Instead of asking the person directly, you may instead, or in addition, ask someone who knows the person, such as a friend, family member or therapist. This is called using an "informant", a term which has unfortunate connotations of sneakiness. It allows you to get the views of someone who knows the person well and who has greater opportunity than you to observe him or her in a natural setting. It is also useful when the respondent cannot give you reliable information. For example, in research with children it is often useful to have the parents' and the teacher's views of the relevant behaviour. This is why, as we discussed in the previous chapter, a more accurate term would be verbal-report rather than self-report. However, self-report is commonly used to cover reports from both the person of interest and other informants and we will retain that usage here.

Advantages and Disadvantages

The main advantage of self-report is that it gives you the respondents' own views directly. It gives access to phenomenological data, that is respondents' perceptions of themselves and their world. Many psychologists, e.g. Harré (1974) and Kelly (1955), argue that researchers should ask the participant for his or her own view unless there are compelling reasons not to do so. An important principle in Kelly's development of Personal Construct Theory was "If you do not know what is wrong with a person, ask him, he may tell you" (quoted in Fransella, 1981, p. 166). Furthermore, self-report methods can be used to obtain information in situations where observational data are not normally available, e.g. for studying life histories or behaviour during a major disaster.

The disadvantage of self-report is that there are a number of potential validity problems associated with it. The data are subjective and may bear little relationship to "reality", as seen by you or others. People are not always truthful. They may deceive themselves, such as when alcoholics cannot admit their dependency to themselves, or they may deceive the researcher, such as when they do not want to reveal undesirable thoughts or behaviour. Furthermore, they may not be able to provide sufficient detail, or use the concepts in which the researcher is interested.

Arguments arising in two separate fields, psychoanalysis and social psychology, cast doubt on the validity of self-reports. Psychoanalysts emphasise the limits to the person's conscious self-knowledge. They argue that many important feelings and experiences are unconscious, and are prevented by defensive mechanisms such as repression or denial from becoming conscious. Thus a person's accounts cannot be taken at face value. Some psychoanalytically oriented researchers prefer projective measures, principally the Thematic Apperception Test (TAT), the Rorschach and sentence completion methods (Korchin, 1976), which are designed to assess the person's unconscious thoughts and feelings, although the validity of these measures is also hard to establish.

From the social psychological perspective of attribution theory, Nisbett and his colleagues (e.g. Nisbett & Ross, 1980; Nisbett & Wilson, 1977) have argued that people often do not know what influences their behaviour, and that there are pervasive biases in the way that we account for our own and others' behaviour. One common source of bias, known as the actor–observer effect, is the tendency for people to say that their own behaviour is caused by situational factors and that other people's behaviour is caused by dispositional factors (Fiske & Taylor, 1991; Jones & Nisbett, 1971). For example, a student might say that she failed an exam because she did not sleep well the night before, whereas she might say that her colleague failed the exam because of lack of ability. Another related type of bias, known as self-serving bias, is the tendency to take credit for success and deny responsibility for failure (Fiske & Taylor, 1991).

These strictures about the limits of self-report methods are important to bear in mind. However, they do not mean that we should abandon this method of data collection, although it is usually advisable to supplement self-report data with observational data (or at least self-report data from other perspectives). As with other measurement methods, the potential limitations of the data must be considered at the analysis and interpretation stage (see Chapter 11).

Constructing an interview or questionnaire may appear to be straightforward, but the apparent simplicity is deceptive. Most people have been on the receiving end of an irritating, poorly designed questionnaire or interview, often in the context of market research. Designing good self-report measures is an art and a craft. For this reason, it is preferable where possible to use established measures rather than attempting to design your own from scratch. There is a huge literature on research interviews and questionnaires, including several entire books (e.g. Brenner, Brown & Canter, 1985; Kvale, 1983; Moser & Kalton, 1971; Oppenheim, 1966; Patton, 1990; Payne, 1951; Rossi, Wright & Andersen, 1983; Sudman & Bradburn, 1982).

Terminology

An interview is a special type of conversation aimed at gathering information, although the interviewer usually has a written guide, known as an interview protocol or schedule. (Note that this is not the same as the research protocol, which refers to the plan for the study as a whole, including the research design and the sampling procedure, for example.) Interviews are usually conducted face to face, although occasionally they may be done over the telephone.

A questionnaire, on the other hand, refers to a structured series of written questions, which usually generate written responses. Checklists and inventories (the terms are used almost interchangeably) are a type of questionnaire, which present a list of items in a similar format and ask respondents to rate all that apply to them. Two widely used examples of inventories are the Beck Depression Inventory (Beck, Steer & Garbin, 1988), a 21-item scale assessing the severity of depression; and the Symptom Checklist-90 (SCL-90: Derogatis, 1977), a 90-item checklist measuring the number and severity of psychological symptoms. The questionnaire may be composed of several subscales, each of which measures an internally consistent construct (such as the Somatization, Depression and Hostility subscales of the SCL-90).

The term "survey" is widely used but imprecisely defined. It usually denotes a systematic study of a medium to large sample done either by interview or postal ("mail-out") questionnaire. A census means a survey of the whole population (as opposed to a sample from that population; see Chapter 9); the best known example is the government population census.

Mode of Administration

Since self-report data may be gathered either by written questionnaires or by interview, researchers need to consider which mode of administration would better suit their purposes. The advantages of written questionnaires are that:

- They are standardised (i.e. the wording is exactly the same each time).
- They allow respondents to fill them out privately, in their own time.
- They can be used to ensure confidentiality, via a code numbering system, and so they can potentially cover embarrassing, socially undesirable or illegal topics (e.g. sexual behaviour or drug use).
- They are cheaper to administer.

The advantages of interviews are that they can use the rapport and flexibility of the relationship between the interviewer and the respondent to enable the interviewer to:

- ask follow-up questions, in order to clarify the respondent's meaning, probe for material that the respondent does not mention spontaneously and get beyond superficial responses;
- ensure that the respondent answers all the questions;
- give more complicated instructions and check that they are understood;
- vary the order of the questions;
- allow the respondents to ask their own questions of the interviewer.

Clinical and counselling psychologists also find interviews appealing because they can use their interviewing skills. These skills are often envied by psychologists who do not have clinical or counselling training. However, clinicians and counsellors also have some unlearning to do, as conducting a research interview is quite different from conducting a therapeutic interview (we will elaborate on this point below).

Open-ended and Closed-ended Questions

Self-report methods can yield either qualitative or quantitative data, depending largely on whether open-ended or closed-ended questions are used.

Open-ended questions are those that do not restrict the answer, which is usually recorded verbatim. For example, the question "How are you feeling right now?" might yield the responses "Fine, thanks", "Like death warmed up" or "Better than yesterday, at least". However, content analysis may be used at a later stage to classify the responses (e.g. into positive, negative or neutral). Also, some open-ended questions may yield quantitative data (e.g. "How old are you?").

The advantages of open-ended questions are that they enable the researcher to study complex experiences: respondents are able to qualify or explain their answers, and also have the opportunity to express ambivalent or contradictory feelings. Furthermore, their initial responses are less biased by the researcher's framework. Respondents are free to answer as they wish, using their own spontaneous language. However, it is worth considering that data analysis may anyway impose the researcher's framework later and so it may respect respondents' opinions more if you allow them to choose which of your categories their response falls into (Sommer & Sommer, 1991).

The main disadvantage of open-ended questions, from the researcher's point of view, is that it is more difficult to assess the reliability and validity of the data. It is hard to ascertain the extent of such potential problems as interviewer bias and variability, and informant deception, exaggeration, fabrication and forgetting. It is not that the reliability and validity of qualitative self-report measures are inherently lower, they are just harder to evaluate, so that both the researchers and the readers are more likely to feel on shaky ground.

A second issue is that open-ended questions typically generate large amounts of data (the "data overload" problem: Miles & Huberman, 1984), which are usually time consuming to analyse. For a start, most qualitative interviews need to be transcribed, which often takes considerable effort (this is where having sufficient funding to pay for transcription can save the researcher time and frustration). Furthermore, the analysis itself requires considerable effort and skill. This will be considered further in Chapter 11, where we cover analysis and interpretation of qualitative data.

A final issue is that open-ended questions tend to produce a great variability across respondents in the amount of data. Verbally fluent respondents may provide very full answers, while other respondents may find open-ended questions demanding to answer. In particular, open-ended questions in written questionnaires are often left blank, because they require more effort to complete.

Closed-ended questions constrain the answer in some way. Answers are usually recorded in an abbreviated form using a numerical code. For instance, the possible responses to the closed question "Are you feeling happy, sad, or neither, at the moment?", might be coded as 1 "happy", 2 "sad" and 3 "neither/don't know". Responses can be made in the form of a dichotomous choice (i.e. when there are two possible responses, such as yes/no), a multiple choice (i.e. where the respondent has to choose one response from several possibilities), a rank ordering (i.e. where a number of alternatives have to be put in order of preference or strength of opinion), or by ticking one or more applicable items on a checklist.

The advantages of closed-ended questions are that the responses are easier to analyse, quantify and compare across respondents. They also help to prompt respondents about the possible range of responses.

The major disadvantages of closed-ended questions are succinctly summarised by Sheatsley: "People understand the questions differently; respondents are forced into what may seem to them to an unnatural reply; they have no opportunity to qualify their answers or to explain their opinions more precisely" (Sheatsley, 1983, p. 197). For example, in research on stressful life events, information from a checklist measure simply tells you whether an event has occurred, but you have no information about the meaning of the event for the individual. "The death of a pet" might mean that the goldfish passed away, or that an elderly person's sole companion has died. A semi-structured life events interview (e.g. that of Brown & Harris, 1978) allows the interviewer to probe further in order to establish the meaning and significance of each reported event. Furthermore, interview or questionnaire studies that consist entirely of closed questions can be an annoying experience for the respondents, as they may feel that they are not getting a chance to get their views across and may resent being controlled by the format.

The following sections examine qualitative and quantitative methods in turn. This structure is mainly for didactic purposes: we do not wish to polarise the two types of methods artificially. In practice, there is a continuum, ranging from unstructured, open-ended methods, through semi-structured interviews or questionnaires, to structured quantitative methods. As we will say repeatedly, it is possible, and often desirable, to combine both qualitative and quantitative procedures within the same study.

QUALITATIVE SELF-REPORT METHODS

For illustrative purposes, we will discuss qualitative self-report methods mostly in the context of the qualitative interview, since the interview is the most commonly used method within the qualitative tradition. However, there are a number of other qualitative self-report methods, such as:

1. *Open-ended questionnaires,* e.g. the Helpful Aspects of Therapy form (Llewelyn *et al.,* 1988).

2. *Personal documents approaches,* which use pre-existing written records, such as personal journals (Taylor & Bogdan, 1984).

3. *Structured qualitative questionnaires,* e.g. the repertory grid (Kelly, 1955), although repertory grids are often analysed quantitatively (see Winter, 1992).

The Qualitative Interview

In addition to using open-ended questions, qualitative interviews are usually loosely structured, intensive and non-directive: the "in-depth/intensive interview" (Kvale, 1983; Patton, 1990; Taylor & Bogdan, 1984). They have similarities to psychological assessment and to journalistic interviews (but also important differences, which we will discuss below).

There are a number of different forms of qualitative interview (Patton, 1990). The most common is the semi-structured interview with interview guide. Such interviews vary widely in length, from a few minutes to many hours, and take place on one occasion or across many occasions. Most qualitative interviews are one to two hours in length. This is referred to as a long interview by McCracken (1988), but it is short in comparison to the intensive life story interviewing described by Taylor and Bogdan (1984), which may involve up to 50 or even 120 hours of conversation.

Alternatives to the semi-structured interview include:

1. *The informal or unstructured conversational interview,* which is most common as an element of participant observation.

2. *The standardised open-ended interview,* which consists of a uniform set of questions which are always administered in the same order, often with fixed follow-up questions.

3. *The questionnaire-with-follow-up-interview method* favoured by phenomenological researchers of the Duquesne school (e.g. Giorgi, 1975; Wertz, 1983). In this method, open-ended questionnaires are used to identify promising or representative respondents who are then interviewed in detail.

A note on terminology: we will tend to use the terms respondent or interviewee to refer to the person on the receiving end of the interview. Other possibilities are informant or participant. We avoid the term "subject" because of its connotations of powerlessness (see Chapter 9). Likewise, there are a number of models of the relationship between the interviewer and interviewee. These range from traditional "subject" models, in which the interviewee is seen as a passive information provider responding to the researcher's questions, to "co-researcher" models, as in feminist (Oakley, 1981; Wilkinson, 1986) or new paradigm (Reason & Rowan, 1981) research, in which the informant is seen as an equal partner in the enquiry.

Sample interview

The following sample transcript of a semi-structured interview is taken from a larger study investigating factors contributing to the psychological well-being of women recently treated for breast cancer (see Pistrang & Barker, 1992). The interview here focused on patterns of help-seeking, i.e. whom the woman talked to about her concerns and feelings about the illness. The interviewer (I) was Nancy Pistrang; the respondent (R) was a married middle-class woman in her late forties.

The interview begins as follows:

I: What I'm interested in knowing about, is how did you decide who to talk to about the concerns and feelings you had? How did you come to talk to one person over another?

R: Um, I suppose it just happened. This particular friend having just been through it, she was the obvious one to speak to. I have another friend, who'd been through the same thing, but I wasn't very close to her at the time. I mentioned it to a lot of people, my sister for example, and I didn't get the answer I wanted, so

I didn't speak to her again. It was more or less a process of elimination, really.

I: When you say you didn't get the answer you wanted from her, what do you mean?

R: This was all *before* I went for the treatment, when they first wanted to investigate. I telephoned my sister and I said, "Well, I don't know why I ever went for the mammogram. I don't know if I want treatment." And she said, "Oh, you must go and have every treatment." And a couple of people I spoke to said, "There's no question about it, you must have all the treatment that they offer." And I was feeling at that time that I didn't know whether I wanted the treatment, I didn't want to find out. And because it was done in such a positive way, "Oh, you must do this", so I crossed those people off because they weren't going along with how I felt at that moment. But this was, as I say, all before. And afterwards, it just boiled down to this friend who had had the treatment before . . .

I: When you say that it was sort of a process of elimination, and people weren't giving you the answer you wanted, what were you wanting at that point? What would you have liked their response to be?

R: Um, really, to, to go along with me a bit more. Um, with what I wanted to do.

I: Would that have meant just listening to what you were feeling?

R: Yes, yes, I think so, rather than just say, "Do this, do this."

The next excerpt occurs about ten minutes into the interview:

I: Getting on to your husband: you've mentioned a few things about talking to him. To what extent did you feel you could really tell him about what you were feeling, what your concerns were?

R: Anything practical, um, he would help me in any practical way, with any practical concerns. Not so much with feelings. Um, but that sounds—I couldn't talk about them, but he was very considerate of my emotional reactions, my ups and downs. He was very considerate, but I couldn't talk round the feelings to him. We're very different, he's very much a fatalist: you do what you can practically and then you get on with it. I mean, since my treatment's ended, I did say to him, I've been reading about [a well-known actress] going off by herself, and I said, "Perhaps I'd like to go away just for a weekend to a retreat," and he'd go along with all that.

I: So it's not that he's unsympathetic . . .

R: Oh, no, not at all.

I:. . . but his style of dealing with it is to be very practical.

R: Yes, he's very helpful and supportive. [Inaudible] I mean, he *would*, if I said, "I really must talk about my feelings", he would. But I think he would probably feel that he couldn't help much, he likes to feel there's something practical he can do.

This transcript illustrates the richness of the data that can come from a qualitative interview, and also gives a foretaste of the "qualitative overload" problem that is involved in analysing the material (see Chapter 11). It also gives a picture of how the interviewer carries out her aim—to understand the participant's experience—by using questions to clarify and explore, and reflections to confirm understanding. In the following sections, we will look in more detail at the procedures used in conducting qualitative interviews.

The interview guide

The first step is to prepare an interview guide which lists the important areas to be addressed and may have some standard questions to be asked. It is usually a good idea to structure the interview around some sort of framework, which could be, for example, conceptual or chronological. The interview typically starts with general questions, as a warm-up. The standard questions need not be covered in a fixed order, but the guide serves as an *aide-mémoire*, to remind you what needs to be asked. It is vital to pilot test the interview protocol on a few respondents and revise it accordingly.

Young and Willmott (1957), in their classic study *Family and Kinship in East London*, describe the use of their interview guide:

> We used a schedule of questions, but the interviews were much more informal and less standardized than those in the general survey. Answers had to be obtained to all the set questions listed (though not necessarily in the same order), but this did not exhaust the interview. Each couple being in some way different from every other, we endeavoured to find out as much as we could about the peculiarities of each couple's experiences and family relationships, using the set questions as leads and

following up anything of interest which emerged in the answers to them as the basis for yet further questions.

(Young & Willmott, 1957, p. 207)

Interviewing style

The interviewer's general stance should be one of empathic and non-judgemental attention, giving the respondent plenty of space to think and talk, and avoiding bias by not suggesting possible responses. If you are unclear about anything, probe further, although legal-style interrogation is obviously to be avoided.

In order to be an effective qualitative interviewer, you must start with an attitude of genuine interest in learning from others, in hearing their story, and you must be able to listen to them with tolerance and acceptance. The schizophrenia researcher John Strauss (Strauss *et al.*, 1987) realised after 30 years of quantitative research that he had learned very little about the nature of schizophrenia; he felt that he had only really begun to learn when he started to listen to what the patients had to say when he asked them about their experiences.

Your counselling skills, such as empathy and clinical intuition, are very much to the fore here. However, there must be a clear distinction between research and therapy interviews, as almost all therapeutic orientations involve interventions which are inappropriate for qualitative interviewing. For instance, it would be wrong to conduct a qualitative interview in cognitive–behavioural style, as this approach, like most therapies, is ultimately interested in changing the client's thoughts and experiences rather than finding out about them. Even client-centred therapists may engage in too much paraphrasing, which can easily end up putting words in the client's mouth. Perhaps a better clinical analogy is the enquiry phase of projective testing (e.g. "What was it about the card that made you think of a flying pig?"), although this style of questioning does tend to fall into the traditional, detached interviewer model.

Tape-record the interview if at all possible, since extensive note-taking runs the risk of distracting the informant and interrupting the flow of the interview. Therefore, note-taking should be kept to the minimum needed to run the interview efficiently (e.g. topics covered, important things to follow up). However, if you have to interview without a tape-recorder, you then need to take verbatim notes, putting quotation marks around everything said by the respondent. Also, as we suggested in Chapter 3, it is worth keeping a research journal to record your impressions of each interview.

Qualitative interviewing skills

If one is motivated to understand and learn about people by interviewing, then a number of technical skills in information gathering and listening become useful. One useful way to describe these skills is in terms of what are called "response modes" (Goodman & Dooley, 1976), that is, basic types of interviewer speech acts or responses. These can be divided into three headings: responses which are essential for qualitative interviewing; responses which are sometimes useful; and responses which should generally be avoided.

Essential response modes. These lean heavily on the "active listening" responses such as those made famous by client-centred therapy. Thus two key responses are open questions—to gather information and to encourage the informant to elaborate—and reflections—to communicate understanding and to encourage further exploration of content. Process suggestions to guide the discussion ("I wonder if you could tell me about . . .") are also essential for beginning and structuring the interview, while brief acknowledgment responses (e.g. "I see" or "Uh-huh") build rapport and help the informant to keep talking. If a more active, paraphrasing style is used, you are more likely to need to account for the interviewer's possible influence on the data when you do your analysis.

Supplemental response modes. In addition, several other types of response are sometimes useful, although they should not be overused. These include the following: closed questions, to test hypotheses near the end of the interview; self-disclosures, which allow the interviewer to explain his or her goals for the interview and to build rapport by answering questions about him- or herself; and reassurances or sympathising responses ("It's hard"), to encourage openness in the informant.

Responses to be avoided. These include problem-solving advice (telling informants how to solve their problems); interpretations, which try to tell informants why they did something or what they actually felt; disagreements or confrontations, which cut off communication by criticising or putting the informant down (e.g. do not try to "catch" informants in contradictions); and giving informants information (other than information about the structure and purpose of the interview itself).

Useful types of questions. Because questions are so important for organising and structuring qualitative interviews, it is worth describing some of the most important types, in the order in which they typically occur in a qualitative interview.

1. *Entry questions* set the interview up and help the informant to find a useful focus for describing his or her experiences (e.g. "Can you think of a particular time when you were afraid of the dark?", "Can you give me a flavour for what it was like for you to go through that?").

2. *Unfolding questions* request information that will help the informant to unfold his or her story for the researcher (cf. Rice & Sapiera, 1984), including questions about activities ("What were you doing at that moment?"), intentions ("What did you want to accomplish?"), feelings ("What did that feel like, when you were standing there, listening to them talk?"), or sensory perceptions ("What were you noticing as you sat there?").

3. *Follow-up probes* are questions which seek further information or clarification about something which the informant has said. They may be standardised requests for elaboration; if the interviewer listens carefully to what the informant says, he or she can probe more selectively when the informant fails to answer a question clearly or says something which is unclear ("What do you mean when you use the word 'gnarly'?").

4. *Construal questions* are usually saved for later in the interview, because they ask the informant for explanations and evaluations and thus move away from the predominant emphasis on description ("How do you make sense of that?").

5. *Hypothesis-testing* questions are best saved for the end of the interview, in order not to "lead the witness". They can be useful for following up hunches or confirming the interviewer's understanding ("Are you saying that not knowing your diagnosis is what frightened you the most?").

It is also good to keep validity considerations in the back of your mind while interviewing. During the interview, you may become aware of possible inconsistencies which could be:

- *internal*, between different parts of the story;

- *external*, with another source, e.g. a document or another respondent;

- *between manifest and latent content*, e.g. between the words and the tone of voice.

Gently and tactfully enquire about these inconsistencies if they arise. It is obviously counterproductive to take an attitude of attempting to ferret out discrepancies or to accuse the respondent of lying. Discrepancies may not reflect invalidity, they often represent different perspectives or conscious versus unconscious thoughts.

QUANTITATIVE SELF-REPORT METHODS

The literature on quantitative self-report methods is enormous, and we can only hope to skim the surface here. More extensive treatments can be found in Bradburn & Sudman, 1979; Dawis, 1987; Moser & Kalton, 1971; Oppenheim, 1966; Rossi, Wright & Andersen, 1983; and Sudman & Bradburn, 1982. For convenience, we will take written questionnaires and rating scales as our running example; however, everything that we have to say applies equally well to interviews designed to yield quantitative data.

As in other places in this book, we will describe the process from the point of constructing a measure, in order to give readers a better feel for the difficulties that are involved. (These difficulties are, in fact, so great that we strongly advise using an existing measure where at all possible.) The central point is that it is not just reliability and validity considerations that need to be taken into account when appraising a measure; it is worth looking closely at the fine detail of how the measure is put together.

Steps in Measure Development

If you are doing research involving a variable that no existing self-report instrument seems to measure satisfactorily, you may need to construct your own measure. This is not a step to be undertaken lightly, as it is very time consuming and it is also harder to publish work with new or unfamiliar measures. However, because many areas are either undermeasured or are poorly measured, this is a common type of research. One often approaches a new research area only to find that no good measures exist, and then ends up by reformulating the research toward developing such a measure. (A common experience of researchers is to discover that such studies are often widely cited and more influential than their other research.)

If you need to construct a measure, the steps are roughly as follows:

1. Having done a literature search to make sure that no existing instrument is suitable, develop a first draft of the scale based on theory, pilot qualitative interviews or analysis of existing questionnaires.

2. Progressively pilot the scale on respondents nearer and nearer to the intended target population (known as "pretesting"), modifying it accordingly. Expect to take it through several drafts, e.g. first to colleagues, second to friends or support staff (ask them to point out jargon or awkward phrasings), third and fourth to potential respondents. It is often worth while running small, informal reliability and possibly factor analyses on a pilot sample of 20 or 30 respondents to see whether any items should be dropped or added before doing the larger, formal study.

3. Once a satisfactory version of the scale has been developed, do a formal reliability study by giving the measure to a large sample (e.g. over 120 respondents) drawn from a population which approximates the population you are interested in. You can then examine its item characteristics (e.g. means and standard deviations), internal consistency and factor structure. It is also typical to administer the measure twice to some of the participants, in order to assess its test–retest reliability.

4. If the reliability and factor structure are satisfactory, you can conduct appropriate validity studies (see Chapter 4), which

examine the measure's correlations with other criteria or constructs. (These studies may also be combined with the previous step.) The new measure is administered, along with a set of similar and different measures, such as a social desirability measure and measures which should not correlate with the new measure (to establish discriminant validity). It is also important to use measures from more than one type or perspective, in order to reduce the problem of method variance (e.g. to use self-report measures plus observer ratings). The goal is to see whether the measure fits in with the pattern of correlations that would be predicted by the theoretical framework from which it was derived.

Questionnaire Design

Designing a questionnaire involves deciding on the topics to be covered and their sequence, writing the questions or items and selecting an appropriate response scale. We will deal with each of these in turn.

In all aspects of questionnaire design, the golden rule is "take care of the respondent". Put yourself in his or her shoes: ask what the experience of being on the receiving end of the questionnaire is like. Make it as easy and free from frustration as possible. As part of the pilot testing, it is a good idea to fill out your questionnaire yourself (often a salutary experience) and give it to a few friends who will be able to give you constructive criticism.

The goal is to not get in the way of respondents being able to communicate their thoughts and experiences. Trying not to alienate your respondents not only makes sense from a general human relations point of view, but it also makes good scientific sense. Irritated people will not give you good data (or even any data at all—they may just throw away your questionnaire).

Topic coverage and sequence

The questionnaire is often broken into subsections representing different topics or variables. The primary consideration is that, as a whole, it should adequately capture all of the concepts needed to answer the research questions. In other words, the data set should yield an answer to each of the research questions or enable each of the hypotheses to be tested. Once this coverage has been achieved, the issue then is how to order the topic areas within the questionnaire.

It is usually better to start off with easy, non-threatening questions that all respondents can answer (Dillman, 1978). This engages the respondents and helps to establish a rapport with them: even a written questionnaire is a form of interpersonal relationship. Demographic questions (i.e. about the respondent's age, sex, etc.) should usually be placed at the end of the questionnaire, as it is better to start with questions relevant to the topic of the interview.

Structured interviews may adopt the so-called "funnel approach", i.e. they start out broadly and then progressively narrow down. This reduces the risk of suggesting ideas to the respondents or influencing their answers. The interview typically begins with open-ended questions then moves in the direction of increasing specificity and closedness. The veteran pollster George Gallup (see Sheatsley, 1983) recommends the following ordering for public opinion research (e.g. to study opinions about sexual harassment): (1) test the respondents' awareness of, or knowledge about, the issue, then (2) ask about their level of interest or concern, then (3) about their attitudes, then (4) about the reasons for these attitudes, and finally (5) about the strength of their opinions.

Item wording

Having established the coverage of topics, the next step is to write the individual questions or items. The wording of an item is of crucial importance. Sudman and Bradburn (1982) illustrate this by the following anecdote, which opens their book *Asking Questions*:

> The importance of the precise wording of questions can be illustrated by a well-known example. Two priests, a Dominican and a Jesuit, are discussing whether it is a sin to smoke and pray at the same time. After failing to reach a conclusion, each goes off to consult his respective superior. The next week they meet again. The Dominican says "Well, what did your superior say?" The Jesuit responds "He said it was all right." "That's funny," the Dominican replies, "my superior said it was a sin." Jesuit:

"What did you ask him?" Reply: "I asked him if it was all right to smoke while praying." "Oh," says the Jesuit, "I asked my superior if it was all right to pray while smoking."

(Sudman & Bradburn, 1982, p. 1)

As getting the wording right is so important, it is worth heeding some key principles, which are described below.

Neutrality. The language of the item must not bias the respondent, i.e. it should not suggest an answer. Possible errors take the form of leading questions (questions which are not neutral, which suggest an answer), questions with implicit premises (built-in assumptions that indicate the questioner's viewpoint) and loaded words or phrases (ones that are emotionally coloured and suggest an automatic feeling of approval or disapproval). Some examples of such problematic questions are:

"Do you think that . . . ?" and *"Don't you think that . . . ?"* These are leading questions that pull for a "yes" response.

"When did you stop beating your wife?" This has become the clichéd example of an implicit assumption; it assumes the respondent has been beating his wife (Payne, 1951). Such questions are usually to be avoided. However, there are times when implicit premises are useful for normalising behaviour, by giving the respondent permission to talk honestly. For example, studies of sexual behaviour may sometimes use questions such as "How old were you the first time you . . . ?", rather than saying "Did you ever . . . ?"

"How often do you refer to a counsellor?" This question is a subtler variant of the implicit premise; it assumes that the respondent does refer to a counsellor. It would be better to include "if at all", or, even better, to have two separate questions, e.g. "Do you refer . . . ?" and "If yes, how often . . . ?"

"Why don't you refer to a counsellor more often?" This question assumes that referring more often is desirable. A better question would be "What factors influence your referral decisions?"

"How often did you break down and cry?" "Break down" is a loaded phrase which gives crying a negative connotation. In this case, it could simply be omitted.

Clarity and simplicity. It is better to use simple, clear, everyday language, adopting a conversational tone. Make sure that it does not demand a reading level or vocabulary that is too advanced for your respondents. In particular, try to avoid psychological jargon (it is helpful to ask a non-psychologist to read your questionnaire to detect this). Psychologists often become so used to their own technical language that they forget that members of the public do not understand it or find it strange. This is another reason why it is vital to pilot the questionnaire on ordinary people.

Specificity. Lack of specificity gives rise to ambiguities, e.g.:

> *"Do you ever suffer from emotional problems?"* The phrase "emotional problems" means different things to different people. Therefore, it is better to define it or use alternatives. On the other hand, you could leave the phrase as it is, if you want to leave it open to people's own interpretations.

> *"Do you suffer from back pain?"* It is better to give a time frame, e.g. "in the last four weeks", and also to specify the anatomical area, perhaps with the aid of a diagram.

> *"Do you like Kipling?"* ("Yes, I kipple all the time.")

Single questions. It is better to ask one thing at a time. Problems arise with double-barrelled questions, i.e. those with two independent parts:

> *"Were you satisfied with the supervision and range of experience at your last placement?"* The respondent could be satisfied with the supervision but not the range of experience.

> *"Were you satisfied with your placement or were there some problems with it?"* The two parts are not mutually exclusive: the respondent could be satisfied with a placement even though there were problems with it.

> *"In order to ensure patients take their medication, psychiatrists should be given more powers of compulsory treatment."* The respondent could disagree with the implications of the initial premise, but agree with the main statement.

Brevity. Short items are preferable. Sentences with multiple clauses are very difficult to process. As a final example of what to avoid, here is a classic of its kind, from no less a figure than John Watson, which violates this and most other principles of item writing:

> Has early home, school, or religious training implanted fixed modes of reacting which are not in line with his present environment—that is, is he easily shocked, for example, at seeing a woman smoke, drink a cocktail or flirt with a man; at card playing; at the fact that many of his associates do not go to church?
> (Watson, 1919, quoted by Gynther & Green, 1982, p. 356)

Constructing the response scale

A rating scale is where the respondent gives a numerical value to some type of judgement. There are a number of different types of scales: Guttman scales, Thurstone scales, rankings, etc. (Nunnally, 1978). Here we will examine by far the most commonly used one, the Likert scale (see Figure 5.1 for some examples).

The major considerations in constructing response scales are as follows.

How many scale points? The number of scale points can range from two upwards. (Scales with two choices are known as "binary" or "dichotomous", with three or more "multiple choice".) There may be logical reasons for using a certain number of responses: e.g. some questions clearly demand a yes/no answer. However, it is more frequently the case that the response scale must be decided by the researcher. The main issues are:

- The reliability increases with more scale points (Nunnally, 1978), although there seem to be diminishing returns beyond five points (Lissitz & Green, 1975). In addition, most people find it difficult to discriminate more than about seven points.

- By and large, people tend to avoid the extreme ends of scales, a phenomenon known as the "central tendency". This means that it is usually better to have at least five scale points, because if you have three or four you tend to get a lot of responses in the middle.

- Instead of using discrete scale points, another approach is to ask respondents to put a mark on a 10 centimetre line (a visual–analogue scale) and then use a ruler to make the measurement (McCormack, Horne & Sheather, 1988). This is commonly used, for example, in pain research, to assess the intensity of the respondent's pain experience (Pearce, 1983).

Unipolar or bipolar? Response scales can either be unipolar or bipolar. A unipolar scale has only one construct, which varies in degree. For example, a scale measuring intensity of pain might range from "No pain at all" to "Unbearable pain". A bipolar scale has opposite descriptors at each end of the scale (e.g. "Active" at one end and "Passive" at the other). In Figure 5.1, the Agreement and the Happiness scales are bipolar; the others are unipolar.

AGREEMENT
How much do you agree or disagree with each of the following statements?

Disagree strongly	Disagree moderately	Disagree mildly	Neither agree nor disagree	Agree mildly	Agree moderately	Agree strongly
−3	−2	−1	0	+1	+2	+3

FREQUENCY
How often do you . . . ?

Never	Seldom	Sometimes	Often	Very often	Always
0	1	2	3	4	5

DEGREE/STRENGTH
How (much) . . . ?

0 Not at all
1 Slightly
2 Moderately
3 Very

QUANTITY/PROPORTION
How many . . . ?

0 None
1 Very few
2 Some
3 Very many
4 All

Figure 5.1 Examples of anchor words for Likert scales

Mid-point. Bipolar scales may or may not have a mid-point, representing such options as "Don't know", "Neutral" or "Neither one way nor the other". In other words, they may have either an odd or an even number of steps.

The argument against having a mid-point is that people usually hold an opinion, one way or the other, which they will express if you push a little. This procedure is known as "forced choice", e.g. "Do you agree or disagree with the following statements?" Forced choice makes data analysis easier, because respondents can be divided into those expressing a positive and those expressing a negative opinion. However, if a question is worded well you should not have a lot of middle responses in the first place.

The argument for having a mid-point is that neutrality represents a genuine alternative judgement and so it is coercive not to allow respondents to express their opinions in the way that they want to.

Anchoring. Anchoring refers to labelling the points of the scale in words as well as numbers. You usually want to define the steps explicitly, so that people are rating to the same criteria. However, this does make two measurement assumptions:

- that the scale has interval properties (see Chapter 4), i.e. that its steps are all equal (for example, that the distance between "not at all" and "slightly" is the same as between "very" and "extremely");
- that people understand the same thing by all the adjectives.

Try to avoid modifiers with imprecise meanings, e.g. "quite" can sometimes intensify (equivalent to "very") and sometimes diminish (equivalent to "somewhat").

Sometimes researchers just anchor the end-points of the scales, as in visual–analogue scales and semantic differentials (which use pairs of bipolar adjectives, such as good–bad, hard–soft, heavy–light). It is also possible to anchor alternate scale points as a compromise between anchoring every point and only anchoring extremes.

Response sets

Response sets refer to the tendency of individuals to respond to items in ways not specifically related to their content (Anastasi,

1982; Bradburn, 1983). They may be conceptualised as personality variables in their own right. The most commonly encountered response sets are acquiescence and social desirability.

Acquiescence. This refers to a tendency to agree rather than disagree ("yea-saying"). The classic example of acquiescence problems is with the California F-scale (Adorno *et al.*, 1950), which was developed to measure authoritarian tendencies (the F stands for fascist). Early item-reversal studies, in which some of the items were replaced by their inverse, seemed to show that this scale was mostly measuring acquiesence rather than authoritarianism (although there is some dispute about this conclusion, see Rorer, 1965).

The way to get around acquiescence problems is to have an equal number of positively and negatively scored items in the scale. For example, in an assertiveness scale, the item "If someone jumps to the head of the queue, I would speak up" would be scored in the positive direction, while "I tend to go along with other people's views" would be scored in the negative direction. Thus when the items are reversed and averaged, any tendencies towards acquiesence would cancel themselves out.

Social desirability. This refers to a tendency to answer in a socially acceptable way ("faking good"), either consciously or unconsciously (Crowne & Marlowe, 1960, 1964). This is especially a problem in occupational testing, as the following humorous advice for aspiring businessmen illustrates (it also unfortunately embodies a sexist assumption that business executives are always men):

> When an individual is commanded by an organisation to reveal his innermost feelings, he has a duty to himself to give answers that serve his self interest rather than that of The Organisation. In a word, he should cheat . . . Most people cheat anyway on such tests. Why then, do it ineptly? . . . When in doubt about the most beneficial answer, repeat to yourself: I loved my father and my mother, but my father a little bit more. I like things pretty much the way they are. I never worry about anything.
> (Whyte, 1959, p. 450, quoted in Crowne & Marlowe, 1964)

Sometimes respondents may attempt to "fake bad". This may occur in forensic contexts, when offenders may be trying to obtain a lighter sentence or a softer prison regime; in the case of insurance claims for psychological trauma, where people may be trying for a larger settlement; or in the context of being on a waiting list for psychological therapy, where clients may be trying to get help sooner.

Possible ways to get around social desirability problems are:

1. Embed a social desirability scale within the main instrument, such as the Marlowe-Crowne (1960) Social Desirability Scale, the L (Lie) scale on the Eysenck Personality Questionnaire (EPQ: Eysenck & Eysenck, 1975) and the Minnesota Multiphasic Personality Inventory (MMPI: Hathaway & McKinley, 1951), and the K (Defensiveness) scale on the MMPI. These provide a direct measure of the extent of socially desirable responding. Factor-analytic studies have found these scales to have two separate components, self-deception and impression management (Paulhus, 1984).

2. Use a forced choice format, where the respondent chooses between alternatives of equal social desirability. For example, the Edwards Personal Preference Scale (Edwards, 1953), which measures personality dimensions such as achievement and affiliation, has paired items balanced for social desirability.

3. Use "subtle items", on which the acceptability of the response is not apparent, e.g. on the MMPI (Weiner, 1948). However, this practice raises questions about the face validity of the scale.

Assembling the questionnaire and looking ahead

Having designed the questions and response scales, the final task is to assemble it all together. Desk-top publishing facilities can help to make the questionnaire attractive by giving it a pleasing layout with readable typefaces (Dillman, 1978).

It is worth reiterating that, in putting the questionnaire together, the maxim "take care of the respondent" should be primary. One aspect of this is to order the topics in a logical sequence, and make the transitions between different topic areas as smooth as possible. Simple things, such as introducing each section with phrases like "Now I'm going to ask you about . . . ", can make the respondent's task easier.

Think about data analysis before the final draft, as you may want to print computer coding instructions on to the questionnaire. If possible, try some quick analyses to examine your main research questions on the pilot sample.

We will deal with sampling in general in Chapter 9, but there are some issues specific to mail surveys. In postal questionnaires, aim for a response rate of over 60%. Send out reminder letters to increase the initial response (Dillman, 1978). Bear in mind that people who return questionnaires are not usually representative of the whole target population: they tend to be higher on literacy, general education and motivation. In order to conceptualise what would lead to bias, ask yourself why someone would not fill out the questionnaire. It is sometimes possible to estimate bias by comparing respondents with non-respondents on key variables. For instance, in a client satisfaction survey, it may be possible to see if the clients who filled out the survey questionnaire differed from those who did not, in terms of severity of problems or length of time in therapy.

INTEGRATING QUALITATIVE AND QUANTITATIVE SELF-REPORT METHODS

It is worth repeating that our separation of interview and written questionnaire, qualitative and quantitative methods was for didactic, not practical, purposes. Our view is that all four combinations of methods have their uses. It is possible to intersperse written questionnaires within verbal interviews and to combine open-ended and closed-ended questions in the same questionnaire or interview. It is often a good idea to begin and end interviews with general open-ended questions. Questions at the beginning give the respondent a chance to talk before he or she has been much influenced by the researcher's framework; questions at the end give him or her a chance to add anything that may not have been addressed within that framework.

FURTHER READING

Moser and Kalton (1971) is a standard text on the social survey approach to questionnaires. Rossi, Wright and Andersen (1983) provide a useful collection of chapters by eminent authorities; the chapters by Bradburn on response effects, Sheatsley on questionnaire construction and Dillman on self-administered questionnaires are well worth consulting (Dillman's material can also be found in his 1978 book). Dawis (1987) reviews scale construction methods in the counselling psychology context. Polkinghorne (1989) gives a brief overview of qualitative data collection methods. Qualitative self-report procedures, and some illustrative studies, are described in the relevant chapters of Taylor and Bogdan (1984) and Patton (1990).

CHAPTER 6   Observation

In the physical and biological sciences, observation is the only possible measurement method, since the objects of study are animals and inanimate objects. In clinical and counselling psychology, however, researchers have a choice: whether to use observation, self-report or a combination of the two.

Observation can take many forms. You may observe the person in his or her own natural setting, such as at home or at school. The ecological psychology studies of Roger Barker and his colleagues (Barker *et al.*, 1978), which provide extensive accounts of behaviour in community settings, are classic examples of this type. Or you may observe under standardised conditions in the clinic or laboratory. For example, the Strange Situations Test (Ainsworth *et al.*, 1978) assesses a child's reactions to being separated briefly from his or her parent under standardised conditions.

Observation is a special activity, which does not come naturally to most people (Bakeman & Gottman, 1986; Patton, 1990). It is different from evaluation (of whether something is good or bad), explanation (of why something happened) or summary report. Observational methods thus require special training.

We are referring here to observation as a measurement method, not as a research design. Correlational research designs are sometimes called passive observation studies (see Chapter 7); this is something of a misnomer, as they may not use observation at all. Observational data may be used in descriptive, correlational or experimental designs: there is no logical link between the measurement method and the design.

Advantages and Disadvantages

The advantage of observation is that it is a direct measure of behaviour, and thus can provide concrete evidence of the phenomenon under investigation. For example, if you are studying couples' communication, the members of a couple may say in an interview that they "can't communicate and always end up getting nowhere". However, if you actually observe them interacting, you usually get a clearer indication of the nature of their problems, for example one member of the couple may be critical and the other may withdraw. Another example is in studying children referred for behaviour problems, where a father might say "my daughter is disobedient". Observing the interaction between the father and his daughter allows you to see for yourself what goes on between them.

Furthermore, observation enables you to assess the behaviour within its context. Observing the child within his or her family and also in the classroom allows the researcher to identify and measure situational variables (e.g. critical remarks from siblings or peers) that might contribute to a problem behaviour.

Observation is also good for studying behaviour that people may not be aware of (e.g. non-verbal behaviour) or behaviour that is inaccessible using self-report methods (e.g. because of denial, distortion or simply forgetting).

The disadvantage of observation is that it can only be used to answer certain research questions, i.e. where you are interested in overt behaviours. Often research questions are more complex than this, and the overt behaviour is only one aspect. Furthermore, observational studies often have problems with reactivity of measurement: people may behave quite differently if they know they are being observed. A potential solution to the reactivity problem is to observe covertly, but this clearly raises ethical issues about deception (which we address below).

Qualitative and Quantitative Observation

Like self-report methods, observational methods have been developed independently within the qualitative and the quantitative traditions. Although the distinction between the two approaches is not always clear, since qualitative material can be analysed in a quantitative way using content analysis, this chapter will look at each of these traditions in turn.

QUALITATIVE OBSERVATION

In qualitative observation, the observer attempts to record a narrative account, which, like a literary description, brings the scene to life. However, unlike a literary description, the account attempts to be explicit and comprehensive rather than metaphorical and selective.

As we discussed in Chapter 4, the historical roots of qualitative methods lie in ancient Greek and medieval histories and travelogues. Systematic qualitative observation as a research method was developed as part of the ethnographic approach in anthropology, e.g. the early work of Malinowski (1929) in the South Pacific. It also was found in medical case studies, Freud (1905/1977) being the outstanding modern example. The data in such case studies are often not purely observational, as the clinician will also draw upon self-report data (to a major extent in the case of psychoanalytic case studies).

A number of different approaches fall under the umbrella of qualitative observation (Good & Watts, 1989). This section examines two major ones: participant observation and discourse analysis. (The analysis of data obtained from such methods is covered in Chapter 11.)

Participant Observation

Participant observation refers to a procedure in which the observer enters an organisation or social group (such as a hospital or a youth gang) in order to gain first-hand experience of its workings. It is characterised by a period of intense social interaction between the researcher and the people being observed, in their own setting, during which the data are collected unobtrusively and systematically (Taylor & Bogdan, 1984). Thus, participant observation involves:

(1) the observer's immersion in the situation, (2) systematic, but unstructured observation and (3) detailed recording of observations, generally from memory. (Note that the term participant is somewhat ambiguous in this context, as it can refer to both the researcher—the participant observer—and the people being observed—the research participants.)

The observer's role in the setting can be anywhere on the continuum from a complete participant (Gold, 1958), such as when Goffman worked as a mental hospital aide to make the observations in *Asylums* (1961), to a complete observer, such as when traditional ethnographers lived in cultures of which they were not a part. Taylor and Bogdan (1984) warn about the dangers of observing a setting with which one is overly familiar (due either to friendship or to expertise), as the study may be compromised by the researcher's inability to take multiple perspectives and by the temptation to censor reports or data which may offend colleagues or friends.

As the object of study is more often an organisation or social group than an individual, participant observation is more compatible with the framework of sociology and anthropology than with psychology. It is particularly associated with the Chicago School of sociology and with the sociology of deviance. Whyte's (1943) *Street Corner Society*, a study of Italian–American youth gangs in Boston, is a classic example of the genre. Whyte, who was a researcher at Harvard University, spent several years living in the community he was studying and talking to several key informants (mostly members of the gang) in order to understand the structure of their organisation. His observations involved joining in their everyday activities, e.g. gambling, bowling, etc. After each period of observation, he wrote extensive field notes which he later analysed with the help of one of the informants in his study.

The psychological case study (see Chapter 8) can also be considered a form of participant observation, at least where the focus is on describing the therapeutic process, rather than on giving an account of the client's history. Studies of individual therapy represent the psychologically interesting situation where one member of a dyad is observing the development of that dyad. There are many such accounts from the perspective of both the therapist and the client, and Yalom and Elkin (1974) interestingly combine their parallel accounts of the same therapy in one volume.

Research questions

In line with the phenomenological approach, most participant observation researchers try to start with no preconceptions about the phenomena under study. They will often go through a process of bracketing, that is, an attempt to identify their preconceptions and set them to one side (see Chapter 4). Anthropologists, in particular, will attempt to set aside their ethnocentric biases when observing other cultures. However, as we have discussed in Chapter 2, disinterested, theory-free observation is an unattainable ideal, since researchers are always observing from within a theory or world-view that says what is important and what is trivial. The issue is to be aware of and minimise, rather than eliminate, the extent of one's bias. In any case, the participant observer usually attempts to start the observation unconstrained by prior hypotheses or specific variables of interest.

In practice, participant observation research usually has a clear focus (e.g. to study the social structure of a psychiatric in-patient ward). The research questions are usually discovery oriented, of the descriptive and definitional type (see Chapter 3). Participant observation is often conducted within the Grounded Theory approach (Glaser & Strauss, 1967; Rennie, Philips & Quartaro, 1988), in which the theory evolves as the study progresses.

Pragmatics

As we have described in Chapter 3, you often gain access to the research setting via a gatekeeper, for example an administrator or senior doctor who decides whether to allow you into the organisation. It is worth starting field notes at this point, since the process of negotiating entry says much about the workings of the organisation that you are entering. Organisations that are conflict ridden, suspicious or highly bureaucratic will each have their characteristic ways of admitting (and excluding) outsiders.

Once in the setting, you may develop a set of key informants who provide in-depth accounts. However, be wary of overreliance on any one informant, or of implicitly selecting informants whose views agree with your own: try to obtain stories from a variety of perspectives.

In the participant observation tradition, the period of observation lasts at least three months. During this time, the researcher is initially passive and works at establishing rapport, and attempts to avoid being forced into roles (e.g. "volunteer"). Some guidelines suggest that the researcher should limit observation sessions (in order to avoid data overload) and observe at different days and times (e.g. nights, weekends).

It is worth paying special attention to any unusual use of language in the setting, as this can often be a clue to important aspects of its structure (Taylor & Bogdan, 1984). The vocabulary used by staff to refer to clients may give important clues about their underlying feelings towards them. For example, do staff in a drug dependency unit refer to their clients as "patients", "junkies", or "addicts", or is there some local terminology by which they distinguish between different types of client?

Field notes

The observations are recorded in the form of field notes, which describe the setting and the people in it (possibly including a diagram), as well as their verbal and non-verbal behaviour (Taylor & Bogdan, 1984). Good field notes bring the scene to life. In addition, things that do not make sense should be recorded for later clarification, and your own actions should also be noted, in order to help to judge your effect. Finally, your own reactions and interpretations should be labelled as "observer's comments" (OC). However, as in all research, try to separate description from evaluation and be aware of how your preconceptions may be influencing your observations.

The researcher does not usually take notes or make tape-recordings during the observation period, as this often distracts those being observed and is more likely to influence their behaviour. Part of the skill of being a participant observer lies in developing your memory. In order to prevent memory overload, limit your time in the setting to an hour or two and write the notes immediately after leaving the field. Remembering key words and drawing a diagram of the setting are useful strategies. The guiding principle (which applies to other areas of life too!) is: "If it's not written down, it never happened."

To illustrate, here is an excerpt from field notes taken during Taylor and Bogdan's (1984) study of institutions for the mentally retarded (i.e. people with learning difficulties):

> As I get to the dayroom door, I see that all the residents are in the room. I can only see two attendants: Vince and another younger man. (O.C. It's interesting how I automatically assume that this other man is an attendant as opposed to a resident. Several hints: long hair, moustache, and glasses; cotton shirt and jeans, brown leather boots. He's also smoking a cigarette, and a resident, Bobby Bart, is buffing his shoes with a rag. Thus this attendant's dress and appearance differ from that of the residents.) Vince, who is 21, is wearing jeans, brown leather boots, and a jersey that has "LOVE" printed on it. He has long hair, sideburns, and a moustache.
>
> I wave to Vince. He half-heartedly waves back. (O.C. I don't think that Vince has quite gotten used to me coming.) The other attendant doesn't pay any attention to me.
>
> Several residents wave or call to me. I wave back.
>
> Kelly is smiling at me. (O.C. He's obviously happy to see me.) I say to Kelly, "Hi, Bill, how are you?" He says, "Hi, Steve. How's school?" "OK." He says, "School's a pain in the ass. I missed you." (O.C. According to the attendants, Kelly attended school at the institution several years ago.) I say, "I missed you too."
>
> I walk over to Vince and the other attendant. I sit down on a hard plastic rocker between Vince and the other atten., but slightly behind them. The other atten. still doesn't pay attention to me. Vince doesn't introduce me to him.
>
> The smell of feces and urine is quite noticeable to me, but not as pungent as usual.
>
> I, along with the attendants and perhaps five or six residents, am sitting in front of the TV, which is attached to the wall about eight feet off the floor and out of the residents' reach.
>
> Many of the 70 or so residents are sitting on the wooden benches which are in a U-shape in the middle of the dayroom floor. A few are rocking. A couple of others are holding onto each other. In particular, Deier is holding onto the resident the attendants call "Bunny Rabbit." (O.C. Deier is assigned to "Bunny Rabbit"— to keep a hold of him to stop him from smearing feces over himself.)

A lot of residents are sitting on the floor of the room, some of these are leaning against the wall. A few others, maybe 10, just seem to be wandering around the room.

(Taylor & Bogdan, 1984, pp. 248–249)

Ethical issues

Two major ethical issues arise with participant observation: whether the observation should be overt or covert, and what to do when you observe illegal or immoral acts. These issues may also occur in quantitative observation, but have been more salient in the participant observation literature. (We discuss ethical issues in general in Chapter 9.)

There are many examples in the literature where the observers concealed the fact that they were conducting research. This was usually done in settings where reactivity of measurement would have been a major problem. Two well-known examples are Humphries' (1970) study of homosexual activity in men's public lavatories, which generated an enormous debate over its ethics, and Rosenhan's (1973) pseudopatient study. Researchers conducting covert observations argue that the nature of their research precludes their asking the consent of those being observed and that their findings bring benefits that justify the deception. However, such deception is contrary to the ethical principle of informed consent and lays the researchers open to charges of being a voyeur or a spy. Proposed research involving covert observation should be subjected to thorough consultations on its ethical status.

A related issue is what to do in cases where you observe illegal or immoral acts. For example, in the above study of state institutions for the mentally retarded, Taylor and Bogdan (1984) observed attendants beating and abusing residents. They argue that stepping out of the observer role could have had some short-term benefits, in that they may have been able to stop the specific instance of abuse. On the other hand, it would have effectively terminated their project, which may have helped to end the abuse by documenting it and possibly leading to permanent changes in the institutional structure to prevent future abuse. In cases like this, researchers face complex dilemmas to which there are no clear-cut answers.

Quality of the data

Finally, participant observation raises some specific issues of reliability and validity:

- *Reliability*. It is hard to check observer accuracy in participant observation. Although it is theoretically possible to have two or more simultaneous observers in the setting, this is rarely done in practice. It is, however, possible to replicate an observation in several settings at once, as in Rosenhan's (1973) pseudopatient study.

- *Observer bias*. As we have discussed above, observers will to some extent be biased: either consciously, for example by theory, or unconsciously, for example, by ethnocentricity or general world-view. These biases may affect how they see things, or they may get their reports from informants or others who share these same biases (Kurz, 1983).

- *Reactivity*. The presence of an observer may alter the behaviour of those being studied. This reactivity problem is not unique to qualitative approaches; it occurs with all types of observation. Participant observers may be able to mitigate it by allowing time for the people in the setting to become accustomed to them. Some researchers try to get around this problem by conducting covert observations, but this of course raises ethical problems (see above).

Discourse Analysis

The second area of qualitative observation, which we will consider only briefly, is discourse analysis. This also comes primarily from within the sociological tradition, although it is strongly influenced by linguistics (Potter & Wetherell, 1987; Sudnow, 1972). Discourse analysis is a loosely organised area: its main feature is a close study of "texts," which are written or other forms of communication. These include conversations (e.g. therapy transcripts), official documents, television broadcasts or newspaper articles. The focus is on the structure, or the underlying assumptions and meanings, of the text, rather than on what the text is supposed to be describing. Discourse analysis differs from self-report in that the intention is to analyse the text as a sample of communication, rather than to understand what the speaker or author is experiencing or trying to communicate.

Two examples taken from psychotherapy process research illustrate how discourse analysis can be used in the clinical and counselling field. The first is Labov and Fanshel's (1977) well-known study: a book-length report which analyses a single 15-minute segment of a psychotherapeutic interview. The authors use microanalytic methods to examine both the content of the speech and also its paralinguistic features, such as voice spectrogram patterns. They reveal how much rich meaning is carried in subtle, barely noticeable variations in speech, and demonstrate the complex nature of the mutual responsiveness between client and therapist.

The second example is Elliott's (1989a) Comprehensive Process Analysis. This is a method for analysing "significant change events" in therapy, which may range from single responses to short episodes within a therapy session. It uses an elaborate conceptual framework, encompassing multiple observers and both qualitative and quantitative procedures, to ensure that all relevant aspects of the event are examined. An application of this procedure to an actual therapy event is given by Labott, Elliott and Eason (1992).

QUANTITATIVE OBSERVATION

The essence of quantitative observation, aside of course from its using numbers, is that it is systematic: the variables being observed and the methods for observing them are explicitly defined. It is characterised by the use of predefined behaviour codes by trained observers (also called raters or judges) of demonstrated reliability (Bakeman & Gottman, 1986). There are usually a few specific target behaviours, although the observation may be more wide-ranging.

For instance, researchers observing aggression on a children's playground must specify precisely what constitutes and does not constitute an aggressive act, e.g. when does a touch become a push or a punch. They must also specify what aspects of such acts will be recorded, e.g. type, frequency or intensity. Thus, compared to qualitative observation, quantitative methods represent a gain in precision at the expense of a narrowing of scope and context.

Quantitative observations can be used to address several different types of research question. For example, they can be used for questions of description (e.g. "What types of verbal response modes are used by Kleinian psychoanalysts?"); for sequential analysis (e.g. "What types of client response are most likely to follow a therapist interpretation?"); and for questions of covariation (e.g. "Are therapists who use more reflections also rated by expert judges as being more empathic?").

Background

Historically, quantitative observation methods developed in three different applied areas: behavioural observation, psychotherapy process research and content analysis in communication. However, despite differences in language and underlying philosophy, many of the same methodological issues apply in all three areas. We will mostly draw on examples from behavioural observation, as that is where the method is most systematically articulated.

Behavioural observation has its conceptual roots in methodological behaviourism, which argues that psychology should restrict itself to observable behaviour (see Chapter 4). Mischel's (1968) argument, that the validity of traditional, trait-based assessment procedures was unacceptably low, also gave an impetus to the development of practical methods for behavioural assessment in the clinical context. These methods attempt to eliminate inferences to internal constructs (Goldfried & Kent, 1972). There is now a substantial practical literature on behavioural observation in clinical work (Barlow, Hayes & Nelson, 1984; Bellack & Hersen, 1988; Ciminero, Calhoun & Adams, 1986). Since, for the behaviourists, research and practice are closely related, many of the procedures can equally well be applied in research.

Psychotherapy process research began with the work of Carl Rogers and the client-centred group in the 1940s and 1950s, the first researchers to study recordings of actual therapeutic interactions, and the first to quantify aspects of the therapeutic relationship, such as therapist empathy (Kirschenbaum, 1979). Subsequent investigators have examined an enormous number of different process variables, ranging from global constructs, such as the quality of the therapeutic alliance, to specific types of responses used by the therapist and client (Greenberg & Pinsof, 1986).

Content analysis arose out of mass media communication research, which uses such material as newspapers or transcriptions of broadcasts as its subject matter (Krippendorff, 1980; Mostyn, 1985). For example, newspaper stories about mental illness might be content analysed according to the underlying etiological model they espoused. However, the raw material need not be restricted to the mass media. Content analysis can be used with self-report data, transcriptions of meetings, etc. For example, Fewtrell and Toms (1985) used content analysis to classify the discussion in psychiatric ward rounds into categories such as medical treatment, mental state and social adjustment. Content analysis provides a useful means of bridging quantitative and qualitative approaches, in that it applies quantitative analysis to verbal (qualitative) descriptions.

Procedure for Conducting Observations

As we discussed in Chapter 5 in the context of self-report measures, it is usually much better to use an existing measure than to attempt to develop your own. Measure development is time consuming and difficult, and it is hard to publish work with unfamiliar measures. This is equally true in the context of quantitative observation: if at all possible, try to use an existing coding manual and rating scheme with established inter-rater reliability. We discuss observational measures here from the viewpoint of the researcher developing a measure in order to clarify the process involved in measure development, rather than to encourage researchers to do it themselves.

Developing the measures

The first step in quantitative observation is to define operationally the behaviour to be observed. The goal is to specify the behaviour sufficiently well, so that it can be observed with high inter-rater reliability. Often this means that the behaviour should be defined so that it can be rated without the raters having to make large inferences, but for some variables this may not be possible. Giving

Table 6.1 Five dimensions of observed clinical process

1. *Perspective of observation*: What is the point of view of the person doing the observation?
   - Researcher (trained observer)
   - Clinician (participant–professional)
   - Client/help-seeker (participant–index person)
   - Significant other (e.g. family member)

2. *Person/focus*: Which element of the clinical process is studied?
   - Client or client system (i.e. individual, family)
   - Clinician or clinical (service) system (e.g. therapist, agency)
   - Interaction of client and clinician (e.g. relationship, "fit")

3. *Aspect of behaviour*: What kind of behaviour or process variable is studied?
   - Intention/form: the intention behind or the grammatical form of what is said or expressed (speech acts, intentions, tasks, response modes)
   - Content: what is said, meant or expressed (ideas, themes)
   - Style: how it is done, said or expressed (e.g. duration, frequency, intensity, paralinguistic and non-verbal behaviour, vocal quality, apparent mood, interpersonal manner)
   - Quality: how well it is done, said or expressed (e.g. accuracy, appropriateness, acceptability, skilfulness)

4. *Unit level*: At what level or "resolution" is the process studied? (selected useful units)
   - Sentence (idea unit): a single expressed or implied idea
   - Action/speaking turn (interaction unit): a response by one person, preceded and followed by actions by another person or different actions by the same person
   - Episode (topic/task unit): a series of action/speaking turns organised by a common task or topic, within an occasion
   - Occasion ("scene" unit): a time-limited situation in which two or more people meet to do something (e.g. session)
   - Relationship (interpersonal unit): the entire course of a relation between two people
   - Organisation (institution unit): a system of relationships organised toward a specific set of goals and located in a setting (e.g. a clinic)
   - Person (self unit: includes a person's system of relatively stable beliefs and characteristics and history of self, other and organisational involvements

5. *Sequential phase*: What is the temporal or functional orientation
   taken toward a unit of process (i.e. towards what happened
   before, during and after the unit)?
   • Context ("antecedents"): what has lead up to a unit of
     process? (e.g. previous speaking turn, earlier relationships)
   • Process ("behaviours"): the process which is targeted for
     study at a given level (unit)
   • Effects ("consequences"): the sequelae of a unit of process
     (e.g. reinforcement, treatment outcome)

(Adapted from Elliott, 1991, by permission of the Guilford Press)

clear definitions is harder than it seems, as even apparently simple
behaviours such as head nods or eye contact, or giving advice in
therapy, pose difficulties in delineation. More inferential constructs,
such as the level of empathy offered by a therapist, are extremely
difficult to define.

Developing a good definition is an incremental process. It is often
useful to start with informal qualitative observation, supplemented
by a review of the literature on the variable of interest and similar
observational measures. The researcher then develops an initial
version of the codes and tries them out on some data. This leads
to revision of the codes and an iterative cycle of testing and revision.
When the researcher has a coding system that he or she can use,
the next step is to attempt to teach the codes to raters, who then
test them out on data. This leads to a further cycle of testing and
revision, which improves the likelihood that others besides the
researcher will be able to use the measure (a form of inter-observer
generalisability referred to as "portability"). Finally, the researcher
utilises the measure in a study, the results of which may suggest
yet more revisions, and so on.

Since many different dimensions of behaviour can be examined,
it is useful to have a framework to help guide one's choices. Table
6.1 gives one such framework, adapted from research on
psychotherapy and counselling processes (Elliott, 1991). Similar
schemes could easily, be constructed for other content areas of
observation, e.g. school classrooms or family interaction. Which
aspects of which dimensions are important depends partly on the
variables being observed and partly on the research questions.

Methods of observation

Having specified the dimensions of the behaviour to be observed, the next step is to choose an observational method. There are several choices (Altman, 1974; Barlow, Hayes & Nelson, 1984; Cone & Foster, 1982).

1. *Narrative recording*, that is writing an account of what happens, is equivalent to qualitative observation. It is used in the behavioural observation and ecological psychology traditions (e.g. Bakeman & Gottman, 1986; Barker *et al.*, 1978). It is useful for hypothesis generation, measure development and for arriving at ideas about causal relationships (in behavioural terms, the antecedents, behaviours and consequences). It is also good for low-frequency behaviours. However, it is difficult to assess the reliability of such observations. Narrative recording is often a preliminary step to developing more structured methods of observation.

2. *Event recording* yields the simplest form of frequency data. The observer counts every occurrence of the behaviour within the entire observation period. For example, if the observation is focusing on counsellor response modes used during a 50-minute counselling session, the final frequency count might be 17 questions, 22 reflections, 4 interpretations and 1 self-disclosure. The advantages of event recording are that it is simple and can be done alongside other activities; the disadvantages are that you can not analyse sequences or other complexities and it is hard to maintain observer attention.

3. *Interval recording*. The observation period is divided into equal intervals (e.g. a 50-minute counselling session might by divided into ten 5-minute intervals) and the number of behaviours is recorded during each interval. In whole interval sampling, the behaviour is only recorded if it is present for the whole of the interval, as opposed to partial interval sampling, when it can be present for any part of the interval. The advantages of interval recording are that it allows sequences to be analysed and gives a rudimentary estimate of both the frequency and the duration of a behaviour. It may be adapted to record several behaviours concurrently. Having timed intervals also helps to keep the observers alert. The disadvantages are that it requires more

observer effort, as timing has to be attended to as well as the behaviour.

4. *Time sampling.* Observations are made at specific moments of time, e.g. every five minutes or every half hour. When observing large groups, scan sampling can be used, where each member of the group is observed sequentially. For example, Hinshaw *et al.* (1989) used scan sampling to observe the social interaction of boys with a diagnosis of hyperactivity or attention deficit hyperactivity disorder. The advantages of time sampling are that it yields a direct measure of the prevalence of a behaviour in a group and is good for high-rate, continuous behaviours. The disadvantages are that low-frequency behaviours may be missed, as they might only occur between the observation times.

5. *Sequential act coding* records events in the order in which they occur. In contrast to event recording, it usually requires a comprehensive coding system to cover all possible events. (Event recording may just focus on one or two events, e.g. specific aggressive acts in a school classroom.) To take a simplified example, researchers may classify events in a therapeutic interaction into client speech (C), therapist speech (T) and silence (S). A sequential act coding record might then look like this: C,T,S,C,S,C . . . This strategy is ideal for sequential analysis, because it relies on natural units (such as talking turns), not artificial units (such as time segments). However, disagreements on where the units begin and end can complicate reliability, and the method is inefficient if you are not interested in sequences.

6. *Duration recording* is similar to sequential act coding, except that the focus is on timing the occurrence of a single behaviour rather than categorising events into codes. You can measure both duration, the interval between the start and the end of each behaviour, and latency, or the interval between behaviours. For example, Brock and Barker (1990) used this method to study the amount of "air time" taken up by each staff member during team meetings in a psychiatric day hospital.

7. *Global rating scales*, in which the observer makes an overall judgement, often of the quality of the behaviour, are usually based on a long period of observation. Clinical examples include the Brief Psychiatric Rating Scale (BPRS: Overall & Gorham,

1962), which rates several dimensions of psychiatric symptomatology, and the Global Assessment Scale (GAS: Endicott *et al.*, 1976; used as Axis V in the DSM–III–R diagnostic system) which rates overall psychiatric impairment. Global ratings, e.g. of empathy or transference, are frequently used in therapy process research (Greenberg & Pinsof, 1986). These are less precise than the behavioural observation methods, in that the observer is being asked to quantify an impression or judgement. On the other hand, global ratings are useful for complex or inferred events and can provide helpful summaries of events. Many global rating scales have acceptable reliability.

8. *Environmental measures.* Finally, an interesting category of observation is where the focus is on the psychological environment as a whole, rather than on specific individuals within it. Procedures include behavioural mapping, where the observers record the pattern of activity in a given environment. For example, Kennedy, Fisher and Pearson (1988) used behavioural mapping to study the patterns of patient and staff activity in a spinal cord injury unit over the course of a single day. Environmental observation may also involve the use of unobtrusive measures (Webb *et al.*, 1966), in which features of the physical environment are used to yield data on patterns of activity. Classic examples of unobtrusive measures are using the wear and tear on a carpet as an index of the popularity of museum exhibits, and using the accretion of graffiti as an index of youth gang activity.

Mechanics

The mechanics of recording the observations need to be as simple as possible, so that the recording does not interfere with making the observations themselves. Possible aids include coding sheets, stopwatches, counters and electromechanical devices. The observations may be conducted in real time, or the interactions may be recorded on audio- or videotape for subsequent observation and analysis.

It is not always necessary or possible for the researchers to do the observations. An alternative is to use self-monitoring methods (Bornstein, Hamilton & Bornstein, 1986). In self-monitoring, participants are taught to carry out the observations themselves. For example, an evaluation of couples' therapy might include the participants keeping written records of the number and type of arguments that they have over the course of several weeks. Self-monitoring can also be done by proxy, e.g. parents could keep records of their child's sleep problems. The advantage of self-monitoring is that it allows the researcher to obtain observational data over long time periods and also from private settings.

If you have sequential data from your observations, e.g. if you use interval or time sampling methods, you can do more complex analyses of how the behaviours develop over time. This is a technical topic involving some advanced statistics; Gottman and Roy (1990) describe some of the options.

Reliability and Validity Issues

An advantage of quantitative observation methods is that they facilitate the calculation of reliability (see Chapter 4 for a discussion of the statistical aspects of assessing inter-rater reliability). One practical problem is observer drift, where observers start out with high reliability, but then tend to develop idiosyncratic rules as the observation proceeds. To prevent this occurring, it is important to monitor the observers' reliability continually.

The main validity issue, aside from problems with the operational definition of the variables, is the reactivity of observation. As we discussed above in the context of qualitative observation, the act of observing may alter the behaviour being observed. The only solution is to make the observations as unobtrusive as possible, and to allow time for the people being observed to become habituated to the observers' presence. This may be easier with qualitative observation, which is usually done to a more leisurely timetable.

Practical suggestions for working with raters

Researchers have various strategies available for maximising the reliability and validity of observer ratings. These include:

* design or selection of measures with clear, well-defined variables and good examples of categories;

- careful selection of an adequate number of raters;
- thorough training and management of raters.

Here we summarise some suggestions from Elliott (1989b; see also Moras & Hill, 1991) on how best to work with raters.

Selection. It is usually better to work with motivated volunteers, such as top students in advanced undergraduate seminars, who are interested in a career in clinical or counselling psychology. Occasionally you may have to drop a rater's data later due to consistent unreliability, so it is best to start out with at least three and preferably four raters.

Training. It is a good idea to begin with a didactic presentation and modelling of the rating process, followed by group rating. This is followed by extensive practice, including weekly feedback on progress and problems. The SPSS Reliability procedure offers very useful analyses for this, providing solid evidence both of progress and of problems which can be shared with the group. For example, reliability checks will tell:

- which categories or dimensions show reliability problems;
- whether a reliability problem is general (spread across all raters) or specific (restricted to one or two raters);
- if a rater has misunderstood a category;
- if two raters have formed a clique which sets them apart from everyone else;
- if particular raters differ greatly in their base rates for a category.

Training should continue until all or almost all scales reach a coefficient alpha (for 3 to 4 raters) of at least .70. (As discussed in Chapter 4, categorical measures can be readily converted into sets of dummy variables, 0 for "absent" and 1 for "present", to provide feedback on specific categories.)

Management. The management and nurturing of raters is at least as important as their selection and training. To foster the research alliance, communicate to the raters that their views will be taken seriously (e.g. encourage them to contribute to the refinement of the rating system and let them know when they rate a particular piece of data more accurately than you do). Regular meetings and feedback during the rating process help to prevent alienation and produce more reliable and valid data. As far as practicable, raters should feel part of the whole research process, including the conceptual framework and the research questions (where it is not necessary to keep them blind), analyses and interpretation; this may occasionally also include co-authorship, if important contributions are made to the study.

FURTHER READING

There is a good treatment of participant observation in many texts (e.g. Friedrich & Lüdtke, 1975; Kurz, 1983; Taylor & Bogdan, 1984). We recommend perusing some of the classic studies using this method, which are mostly stimulating and readable, e.g. Goffman (1961) and Whyte (1943). For more detail on discourse analysis, the volume edited by Sudnow (1972) is an interesting collection of the early work of many of the major figures in the area; Potter and Wetherell (1987) give an up-to-date assessment from a social–psychological standpoint. Quantitative observational methods are reviewed by Cone and Foster (1982; Foster & Cone, 1986) and by Weick (1985). Greenberg and Pinsoff (1986) review measures for use in psychotherapy process research, while Hill (1991) gives an excellent introduction to therapy and counselling process research in general.

CHAPTER 7   Foundations of design

The previous chapters have covered the groundwork and measurement phases of the research process; the current chapter begins our examination of the design phase. This order, first measurement then design, roughly corresponds to how you go about planning an actual research project: you usually begin by thinking about which variables interest you and how to measure them; next you think about design. From now on, we will put measurement behind us, working, for didactic purposes, on the assumption that it is unproblematic, even though we recognise that this is often not the case.

To clarify what we mean by the term design, think of the questions "what?", "when?", "where?" and "who?" about a research project. Measurement is the "what" aspect: what is being studied, what measurements are made. Design, in the sense we are using it here, denotes "when, where and on whom" the measurements are taken: the logical structure which guides the data collection of the study. It covers such topics as the relative merits of large-sample versus single-case studies, what type of control group, if any, is required, and who the participants will be. The terms research design and experimental design are also sometimes used in a broader sense to denote everything to do with planning and executing a research project, synonymous with our use of the term research methods. The more restricted sense of the term design that we are using here is consistent with its use in the statistical literature (e.g. Keppel, 1991; Kirk, 1982; Winer, 1971). Whether the broader or narrower meaning is intended is usually clear from the context.

Research designs can be classified into two fundamental types: experimental and non-experimental designs. Experimental designs involve an active intervention by the researcher, such as giving one type of therapy to some clients and a second type to others, whereas in non-experimental designs, the researcher takes measurements without changing the phenomenon or situation to be measured. These two approaches to design reflect "the two disciplines of scientific psychology" (Cronbach, 1957, 1975). Experimentalists are often more concerned with examining the causal influence of external factors, which are amenable to experimental variation; non-experimentalists are often more concerned about person variables. The remainder of this chapter will elaborate on this experimental/non-experimental distinction and make various important subdistinctions.

NON-EXPERIMENTAL DESIGNS

Non-experimental designs can be classified, according to their aims, into descriptive and correlational designs. As is clear from their name, descriptive designs usually aim simply to describe, whereas correlational designs aim to examine associations, make predictions or explore causal linkages.

Descriptive Designs

Examples of descriptive studies frequently appear in the mass media: public opinion surveys, in which respondents are asked which political party they intend to vote for; the national census, which reports, for instance, the percentage of people living in various types of accommodation; and national unemployment statistics. However, the importance of systematic descriptive research is generally overlooked by clinical and counselling psychologists, although such research is often extremely valuable as a preliminary step in understanding the phenomena of interest. Some examples of descriptive studies are:

- *Descriptive epidemiological research*, which aims to document the incidence and prevalence of specified psychological problems.

- *Consumer satisfaction research*, which assesses clients' satisfaction with a psychological service.

- *Phenomenological research*, which aims to understand the nature and defining features of a given type of experience.

Naturally enough, quantitative descriptive studies report their results using descriptive statistics. This is a technical term covering such statistics as percentage, mean, median, incidence and prevalence. However, it is rare to have a purely descriptive study, as researchers often want to examine the associations between two or more variables of interest. For example, in a consumer satisfaction study you may want to see whether there is an association between client satisfaction and various client demographic characteristics, such as gender or ethnicity. This leads on to the next type of study, the correlational design.

Correlational Designs

Correlational studies aim to examine the relationship between two or more variables: in technical language, to see whether they covary, correlate or are associated with each other. Such studies are also called naturalistic or passive observation studies, in contrast to those studies employing active methods of experimental manipulation. (Passive observation, as a research design, should not be confused with participant observation, which is a data-gathering method.) In correlational studies, researchers measure a number of variables on each participant, with the aim of studying the associations between these variables. However, the term correlational design is slightly misleading, as it suggests that the associations between the variables will be assessed using a correlation coefficient. The drawback of correlation coefficients is that they only measure one type of association between variables, that is, a linear association. As we are also including the examination of non-linear associations between variables under this heading (although this is infrequently done by most researchers, who tend to restrict their attention to linear models), the term relational designs is perhaps more appropriate (Elliott, in press). However, we are retaining the term correlational designs for consistency with the established literature.

A well-known example of a correlational design is Brown and Harris's (1978) study of the social origins of depression, which looked at the association between women's depression, their experience of stressful life events, and vulnerability factors (such as low intimacy with the husband and loss of the mother before the age of 11). Correlational designs are often also used to examine individual differences, for example in predicting which clients will respond best to a psychological intervention. Examining such correlations is a common preliminary step in causal explanation. That is, one typically tries to predict what will happen to whom (e.g. in therapy or counselling) in order to understand why it happens (e.g. what are the effective ingredients) or in order to improve an application (e.g. to learn how to enhance its outcome).

Measure development research, which aims to develop, evaluate or improve measures, uses both descriptive and correlational designs. As we discussed in Chapter 5, developing a new measure involves extensive testing of reliability and validity, which uses a correlational framework, as well as providing normative data for the measure, which is a form of descriptive study.

Correlational designs may be cross-sectional, in which all observations are made at the same point in time, or they may be longitudinal, in which measurements are made at two or more different time points. Correlational studies may use simple statistical measures of association, e.g. chi-square and correlation coefficients, or multivariate methods, such as multiple regression, factor analysis and log-linear procedures. They may also use more advanced techniques which aim to map the underlying structure of complex data sets. These go under various names: path analysis, latent structure analysis, causal modelling or structural equation modelling (e.g. Bentler, 1980; Fassinger, 1987; Hoyle, 1991; Kenny, 1979). They are used for evaluating how well conceptual models generated from previous research or theory fit the data.

Path analysis is both a method of conceptual analysis and a procedure for testing causal models. Its framework is a useful tool for planning research, even if you never actually carry out a formal path analysis, in that it forces you to spell out your theoretical model. It is also useful for trying to conceptualise the results of correlational studies. The essence of path analysis is to tell a story in diagrammatic or flow-chart form, showing which variables influence which others: the examples of different kinds of causal linkages that are given in the next section are depicted in the form of elementary path diagrams.

Correlation and causation

The main drawback of correlational studies is that they cannot be used to make unequivocal causal inferences. The golden rule of research design is: *correlation does not equal causation*. Correlations may strongly suggest causal influences, but they cannot firmly establish them. You will see this rule frequently ignored in popular journalism and sometimes in the professional literature too.

The existence and nature of causal relationships involve some difficult philosophical problems (Cook & Campbell, 1979; White, 1990). When we say that A causes B we imply four conditions: (1) that A and B covary, i.e. that they tend to occur jointly, (2) that A precedes B, (3) that the relationship between A and B is not spurious, i.e. that it is not explained by other variables and (4) that if A changes then B will also change. In psychology and epidemiology we are often dealing with probabilistic rather than deterministic causes. Thus, when we say that smoking causes lung cancer or that poverty causes ill health, we are not talking about certain causation (there are always exceptions) but about increased risk.

Correlational studies will often establish the first condition, that two variables, A and B, covary. Information relevant to the second condition, how they are ordered in time, will usually also be known. The third condition, that of eliminating spurious explanations, can be addressed to some extent with a correlational framework. Let us take a simplified example, derived from client-centred theory (Rogers, 1957). Suppose that variable A represents counsellor empathy and variable B represents the client's outcome at the end of counselling. A number of inferences about their causal relationships are possible, as depicted in the following simple path diagrams (in which an arrow indicates the direction of a causal relationship):

1. $A \longrightarrow B$

That is, A causes B: higher counsellor empathy brings about better client outcomes.

2. $B \longrightarrow A$

That is, B causes A: clients who are improving in counselling tend to generate more empathic responses from their counsellors.

3.

A and B are both caused by a third variable, C, e.g. client psychological-mindedness. Clients who are more psychologically minded could possibly have better outcomes in counselling and also generate more empathy in their counsellors. Thus the apparent causal relationship between A and B is spurious: it is entirely explained by the third variable C. The presence of such third variables which provide competing causal explanations prevents the researcher from drawing accurate causal inferences and thus reduces the study's validity.

4. $A \longrightarrow D \longrightarrow B$

A does not influence B directly, but indirectly via D. Higher counsellor empathy could lead to increased client self-exploration, which could then lead to better client outcome. Variables such as D are known as "mediating variables" (Baron & Kenny, 1986).

5. $A \longrightarrow B$
$\uparrow$
E

The relationship between A and B differs according to the value of E. E could represent the type of client presenting problem, e.g. anxiety or depression, or a demographic variable such as age or gender. Variables such as E are known as "moderator variables" (Baron & Kenny, 1986).

The art of research design is to collect data in such a way as to examine the influence of third variables and of mediating and moderator variables, in order to be able to draw clear inferences about the relationships between the variables under study. This helps to address the third of the above conditions for inferring causality, that the apparent causal relationship is not spurious.

However, correlational designs are less good at addressing the fourth of the above conditions, that changing variable A produces a corresponding change in variable B. This is the essence of experimental designs: to manipulate systematically one or more variables at a time. It is done in order to demonstrate that influencing one variable influences another, and also to rule out possible competing causal explanations.

EXPERIMENTAL DESIGNS

The word experiment has the same root as the word experience: both derive from the Latin for try or test. Psychologists usually think of an experiment as a study involving random assignment to two or more groups or conditions. However, this view is a recent development (within the past 30 to 50 years) and represents a methodological narrowing under the influence of positivism and biomedical research. Previously, and today in its ordinary usage, an experiment refers to "the action of trying anything, or putting it to proof; a test, trial", or "an action or operation undertaken in order to discover something unknown, to test a hypothesis or establish or illustrate some known truth" (*Oxford English Dictionary*). Thus an experimenter interferes with the natural course of events, in order to construct a situation in which competing theories can be tested. These theories often concern causal influences between variables. In physics, formal experimentation began with Galileo, who attempted to test his theories of dynamics by rolling balls down inclined planes (Chalmers, 1990), initiating what we now call the hypothetico-deductive method. Before Galileo, science had relied on drawing generalisations from passive observations and from informal trial-and-error experimentation.

Experimental designs are of particular interest to clinical and counselling psychologists because therapeutic work itself can be thought of as an experimental intervention. The therapist considers a problematic situation in the client's life, forms a hypothesis about what is causing it and what might be done to improve it, attempts to change something about it and then observes the results. Here the tentative connotation of experiment is apt: if the intervention does not work, the therapist then repeats the cycle by reformulating the problem, trying something else and once more observing the results. This experimental approach to therapeutic work lies at the core of the applied scientist model (see Chapter 2).

As an example, most psychotherapy outcome studies use an experimental design. For instance, Sloane *et al.*'s (1975) classic comparative outcome study randomly allocated clients to receive either psychodynamically oriented psychotherapy or behaviour therapy from therapists who were experts in each orientation, or to be on a wait-list control group. (The results showed that both groups of therapy clients improved more than the controls, and that the behaviour therapists showed a marginal superiority over psychodynamic psychotherapists on some of the outcome measures.)

Terminology

There is a considerable amount of terminology in the experimental design area. The treatment that is varied by the experimenter is known as the independent or experimental variable; the measure of the experimental variable's effect is known as the dependent or outcome variable. In the Sloane *et al.* study, the independent variable is the experimental condition (psychodynamic therapy, behavioural therapy or control group) and the dependent variables are the measures of psychological symptoms, severity of distress, social functioning, etc. that were used to assess client improvement. (Note that the term "group" is often used to denote one of the experimental conditions; it is potentially confusing in this application, as it wrongly suggests that group rather than individual therapy was used.) Frequently, one or more of the groups in the design is subjected to an experimental intervention or manipulation, while another group provides a control group, because it is used to rule out or control for the influence or one or more third variables. For example, the wait-list group in the Sloane *et al.* (1975) study was used to control for the potential therapeutic benefits of the assessment interviews and also any effects of client expectancies on outcome.

Many types of experimental designs are covered in the specialist statistical literature (e.g. Keppel, 1991; Kirk, 1982; Winer, 1971), such as factorial designs, repeated-measures designs and Latin squares; here we will look at some of the simpler ones. The statistical method used in experimental studies is usually the analysis of variance (ANOVA), or related methods such as the t-test, multivariate analysis of variance (MANOVA), the analysis of covariance (ANCOVA) or discriminant analysis. However, before examining some specific examples, it is helpful to consider some general principles of validity, in order to provide a framework for thinking about the strengths and weaknesses of any given design.

Cook and Campbell's Validity Analysis

The influential work of Campbell and his collaborators (Campbell & Stanley, 1966; Cook & Campbell, 1979) is indispensable: Cook and Campbell's (1979) book is required (although sometimes difficult) reading for all applied psychology researchers. Their ideas were developed in the context of designs that attempt to infer causality, which is why we are addressing them here under experimental designs. However, the concepts can be applied to all designs, descriptive and correlational as well as experimental. They are invaluable both for planning one's own research and for evaluating other people's.

The central thrust is an analysis of different types of validity. We are now using the concept of validity in a broader sense than in Chapter 4, when we discussed the reliability and validity of measures; we will be talking about the validity of the conclusions you can draw from the study as a whole. Campbell and Stanley (1966) introduced the fundamental distinction between internal and external validity. Internal validity refers to the degree to which causality can be inferred from a study: i.e. in the language of experimentation, is the independent variable producing the changes in the dependent variable? External validity, which is sometimes called ecological validity, refers to the degree to which the results of the study may be generalised over time, settings or persons to other situations, e.g. whether an intervention in a clinical trial was delivered in a realistic or an artificial way.

Cook and Campbell's (1979) expanded treatment considered statistical conclusion validity in addition to internal validity (both of which concern interpreting covariation) and construct validity in addition to external validity (both of which concern the generalisability of the study—construct validity can be seen as assessing generalisability across different measures). Here, we shall just look at internal validity. Construct validity, which derives from the work of Cronbach and Meehl (1955), is covered in Chapter 4. External validity is covered in Chapters 9 and 11, and statistical conclusion validity is covered in Chapter 11.

The central dilemma is that there is often a trade-off between internal and external validity. It is possible to achieve high internal validity in a laboratory, where the researcher can exert considerable control. A common criticism of social psychology experiments of the 1960s and 1970s was that, although they had achieved high internal validity by being conducted in a controlled laboratory setting with a homogeneous population (often male American undergraduates), they had in so doing sacrificed their external validity, i.e. their generalisability or real-world relevance: in a nutshell, the designs were clever but artificial (Armistead, 1974; McGuire, 1973). The same criticism also applies to early analogue studies of behaviour therapy, which were conducted in artificial laboratory conditions with volunteer clients (Shapiro & Shapiro, 1983). Conversely, field research, which is conducted in natural settings with clinical populations, usually has high external validity. Unfortunately, this is often at the expense of internal validity, since experimental control is much more difficult to obtain in field settings, for a variety of reasons which we discuss below.

The thrust of Cook and Campbell's work is that every design is imperfect, but that it is possible to analyse systematically the potential consequences of these imperfections, which are known as "threats to validity". The researcher's task is to try to achieve an optimal design given the aims and constraints of the research. To quote one prominent psychotherapy researcher, "The art of outcome research design then becomes one of creative compromises based upon explicit understanding of the implications of the choices made" (Shapiro, 1989, p. 164). Cook and Campbell's framework is an indispensable tool for thinking about the consequences of such compromises.

Cook and Campbell's Classification of Research Designs

In addition to analysing validity issues, Campbell and his collaborators (Campbell & Stanley, 1966; Cook & Campbell, 1979) also proposed a taxonomy of designs. They introduced the fundamental distinction between quasi-experimental and experimental designs. Quasi-experiments are defined as "experiments that have treatments, outcome measures, and experimental units, but do not use random assignment to create the comparisons from which treatment-caused change is inferred" (Cook & Campbell, 1979, p. 6). However, in the light of our earlier discussion about the term experiment being too narrowly defined within psychology, it seems preferable to use the more precise terms non-randomised and randomised designs instead of quasi-experiment and experiment (cf. Rossi & Freeman, 1985). Cook and Campbell give an extensive listing of possible non-randomised and randomised experimental designs. Here we will consider the most commonly used ones as illustrative examples.

Non-randomised Designs

One-group posttest-only design

This design can be depicted in the following diagram:

$$X\ O$$

The notation is that X stands for a treatment, that is, something that is done to the participants, for example, a clinical intervention. O stands for an observation or measurement, of one or of several variables. The diagram can also be used to depict designs where X is not an experimental treatment, but rather some other event that occurs to the participants, such as a disease or a disaster.

The one-group posttest-only design, originally labelled the one-shot case study by Campbell and Stanley (1966), is the simplest possible design. It is characterised as a quasi-experimental design because of the experimental intervention, X, although it can also be conceptualised as a type of descriptive study. One common application is in consumer satisfaction studies, in which clients are surveyed during or after a psychological intervention to find out how they felt about it. This design is useful for generating hypotheses about causation. However, it is almost always insufficient for making inferences about causal relationships, because it assumes *post hoc ergo propter hoc* (because B happens after A, B must result from A).

However, as Cook and Campbell (1979) note, this design should not be dismissed out of hand in research aimed at testing causal explanations. It can be rescued if enough contextual information is available, and especially if one takes a detective-work approach, looking for signs or clues to causality—what Cook and Campbell (1979) call "signed causes". In the clinical and counselling context, such signs might include posttreatment ratings of perceived change or retrospectively completed estimates of pretreatment levels of functioning. (The detective metaphor is appropriate here, since Sherlock Holmes and his successors based their causal inferences— concerning whodunnit—on *post hoc* data.)

One-group pretest–posttest design

$$O_1 \; X \; O_2$$

This design is like the previous one with the addition of a premeasure, which then allows a direct estimate of change over time. For example, this design is commonly used in evaluating the outcome of a clinical service. The psychologist might administer a measure of problem severity, such as the Beck Depression Inventory (Beck, Steer & Garbin, 1988), to all clients before and after therapy.

However, it is not immediately possible to attribute any change in the outcome variables to the experimental treatment, X. This is because, as in the previous design, it is not possible to infer *post hoc ergo propter hoc*. For example, a newspaper headline in a feature on mental health stated: "Despite being the target of suspicion, the evidence that antidepressants work is indisputable: more than two-thirds of people taking them recover" (*Observer*, 12 January 1992). The inference appears to be that since taking antidepressants is associated with a good chance of recovery, therefore they must cause that recovery. (To see the logical fallacy more clearly, try substituting taking antidepressants with some less obviously psychotherapeutic activity, such as brushing one's teeth.) In addition, the implication that the antidepressants cause recovery is further called into question since the recovery rate of depressed people who did not take antidepressants is not supplied—perhaps two-thirds of them recover also. The availability of such data would result in a non-equivalent groups pretest–posttest design, described below.

Cook and Campbell (1979) provide a checklist of possible threats to internal validity in this design. For researching the effects of psychological interventions, the most important ones are:

- *Endogenous change*, which refers to any kind of change within the person. The most important instance is spontaneous recovery, also called spontaneous remission, which means recovery occurring with no apparent external reason (such as a formal psychological intervention).

- *Maturational trends* refer to the growth or maturation of the person. This is a special case of endogenous change. It is, of course, especially relevant to research with children, who may often "grow out" of their psychological problems.

- *Reactivity of measurement*, where the act of making a measurement changes the thing being measured (see Chapter 4). For example, there may be practice effects on a psychological test, where participants perform better on a second administration of a test because they have learned how to respond. As a second example, clients in the wait-list control group in the Sloane et al. (1975) study were extensively interviewed as part of their initial assessment, which may well have had clinical benefits.

- *Secular drift*, i.e. long-term social trends, such as a general reduction in smoking over the years.

- *Interfering events*, i.e. events other than the experimental intervention that occur between the pretest and the posttest. For example, fiscal changes such as increased cigarette or alcohol taxation; crisis; or war.

- *Regression to the mean*. A group of participants in a study may be selected on the basis of extreme scores on some measure, e.g. clients for a therapy study might be selected on the basis of high scores on an anxiety scale. If that measure is unreliable, then the scores on the posttest will tend to move closer to the mean even if the therapy was ineffective, i.e. they will tend to show that clients have improved. This is because the extreme scores on the pretest will have partly reflected measurement error, which will tend not to be as extreme on the posttest.

One further problem in interpreting the findings from this and other experimental designs has to do with the construct validity of the experimental intervention (Cook & Campbell, 1979). It is important to note the distinction between internal validity and the construct validity of the experimental intervention. The question of internal validity asks whether change can be attributed to the intervention, X, or to something else; whereas the question of the construct validity of the experimental intervention accepts that X is producing the change and asks what about it (what construct) actually accounts for the change? Some possible construct validity problems are:

- *Confounding variables*. Confounding means occurring at the same time as, and thus inextricably bound up with. In the Sloane et al. (1975) study discussed above, the type of therapy was confounded with the person of the therapist, since each of the two interventions (behaviour therapy and psychodynamic therapy) was delivered by two different sets of therapists. It is possible that the differences between the therapies could simply have reflected differences in the personality or skill of the therapists who delivered them.

- *Expectancy effects*. Clients may benefit from a service simply because they expect to, rather than as a direct result of what the service actually delivers. This expectancy effect is related to the placebo effect in drug studies, where patients may benefit from pharmacologically inert treatments.

- *Hawthorne effect*, where the introduction of a new procedure, whatever it is, produces a beneficial change. This effect takes its name from a study in occupational psychology, in which decreasing the level of illumination in a factory was found to increase industrial output, but so also was increasing the level of illumination (Roethlisberger & Dickson, 1939).

The difference between O_2 and O_1 (i.e. the total pre–post change) is sometimes called the gross effect of the intervention (Rossi & Freeman, 1993). The net effect is defined as the effect that can reasonably be attributed to the intervention itself, that is, the gross effect minus the effect due to confounding variables and error. In clinical research it is often a good first step to use a simple design such as the one-group pretest–posttest to demonstrate that a gross effect exists at all. Subsequent studies can then use more sophisticated designs with control or comparison groups to estimate the net effects, rule out the effects of possible confounding variables and examine which components of the intervention are actually responsible for client improvement.

Non-equivalent groups posttest-only design

$$NR \quad X \quad O$$
$$NR \qquad\quad O$$

In the notation *NR* stands for a non-randomised assignment to experimental groups.

This commonly used design is like the one-group posttest-only design, except that the group receiving the experimental treatment is compared to another similar group that did not receive the treatment. For example, an intervention could be instituted on one hospital ward and another ward be used as a comparison group. Unlike the previous and the following design, this provides no direct estimate of pre–post change. It can be used for retrospective studies, where there is no premeasure and postmeasures are all that one can manage in the circumstances. (This design can also be regarded as correlational, since what is being studied is the association between the group membership variable and the outcome variable.)

In clinical and counselling applications, *X* usually represents an intervention. However, the conceptual framework of the design can also be used for comparing groups who differ in having experienced some life stressor, a kind of negative experiment. The effects of this stressor or experience (e.g. childhood sexual abuse, adoption, parental divorce) can then be evaluated and causal hypotheses generated. Similarly, some epidemiological case-control studies can also be considered under this category, where *X* would represent having some illness or predisposition to illness, e.g. being HIV positive (Schlesselman, 1982).

The major threat to internal validity in this design (and equally in the following design) is uncontrolled selection. That is, since the assignment to groups is not random, one cannot assume that the two groups were the same before the treatment, *X*. Participants in the different groups may differ systematically on, for example, motivation, problem severity or demographic characteristics. Even if the researcher is able to compare the groups on these variables, there still may be other important systematic differences that are not tested for.

Non-equivalent groups pretest–posttest design

$$NR \quad O \quad X \quad O$$
$$NR \quad O \quad\quad\quad O$$

This commonly used design combines the features of the previous two, and helps to rule out some of the associated internal validity threats. The group in the lower part of the diagram that does not receive the experimental intervention is called a control group. Several different types of control are possible, ranging from no treatment at all to an alternative comparison treatment. The type of control group depends on the research question: whether you are trying to show that the experimental treatment is as good as or better than an established treatment, or simply better than nothing at all. We will discuss these issues more fully below under the heading of the randomised groups pretest–posttest design.

The design can easily be extended to encompass two or more experimental or control groups. A well-known example of the design in practice is the Stanford three community study (Farquhar *et al.*, 1977), which studied the effects of the mass media and community interventions on the prevention of heart disease. It was conducted in three small towns in California. One town received only the pre–post measurement, another a sustained mass-media campaign, and a third mass media plus community intervention in the form of face-to-face instruction. The results showed encouraging effects for the mass-media condition, which were augmented in the community support condition.

Eysenck's (1952) review of early psychodynamic psychotherapy outcome studies can also be considered within the framework of this design. Eysenck compared studies of patients treated with psychoanalysis or psychodynamic psychotherapy with other studies of the spontaneous remission rates of broadly comparable groups of untreated patients. The outcome variable was the patient's rated improvement at the end of therapy, or about two years after diagnosis in the case of the comparison groups. Eysenck famously concluded that no effect for psychotherapy could be demonstrated, since the two-thirds improvement rate of therapy clients was much the same as the two-year spontaneous remission rate of untreated clients. This quasi-experimental design, as Eysenck acknowledged at the time, has many weaknesses: his conclusions were subsequently much argued over (Bergin & Lambert, 1978), and led to the refinement in research designs that culminated in Sloane *et al.* (1975) and other more recent studies.

Prospective case-control studies, where a cohort of individuals is studied longitudinally to study the impact of a disease or of stressful life events, can also be considered under this category (Schlesselman, 1982). Because participants are being studied prospectively, then measures are obtained before the event of interest. For example, a cohort of elderly people might be studied at one-year intervals to examine the psychological impact of bereavement by comparing the individuals who were bereaved with those who were not.

As in the previous design, the main threat to internal validity is uncontrolled selection: that the two groups may differ systematically in ways other than the presence or absence of the experimental treatment. Sometimes experimenters try to compensate for differences in the two groups by statistical methods, e.g. analysis of covariance or multiple regression (Cook & Campbell, 1979). For example, if the experimental group turns out to be younger than the control group, age might be used as a covariate in the analysis (often described as partialing out the effects of the covariate, in this case age). This can be misleading when the non-equivalent groups are drawn from two different populations: it is like trying to equate an elephant and a mouse by adjusting for their relative weights. However, such analyses may be performed in randomised designs, when the groups are drawn from the same population. Another approach, which Rossi & Freeman (1993) refer to as "constructed controls", is to try to match participants in each group on key variables, such as age, gender and problem severity. However, this is difficult to accomplish and again can be misleading if the groups represent two different populations.

The interpretability of this and other non-randomised experimental designs can be enhanced by adding pretests and later assessments to examine the process of change more closely and also by adding specific control groups to deal with specific internal validity threats.

Interrupted time-series design

$$O_1 \quad O_2 \ldots O_{20} \quad X \quad O_{21} \ldots O_{40}$$

This design extends the one-group pretest–posttest design to cover multiple measures over time. It has a different rationale to the previous designs, in that it attempts to pinpoint causal influences by looking at discontinuities between a series of baseline measures and a series of follow-up measures (we have arbitrarily depicted 20 baseline and 20 follow-up points; in practice there may be considerably more). It is good for studying naturally occurring chronological data and can be used to analyse existing data from large samples, e.g. to look at changes in national alcohol or tobacco consumption following taxation changes, or reductions in injuries following legislation on car seat-belt legislation (Guerin & MacKinnon, 1985). It can also be used in single case designs, in which participants serve as their own controls (see Chapter 8). The main threat to internal validity is the presence of interfering events: that something else may occur at the same time as the treatment, X, that will produce changes in the outcome variable.

Randomised Designs

Randomised experimental designs (as opposed to quasi-experimental or non-randomised designs) are characterised by the random assignment of participants to experimental conditions. The main advantages of randomisation are that it rules out selection bias as a threat to internal validity and that it allows the use of the statistical theory of error. Randomised experimental designs enable the experimenter to manipulate a single variable at a time, and thus any relationships established between the independent and dependent variables are more likely to fulfil the four conditions for inferring causality discussed above.

The theory of experimental design was developed by Fisher in the 1920s. The early work was mostly done in agriculture, looking at how crop yields were affected by different fertilisers or different varieties of grain. This agricultural origin accounts for some of the terminology which is still used to describe different experiments (e.g. split plots or randomised blocks refer to parts of fields); it also provides another area of application in which to picture specific designs. Here we will tend to focus on designs in therapy outcome research; it is the area we know best, it is one in which a lot of work has been done and it is of interest to most clinical and counselling psychologists. The statistical textbooks (e.g. Keppel, 1991; Kirk, 1982; Winer, 1971) cover many different experimental designs. We will illustrate the issues in the context of a commonly used design in clinical research, the randomised groups pretest–posttest design:

$$R \quad O \quad X \quad O$$
$$R \quad O \qquad\;\; O$$

In the notation, R denotes a randomised assignment of participants to experimental conditions. Such assignment needs to be done without bias, in order to ensure that each participant has an equal chance of being in each condition. This may be done in several ways, e.g. by using random number tables, by flipping a coin or by drawing lots. On the other hand, non-random methods of allocation, e.g. by assigning the first ten participants to the experimental group and the next ten participants to the control group, may introduce systematic error (Cook & Campbell, 1979). One common example of this design is in clinical trials (often referred to as randomised controlled trials or RCTs), in which a new therapy or drug is tested against a pill placebo or a no-treatment control (Schwartz, Flamant & Lellouch, 1980).

The independent variable, i.e. whether or not the participants receive the experimental intervention, is known as a "between-groups factor" (since it divides the participants into groups). The design depicted above is said to have a between-groups factor with two levels (i.e. the experimental group and the control group). This basic design may be extended in several ways. Some examples are described below.

More than two levels. There can be more than two levels of the between-groups factor, i.e. there may be more than one experimental group or more than one control group. For example, the type of intervention factor in the Sloane *et al.* (1975) study had three levels: psychodynamic therapy, behaviour therapy and a wait-list control group.

Multi-factorial designs. In these designs there is more than one between-groups factor. For example, the second Sheffield Psychotherapy Project (Shapiro *et al.*, 1994) had two between-groups factors: a two-level therapeutic orientation factor (psychodynamic-interpersonal versus cognitive-behavioural forms of therapy) and a two-level length of intervention factor (8 sessions versus 16 sessions).

Repeated-measures design. The pretest–posttest design is an example of a repeated-measures design, i.e. one in which the same individuals are assessed at two or more points in time. Additional levels of the repeated-measures factor may be introduced, e.g. there may be a follow-up assessment six months or a year after the intervention has ended.

Blocking factors. These are factors that represent participant individual difference variables (e.g. type of presenting problem) within the overall research design (this is also referred to as stratification). Such factors are included in order to examine their effect as potential moderator variables or in order to ensure that the experimental groups are balanced on crucial variables. The procedure is that participants are grouped into the relevant categories before the randomisation to experimental treatments takes place. For example, the Sloane *et al.* (1975) study had two blocking factors: client gender and the client's initial level of distress. The researchers first allocated potential clients to the appropriate cell in a 2×2 table (men/women by high/low distress). Then they randomly assigned groups of clients from the same cell to the therapists within each of the two experimental treatment conditions (behaviour therapy or psychodynamic therapy) or to the wait-list control group.

In the educational context, analyses addressing the question of which interventions work best for which students are referred to as aptitude–treatment interaction studies (Snow, 1991), and this terminology has been adopted in the study of the psychological therapies (Shoham-Salomon & Hannah, 1991). Designs that incorporate many treatment and client factors can attempt to analyse what treatment works best in what circumstances, or as Paul's (1967) question states: "*What* treatment, by *whom*, is most effective for *this* individual with *that* specific problem, and under *which* set of circumstances" (p. 111). However, such large-scale designs, within what has been called the matrix paradigm (Stiles, Shapiro & Elliott, 1986), have serious practical limitations, not least because of the number of participants required.

Analysis of covariance designs. These are similar to blocked designs, but are used when it is known that the individual difference variable being investigated, e.g. psychological-mindedness or severity of symptoms, has a linear relationship to the outcome variable. Analysis of covariance is a more powerful procedure than blocking, but the statistical assumptions that must be met before it can be employed are more restrictive. Keppel (1991) gives a useful discussion of the relative merits of the blocking versus the analysis of covariance approach.

Control and comparison groups

The terms control and comparison group are rather loosely defined. The implication of the term control group is that some active ingredient in the experimental group is missing (as in agricultural experiments, where the experimental groups might be given various fertilisers and the control group none), whilst the term comparison group implies that a viable alternative treatment is given. We will use the term control group as a shorthand for control or comparison groups. As we discussed above in the section on the non-equivalent groups pretest–posttest design, several types of control are possible, depending on the research questions, although the selection of suitable control groups for psychotherapy research (and other applications) raises ethical, scientific and practical problems.

No-treatment controls. These, in which the control group receives no treatment at all, are used to provide a maximum contrast with the therapy under investigation. However, there are serious ethical issues in withholding treatment from clinically distressed clients. Researchers must balance the possible harm resulting from an untested treatment with the denial of benefit resulting from a potentially effective one. This problem may not arise in a quasi-experimental design, since a group of clients who might be unable (for geographical or other reasons) to receive the experimental treatment could be used as a control group. Furthermore, given that the effectiveness of established psychological therapies has been demonstrated (Stiles, Shapiro & Elliott, 1986), no-treatment controls are scientifically uninteresting (Parloff, 1986): they are only useful in the early stages of a research programme.

Wait-list controls. This kind of control often provides a workable compromise, particularly with short-term treatments or mildly distressed clients. Clients who are randomly assigned to the wait-list group are given the same initial assessment, and then placed on a waiting list to receive the intervention once the experimental group has completed it (e.g. Sloane *et al.*, 1975). Thus they control for the reactivity of the initial assessment.

Expectancy and relationship control groups. These control for expectancies of benefit or instillation of hope and also for the effects of contact with the therapist. In drug trials, where patients are given a sugar pill or other pharmacologically inert substance, they are known as placebo control groups. However, this terminology is too imprecise for the psychological context: it is better to be specific about what the control group is intended to control for. In pharmacology, clinical trials are ideally done in a double-blind study, where neither patients nor experimenters know which experimental condition each patient is in. However, even in drug trials, this is not always practicable because patients may be able to distinguish between active drugs and placebos, e.g. by their side effects. In psychological applications, any control treatment should appear as credible to clients as the experimental one. Expectancy or relationship controls generally work well for clinical trials in drug research, but are questionable for psychotherapy research, where relationship factors or aspects of the therapeutic alliance (so-called "non-specific factors" or "common factors": see Frank, 1973) are generally the best predictors of outcome.

Comparative treatment groups. These use an established comparison treatment, rather than a placebo, that might be expected to have a benefit equal to that of the experimental treatment (Parloff, 1986).

They provide an ethical way of doing research. Given the broad equivalence of most major forms of therapy, they are unlikely to produce statistically significant effects unless the sample is quite large (over 60 clients per group), but often the researchers' concern is to show comparability rather than differences.

Practical limitations of randomisation

Although randomised experiments are scientifically valuable, they may be hard to carry out in practice, for several reasons (Rossi & Freeman, 1993):

- Random assignment to experimental groups does not ensure that the groups will be equivalent or that they will stay equivalent. Randomisation is by definition a chance process, and will thus occasionally produce some unusual distributions. Problems of non-equivalence become more acute if the sample sizes are small or if there are a large number of "nuisance variables" on which the researcher is trying to equate the groups (Hsu, 1989).

- Many experiments suffer from attrition, that is, some participants may drop out of the experiment before the treatment is completed and the post-measures are collected. Attrition reduces the equivalence of the experimental and control groups (Flick, 1988; Howard, Krause & Orlinsky, 1986).

- There may be leakage between the conditions. For example, if half of the patients on a hospital ward are taught a social skill, e.g. relaxation, they may then teach it to other patients in the control condition. In drug trials, there is anecdotal evidence that patients in the experimental group may sometimes share their medication with patients in the control group who have been deprived of it.

- Other staff may not understand the need for randomisation, seeing it as antithetical to the principle of giving individualised care to each client, and thus it may be hard to obtain the necessary cooperation for the study.

- Randomised experiments are costly and time consuming, and should therefore only be used where there is prior evidence that the experimental treatment is beneficial.

- Randomisation cannot be used ethically to study the impact of negative experiences, e.g. smoking, drug use, disasters or psychological trauma. In these cases, non-randomised experimental designs or correlational designs must be used (which is why there is more scope for interested parties, such as tobacco companies, to dispute the results).

- Randomised trials do not take account of patient choice (Brewin & Bradley, 1989). Outside of research studies, clients will select a treatment based on their individual preferences: randomised trials may thus give clients a treatment they do not want and with which they may consequently fare less well.

The realisation that these problems exist with randomised experimental designs, which for a long while were regarded as a scientific panacea, has shaped the growing interest in non-randomised experimental designs and in correlational designs.

CONCLUSION

The central issue is to choose a design appropriate to the research questions and to the stage of the research programme. In the early stages of an investigation, or where there has been little previous research, you are probably unsure of the nature of the phenomena you are looking at. Furthermore, a newly established clinical service may not be stable: its operational policies and modus operandi may be chopping and changing (Rossi & Freeman, 1993). In these cases, a simple descriptive or correlational design is better. Later on, when you are clearer about what the important variables are and how they interrelate, and are more able to specify the nature of the treatment, you can use more sophisticated designs to pin down the effects of crucial variables and test competing theoretical models. Also, several studies taken together can often help to eliminate specific competing theoretical explanations.

We have drawn heavily on Cook and Campbell's (1979) analysis of threats to validity. Their central theme is that no research design is perfect: the important thing is to be aware of the strengths and weaknesses of whatever design you decide to adopt. It is important not to read Cook and Campbell as saying that designs have to have no validity problems at all. Their message is to do the best that you can in the circumstances, but to be aware of potential problems that may arise later on in interpreting the findings. Thus research designs require careful planning in order to anticipate the potential results and competing explanations.

FURTHER READING

Cook and Campbell's (1979) ideas on validity and on the different experimental and correlational designs are essential reading. A more statistical treatment of randomised designs is given in the standard texts, such as Winer (1971), Keppel (1991) and Kirk (1982). Christensen (1991) and Kerlinger (1986) give an overview of design from the standpoint of experimental psychology. Shapiro (1989) illustrates the issues in the context of psychotherapy outcome research.

As in other areas of research, it is worth reading some classic studies. The two that we have looked at in this chapter provide a good starting point: Brown and Harris (1978) for a descriptive, correlational design, and Sloane et al. (1975) for a randomised experimental design.

CHAPTER 8   Small-N designs

Small-N designs, such as systematic case studies and single-case experiments, are a potentially appealing way of blending science and practice, since they enable clinicians and counsellors to integrate formal research methods into their everyday work (Barlow, Hayes & Nelson, 1984). From the practitioner's point of view, the advantages of small-N research are that it is usually inexpensive, not very time consuming and, more importantly, that its underlying philosophy is often congenial to practitioners, since it addresses individual uniqueness and complexity.

Recall the idiographic–nomothetic distinction that we introduced in Chapter 4. Idiographic methods look intensively within the individual; nomothetic methods compare across individuals, looking for general patterns or laws. Nomothetic approaches, particularly the large-group experimental and quasi-experimental designs that we examined in the previous chapter, have been criticised on the grounds that the act of averaging loses the response of the individual within that of the group (Bergin & Strupp, 1972; Dukes, 1965; Kiesler, 1966). In particular, Kiesler (1966) has drawn attention to "uniformity myths" in psychotherapy research: the implicit assumption by researchers that clients are all similar, that different therapists each deliver an identical intervention, and so on. For example, in a psychotherapy outcome study, the overall difference between the pretherapy mean score and the posttherapy mean score on a depression measure may indicate a slight average improvement associated with the therapy under investigation. However, this overall positive change may conceal the fact that, although most clients have improved, a significant minority have deteriorated (Bergin, 1971). Such differential responses would not be discovered without paying attention to the pattern of improvement for each individual client. As a second example, in neuropsychological case-control research, client heterogeneity, with respect to age, premorbid functioning or the size of the neurological lesion, may obscure important effects that will be clearly seen if one looks at the single case (Shallice, 1979). Small-N designs address some of the drawbacks of nomothetic, group comparison designs (Barlow & Hersen, 1984; Kazdin, 1982) and provide a rigorous way to implement an idiographic approach to research.

As Fonagy and Moran (1993) point out, small-N studies were the dominant paradigm in medicine and psychology until the early decades of the twentieth century. Then the influence of Pearson's and Fisher's statistical innovations, such as correlational methods and the analysis of variance, became widespread. As we saw in the previous chapter, these statistical methods were originally developed in an agricultural context, to assess the yields of different fertilisers or strains of wheat. In this context, large samples and group comparison designs work well; examining the response of individual plants is less relevant. However, the agricultural metaphor does not translate easily to clinical and counselling psychology, where individual differences are of major importance. In recognition of this, there has been a resurgence of small-N methods in the past thirty years, deriving its impetus from several different traditions.

Different Traditions

Firstly, there is the tradition of applied behaviour analysis (i.e. operant behaviourism), as guided by Skinner's view that the goal of behavioural science is "to predict and control the behaviour of the individual organism" (Skinner, 1953, p. 35). Single-case experimental designs, aimed at demonstrating such prediction and control, were first developed in the 1950s and 1960s (Davidson & Costello, 1969), and studies using these designs proliferated in the 1970s. The *Journal of Applied Behavior Analysis* is devoted to publishing examples of this kind of work.

Secondly, innovative measurement methods for single-case designs were pioneered by M. B. Shapiro, who developed a measurement technique known as the Shapiro Personal Questionnaire which enables each patient's problems to be quantified and monitored on a day-by-day or week-by-week basis (Shapiro, 1961a, 1961b; Phillips, 1986). In contrast to the operant work, Shapiro's approach takes a more phenomenological stance, being tailored to the individual client's view of his or her problems, and is less concerned with experimental manipulation of treatments.

Thirdly, there is the single-case tradition in neuropsychological research. Luria (1973) dates the birth of scientific neuropsychology to 1861, when Broca described a case of speech impairment that was associated with a localised lesion of the brain. Since that time, case studies have continued to play an important role in the development of the area and currently seem to be enjoying a resurgence of popularity (Shallice, 1979; Wilson, 1987). Methodologically, examples range from qualitative narrative case studies (e.g. Sacks, 1985) to small-N studies using intensive quantitative neuropsychological test data (e.g. Shallice, Burgess & Frith, 1991).

Fourthly, there is the idiographic tradition in personality research. Allport (1962) passionately criticised the almost exclusive reliance on nomothetic methods: "Instead of growing impatient with the single case and hastening on to generalization, why should we not grow impatient with our generalizations and hasten to the internal pattern?" (Allport, 1962, p. 407). Murray (1938) developed an approach to studying personality based on intensive investigation. Proposition one of his theory, which captures the key idea of this chapter, is "The objects of study are individual organisms, not aggregates of organisms" (Murray, 1938, p. 38).

The terminology of the area partly reflects these different traditions. Single-case designs (sometimes referred to as N=1 designs) are characterised by repeated measures of a quantitative variable on a single case. They usually involve an experimental manipulation of a treatment, although there are non-experimental versions, e.g. time-series designs. Single-case designs which do not use intensive repeated measures and do not have an experimental manipulation, for example the classic case history approach, are referred to as case studies (Bromley, 1986; Dukes, 1965), although the boundary between the two approaches is not always clear. This chapter will focus first on experimental designs and then on non-experimental ones. Although the focus is on design, we also include some suggestions about measurement, because small-N designs call for some specific measurement approaches.

EXPERIMENTAL DESIGNS

Single-case experimental designs are ones in which a treatment or intervention is tested on a single individual, in order to see whether or not it is effective. In technical terminology, they are all non-randomised one-group experimental designs, in which the individual participant serves as his or her own control (Cook & Campbell, 1979: see also Chapter 7).

Procedure

As with group comparison designs, the first step is to select the measure or measures to be used. In single-case designs, the measures need to be capable of frequently repeated administration (Nelson, 1981): they must be brief and minimally reactive. The two most common types are observer ratings (e.g. staff ratings of a patient's self-injurious behaviour on an in-patient ward) and client's ratings from self-monitoring (e.g. of obsessional thoughts). Having chosen the measure, the next step is to select an appropriate frequency of measurement: usually it is daily, but it may be, say, hourly or weekly.

All designs start with a series of baseline measures, which continue until the measurements are stable, usually for 10 to 20 observations. After that, the first experimental treatment is introduced. This area has its own notation, based on the first few letters of the alphabet: A stands for the baseline, or no-treatment phase; B, C, D, etc. stand for the various treatments or interventions. There are many possible single-case designs, each of which raises practical and sometimes ethical issues. We will look at four common examples here; more elaborate designs are given in the specialist textbooks (Barlow, Hayes & Nelson, 1984; Barlow & Hersen, 1984; Kazdin, 1982).

AB design

The AB design (see Figure 8.1), in which the baseline is followed by an intervention, is the simplest form of design. For example, the effectiveness of a positive parenting approach to manage a child's tantrums might be investigated. The parents would be asked

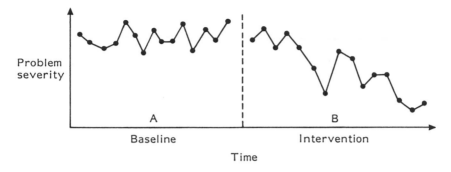

Figure 8.1 The AB design

to observe the number of tantrums (suitably operationalised: see Chapter 6) every day for two weeks. Then they would institute a new way of responding to them, such as time-outs for the tantrums and praise for good behaviour. If the intervention is effective, the B phase of the design will then demonstrate a reduction in the target problem's severity or frequency.

The drawback of the AB design is that it only gives weak evidence for the causal influence of the experimental treatment. It suffers from the same threats to internal validity as the one-group pretest–posttest design (Cook & Campbell, 1979; see also Chapter 7), for example, that an interfering event may occur at the same time as the treatment is introduced. So more elaborate designs have been developed to try to get round this problem.

The reversal (or ABAB) design

The reversal (or ABAB) design is an AB design immediately followed by its own replication (see Figure 8.2). It is frequently used in operant behaviour modification work. For instance, in the child's tantrum example above, once the intervention had been shown to be effective the baseline, no-treatment, phase would be reinstituted, followed finally by the intervention again. The rationale is that these reversals demonstrate experimental control over the target behaviour. There are also more complicated variants, e.g. the ABACAB design in which a second intervention is introduced after the second baseline phase. For example, a token economy on an in-patient ward might have its contingencies modified in the second phase.

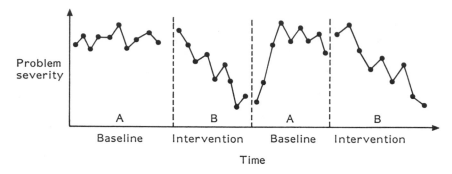

Figure 8.2 The ABAB design

The ABAB design suffers from three major problems. Firstly, the effects of many interventions are not reversible. Permanent learning or personality change may occur, or the problem may not recur once it has been dealt with. This design could not be used to study the effects of psychodynamic or cognitive therapy, for example. Secondly, even if the intervention is reversible, there are serious ethical problems with the withdrawal of treatment in the second and subsequent baseline phases. This is similar to the ethical dilemma faced in having no-treatment control groups in group comparison designs, but more acute because treatment is withdrawn rather than withheld. For example, a child may revert to having tantrums, or psychiatric in-patients may recommence self-injurious behaviours. Thirdly, switching on and off the intervention may have undesirable psychological consequences. It may lead to the client's losing trust in the psychologist, or may even result in the problem behaviour being harder to extinguish because it is maintained on a partial reinforcement schedule.

Multiple baseline design

With several (presumed independent) target behaviours (e.g. a child suffering from tantrums, enuresis and dog phobia) or one target behaviour in several independent settings, you can use a multiple baseline design. Interventions targeted at each behaviour are introduced sequentially and their impact on all the target behaviours is measured (see Figure 8.3). The idea is to demonstrate that the effect of each intervention is specific to a particular problem.

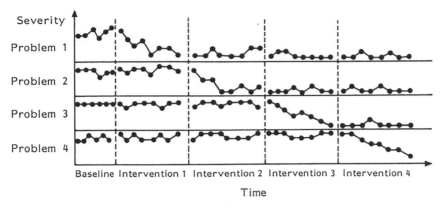

Figure 8.3 The multiple baseline design

Barlow and Hersen (1984) fit the famous early psychoanalytic case of Anna O (Breuer & Freud, 1895/1955) into this schema, since Breuer targeted various separate interventions, such as hypnosis and interpretation, at each of Anna O's symptoms in turn. However, although this design is amenable to non-behavioural therapies, it is much more commonly used within a behavioural framework.

In an interesting application of this design, Bennun and Lucas (1990) investigated the impact of a two-component intervention with couples in which one partner had a long-standing diagnosis of schizophrenia. Using a "multiple single case design" with a sample of six couples, they showed that the first component of the intervention—education—had an impact on the well spouse's perception of their ability to cope, but had no effect on presenting symptoms. The second component of the intervention—problem solving and communication training—had an impact on positive symptoms of schizophrenia.

Changing-criterion design

This design is used to demonstrate experimental control over a single problem behaviour that may be progressively reduced in severity (see Figure 8.4). It is useful in working with clients who are dependent on drugs or alcohol. For example, it may be used in helping a client to stop smoking, where the client progressively cuts down to more stringent targets (criterion 1 would be 20 a day,

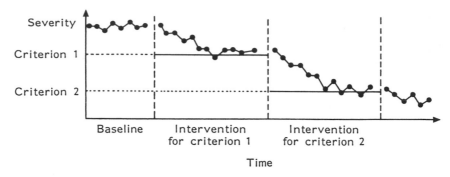

Figure 8.4 The changing-criterion design

criterion 2 would be 15 a day, and so on). Or it could be used with a positive behaviour that is being shaped, e.g. appropriate social interaction in childhood autism.

Data Analysis

Data from single-case designs are normally displayed on a graph (as in Figures 8.1 to 8.4). Part of the appeal of these designs is that the success or failure of the intervention is usually immediately obvious from the graph (Morley & Adams, 1991): it should hit you between the eyes. Such graphs can often be helpful to show to the clients, to enable them to monitor their progress and to demonstrate clearly that the intervention is working (or not, as the case may be).

However, in some cases the changes may be less clear cut, or a measure of their magnitude may be required. This has led some researchers to call for the use of statistical methods. The topic of which, if any, statistical tests to use is too technical to cover here; Morley and Adams (1989) describe some possibilities.

Generalisation

Although single-case studies are essentially idiographic, the investigator often wishes to generalise beyond the specific individuals studied to make broader claims about the effectiveness of the treatment tested. This is usually done by conducting a clinical replication series (Barlow & Hersen, 1984), that is, replicating the study on several individuals. In this way the external validity of the findings are established. The notion of a clinical replication series is derived from Cronbach's (1975) concept of locally intensive observation. As a finding is tested in other settings, varying conditions will test the limits of its external validity and lead to richer theory:

> As [the researcher] goes from situation to situation, his first task is to describe and interpret the effect anew in each locale, perhaps taking into account factors unique to that locale . . . As results accumulate, a person who seeks understanding will do his best to trace how the uncontrolled factors could have caused local departures from the modal effect. That is, generalisation comes late and the exception is taken as seriously as the rule.
>
> (Cronbach, 1975, p. 125)

This approach can be applied equally well in experimental and naturalistic, non-experimental approaches.

NATURALISTIC CASE STUDY DESIGNS

Although behaviourally oriented researchers (e.g. Hayes, 1981) often claim that experimental single-case designs can readily be adapted to non-behavioural treatments, their emphasis on observable events and experimental manipulation makes these designs problematic for studying psychodynamic, experiential and even cognitive therapies. Non-experimental case study designs— the traditional narrative case study, the systematic case study and time-series designs—are more appropriate to these types of therapy.

Narrative Case Studies

The narrative case study is the traditional description of a client or treatment, based on the clinician's case notes and memory. Freud's case histories, e.g. "Little Hans" (Freud, 1909/1955) or "Dora" (Freud, 1905/1953) are classic examples of this genre. Case studies have played an important role in the development of clinical and counselling psychology. They can serve a number of purposes, including documenting the existence of a clinical phenomenon, often a rare one (e.g. early case studies of multiple personality disorder), disproving a universal proposition (e.g. that only women suffer from hysteria), demonstrating a new intervention, and generating hypotheses about causes (Dukes, 1965; Lazarus & Davison, 1971). Valuable information can be gathered from case studies, as long as their nature and limitations are understood. In general, case studies tell us what is possible but not what is typical. Similarly, they can suggest a possible connection or cause, but cannot provide strong confirmatory evidence.

However, Spence (1986) and others have argued that narrative case studies such as Freud's contain too much narrative smoothing: that is, they are too selective and have often been altered to tell a better story. Narrative distortions can be investigated by the following self-experiment. Tape-record a therapy session; do not take notes immediately, instead wait one or two days before writing from memory a summary of at least half a page. Then listen to the tape of the session while taking detailed notes and noting any inaccuracies. In addition to large amounts of missing material, you will also find that you have collapsed things that happened at different times, got some things out of order and may have attributed statements to the wrong speaker or even completely fabricated things.

Like the one-group posttest-only design that we discussed in Chapter 7, narrative case studies can be used to infer possible causal explanations if sufficient additional information is available. For example, in psychohistorical case studies, Runyan (1982) points out that careful consideration of the known facts often allows the researcher to rule out most of the possible explanations for an event.

Systematic Case Studies

Given the problems with case studies (reliance on memory, anecdotal data collection, narrative smoothing), it is worth considering how to improve the quality of information, in order to strengthen the conclusions which may be drawn. Kazdin (1981) lists five characteristics of case studies which improve their credibility:

1. systematic, quantitative (versus anecdotal) data;

2. multiple assessments of change over time;

3. change in previously chronic or stable problems;

4. immediate or marked effects following the intervention;

5. multiple cases.

The combination of these features substantially improves the researcher's ability to infer that a treatment caused an effect (i.e. it increases the internal validity of the study).

Systematic case studies are careful investigations using a variety of non-experimental methods (for a review see Elliott, 1983). They typically address questions about topics of interest to practising therapists and counsellors, such as:

- *Client change*: e.g. "Is this client better?", "In what ways has the client changed?", "When did change occur?"

- *Therapy process*: e.g. "What did the client and therapist typically do or experience in therapy?", "How much do they agree with each other about what happened?", "Did these processes change over time?"

- *Change processes*: e.g. "Did the therapy help the client get better?", "What processes in the therapy were effective or helpful?"

A number of measures and designs, involving varying degrees of time and effort, may be utilised. We address each of the above three questions in turn, giving suggestions for carrying out systematic case studies on your own clients. These suggestions are ordered from least to most time consuming, so that you may begin with a minimum requirement and work up to more elaborate procedures.

Client change

The task here is to improve on anecdotal impressions of client progress or deterioration. There several options:

1. Administer a standardised change measure, suitable for the particular client, before and after therapy. For example, give the Beck Depression Inventory (Beck, Steer & Garbin, 1988) to a depressed client.

2. Add an individualised change measure, before and after therapy (Mintz & Kiesler, 1982). For example: target complaints (Battle *et al.*, 1966) or the Shapiro Personal Questionnaire (Shapiro, 1961a; Phillips, 1986).

3. Use additional standardised change measures, e.g. a global inventory such as the SCL-90-R symptom checklist (Derogatis, 1983).

4. Ask the client: "What has changed since therapy started?", or better, have a third person interview the client for you, e.g. the Change Interview (Elliott *et al.*, 1990).

5. Add more assessment points, for example at mid-treatment (or every 8 to 10 sessions) or at follow-up (e.g. six months or one year after treatment).

6. Add weekly measures of change, e.g. readminister the Shapiro Personal Questionnaire at each session.

7. Add further cases, creating a clinical replication series (Barlow, Hayes & Nelson, 1984).

Therapeutic process

There are also a variety of systematic ways to assess therapeutic process, i.e. what happens in a session and the client's reactions to that session. Many of these methods are reviewed in Greenberg and Pinsof (1986). They include:

1. Audiotaping the session and then taking detailed process notes from the tape, or transcribing some illustrative passages.

2. Periodic therapeutic relationship measures, administered, for example, every three to five sessions. For instance, the Barrett-Lennard Relationship Inventory, the Penn Helping Alliance Questionnaire or the Working Alliance Inventory (all reviewed in Greenberg & Pinsof, 1986).

3. Standard self-report session measures, completed by the client and the therapist. For example, the Session Evaluation Questionnaire (Stiles, 1980); the Session Impacts Questionnaire (Elliott & Wexler, 1994); the Therapy Session Report (see Greenberg & Pinsof, 1986).

4. Treatment-specific measures, completed by the therapist or the supervisor after each session, to assess the therapist's adherence to the treatment model or the client's progress. For example, the Cognitive Therapy Scale (Beck *et al.*, 1979); the Experiential Task Completion scales (Greenberg, Rice & Elliott, 1993); the NIMH treatment adherence scale (DeRubeis *et al.*, 1982).

Change processes

Finally, one can attempt to assess the effective ingredients in the intervention, in order to understand what you did well (and badly) with the client. Possible methods include:

1. Asking the client: use client self-report measures about helpful factors or significant events. These can take the form of a posttreatment questionnaire or interview (e.g. Llewelyn & Hume, 1979).

2. Select a notable treatment success or failure (or both) and analyse or compare them (e.g. Strupp, 1980). Or compare the most and least helpful session, based on client or therapist ratings, or ratings on a weekly change measure (e.g. Parry, Shapiro & Firth, 1986).

3. Select an interesting or important event in therapy; transcribe it and analyse it thoroughly, using either Task Analysis (Rice & Greenberg, 1984) or Comprehensive Process Analysis (Elliott, 1989a).

Parry, Shapiro and Firth's (1986) systematic case study illustrates several of these possibilities, and is a good example of the potential strength of systematic case studies for linking clinical practice and research in non-behavioural treatments.

Time-series Designs

The final example of non-experimental designs is the time-series design. The aim of this design is correlational rather than experimental: you monitor two or more variables over time and look at their interrelationship. A large number of observations are needed in order to meet the assumptions behind the use of the usual statistical methods. These designs originated in econometrics, where, for example, the effect of one year's interest rates on the following year's economic activity may be examined using monthly data over 25 years.

Gottman and his co-workers have promoted these methods within psychology in general and the study of psychological therapies in particular (e.g. Gottman, 1981; Gottman & Roy, 1990). Complex statistical methods are needed to assess the evolving relationships within and between variables (Gottman, 1981; Skinner, 1991). An interesting application was Moran and Fonagy's (1987) use of time-series methods to study the process and impact of child psychoanalysis on an adolescent girl with diabetes. They demonstrated an association between certain psychoanalytic content themes, e.g. the girl's anger with her father, and the study's principal outcome variable, variations in her blood glucose level.

CONCLUSION

Small-N designs thus represent both a way to look at individual uniqueness and complexity, and also a viable method of research for practising clinicians. Like all research methods, they have their strengths and weaknesses. They are good for looking at phenomena in depth, demonstrating that certain phenomena exist, or disconfirming theories by providing counter-examples. They are poor at establishing typicalities or general laws.

In line with our stance of methodological pluralism, we would argue that a thorough investigation of any topic area needs to combine both large-N and small-N approaches. It is possible, even desirable, to examine single cases within the context of a larger group comparison study. Rogers' (1967) classic "silent young man" case is taken from a larger experimental study, as is Parry et al.'s (1986) "anxious executive" case. These two examples both give a human dimension that is lacking in the predominantly statistical reports from the larger projects.

FURTHER READING

Most of the references on experimental single-case designs cover similar ground. Barlow and Hersen (1984) and Kazdin (1982) are the two standard textbooks; there are good chapter-length treatments by Morley (1989) and Peck (1985). Barlow, Hayes and Nelson (1984) set these designs against a background of scientist/practitioner professional issues.

Bromley (1986) and Yin (1989) discuss case studies as a general research method. It is worthwhile reading some of the classic narrative case studies, both from a research and from a clinical point of view. Any of Freud's are worthwhile; "Little Hans" (Freud, 1909/1955) or "Dora" (Freud, 1905/1953) provide good starting points. On the behavioural side, there is Watson and Rayner's (1920) famous (and ethically dubious) case of "Little Albert". Carl Rogers pioneered the application of audiotape to client–therapist interaction in single cases: the case of "a silent young man" (Rogers, 1967) is an excellent example of a process-oriented study. Parry *et al.* (1986) and Moran and Fonagy (1987) are interesting contemporary examples of case studies using more intensive quantitative methods.

CHAPTER 9   The participants: sampling and ethics

The final aspect of design concerns the participants in the research. It addresses the "who?" question that we posed in Chapter 7: who will you be studying, and to whom do you intend to apply the findings of the study? We will also consider ethical issues here, since they concern the researcher's relationship with the participants.

We usually prefer the term participants to the old-fashioned, but still current, subjects. The latter term, with its monarchic connotations, has undesirable implications of powerlessness and passivity. The stock phrase "running the subjects" is especially to be avoided: one of our students once wrote something like "the subjects were run in their own homes", which conjures up an image of indoor jogging. For interviews and questionnaires, you can speak of respondents or interviewees. (For observational research, the term observees does not yet exist!) In ethnography, the term informants is typically used, although this has unfortunate connotations of surreptitiousness. New paradigm researchers (e.g. Reason & Rowan, 1981) may use the term co-researchers, to emphasise the idea of the participant as an equal partner in the research enterprise.

The chapter has two separate sections: sampling and ethics. We have placed this material here, after the chapters on measurement and the first two chapters on design, because some of the issues to be considered depend on a knowledge of those topics. Furthermore, new researchers often focus on the population and how it will be sampled before they have formulated what they will be studying. However, it is worth thinking about some of the issues concerning the participants during the groundwork stage of the project, after choosing the problem and developing the research questions (see Chapter 3). Problems of access to populations are bound up in some of the organisational and political issues that we discuss in that chapter. At an extreme, if there is no sample available, there is no study.

SAMPLING

Sampling refers to the process of specifying and obtaining the participants for the study. In chronological order, the practical steps involved are (1) specifying the target population, (2) choosing the sampling procedure and (3) determining the sample size. We will deal with each of these in turn, and then consider some alternative approaches. Although we will mainly be using language associated with the quantitative research tradition, we intend our discussion to have a general application. Qualitative researchers may sometimes appear less concerned about representativeness, going instead "for the people who will tell you the story", but we contend that all researchers must decide, implicitly or explicitly, how to respond to these sampling issues.

It helps to think in terms of three nested sets (see Figure 9.1):

1. The *universe* is the broad population to which eventual generalisation of the findings is desired.

2. The *target population* is the defined group from which the participants in the study are to be selected.

3. The *sample* is the subset of the target population consisting of those participants who actually take part in the study. There may be a gap between the ideal and the actual sample: the terms "intended" versus "achieved" sample can be used to denote this.

For example, you may be interested in the incidence of depression in British women who consult their general practitioners (family doctors). In this case, the universe may be all British women who visit their general practitioners, the target population all women who consult 10 specific doctors in February 1994, and the intended sample 1 in 20 of those women. The achieved sample will be the subset of women actually interviewed. In the case of a census, the

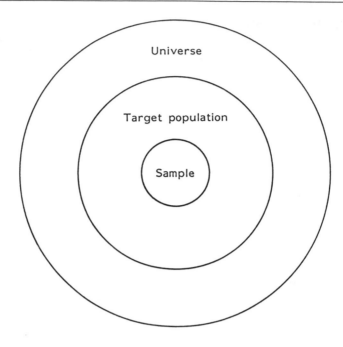

Figure 9.1 The universe, the target population and the sample

universe, the target population and the intended sample are one and the same (e.g. in a national census they consist of all members of that country's population), although the achieved sample will fall short of this, as some people are inevitably missed out.

A quantitative measurement made in a sample is called a statistic; it is usually done to estimate a population parameter. For instance, the prevalence of depression in a sample of women visiting their general practitioners is a statistic; this may be used to estimate the overall prevalence of depression in the target population of women users of those practices, which is a parameter.

Generalisability

Usually researchers are not just interested in the specific sample itself, rather they want to generalise the findings to other groups. The extent to which this is possible is referred to as the external validity of the study (Cook & Campbell, 1979). External validity is captured by the question, "To what extent do the results of my study apply beyond the specific people, situations or incidents in the sample, to others like them?" Of course, generalisability is not just a matter of sampling, since it also involves consideration of the setting, the time, the measures and so on. We consider these aspects of external validity later on, when we discuss analysis and interpretation in Chapter 11.

From a purely sampling point of view, there are two types of generalisation, corresponding to the transitions from one subset to the next in Figure 9.1. The first type is generalising from the sample to the target population. In quantitative research this is known as statistical inference, and there is a well-established set of procedures to accomplish it. However, these procedures make certain assumptions, such as unbiased sampling from the target population, which we will examine below. The second type is generalising from the target population to another population or to a larger universe. This is done on the grounds of general plausibility, rather than any statistical argument. For example, can the results of a study of back-pain patients seen at hospital X be generalised to hospital Y? To people with back pain who do not seek help? To other countries or cultures? If these groups of people are plausibly similar enough, then the results can be generalised across them; if not, then the findings must be considered as specific to the original target population until replications in other populations are conducted.

In the case of qualitative and small-N research, the argument for generalisability always depends upon plausibility, in a similar way to the second step of generalisation in quantitative methods.

The importance of external validity depends on the type of research. Basic research on general human processes, including qualitative research of the definitional kind, places a high value on external validity, since it seeks universal generalisability. Applied research may also seek to generalise, although often less widely, for example to a particular client group. For evaluation and action research, external validity is often less important, since the research seeks an understanding of, and solutions to, a particular problem in a particular setting, and seeks generalisability only to the immediate future.

The Target Population

The first step in sampling is to specify the target population. It can be defined in terms of, for instance, gender, social class, problem type or problem severity. It may be defined narrowly (e.g. married women aged 35–45 living within the Liverpool city boundaries with no significant medical or psychiatric history) or broadly (e.g. all British women aged 18 and over). Narrowly defined populations are called homogeneous, broadly defined ones heterogeneous.

Researchers must make a trade-off when deciding on the breadth of the target population. A homogeneous sample has the advantage of reducing the degree of extraneous variability (i.e. statistical noise) in the sample, which gives more power in detecting effects that you are interested in, and more precision in estimating the magnitude of those effects. In analysis of variance terms, homogeneity reduces the proportion of error variance to total variance. For example, if you are researching the influence of life events on depression, any relationship will be harder to detect in a more heterogeneous sample, since depression is a function of many variables other than life events.

On the other hand, the increase in precision from a narrow definition of the target population is bought at the expense of the following costs:

1. There will be reduced generalisability to a larger universe (e.g. if you are studying women in their thirties, the findings will not necessarily apply to women of all age groups).

2. Practical difficulties will result, including the problem that the more stringent are the inclusion criteria, the harder it is to find participants, since more people have to be screened or you have to obtain referrals from more specialised services. Mintz (1981) has called this Waskow's Law: "As soon as you completely specify a population, it will disappear."

3. Having a homogeneous sample precludes examining individual differences, e.g. if there is little variability in age within your sample, you cannot look at age as an individual difference variable (Shapiro, 1989).

Sampling Methods

In order to make inferences from the sample to the target population from which it is drawn, the sample should ideally be unbiased. This means that every member of the target population should have an equal chance of being selected for the sample. A number of sampling techniques may be used to generate a representative sample (Cochran, 1977; Sudman, 1976). For example, in probability sampling, every member of the target population has a given chance, say one in ten, of being included in the study; whereas in stratified sampling, the target population is first subdivided into groups, e.g. according to social class or diagnostic variables, before making the allocation to the study. Psychologists are typically careless about sampling methods: they tend to rely on convenience sampling (i.e. whoever they can get) and hope that their results will generalise, if the sample is large enough. However, it is wrong to assume that a sample large enough to detect statistical significance is large enough to ensure generalisability. No matter how large the sample is, you can only generalise safely if the sample is representative of the target population.

However, eliminating bias is not always feasible. Even with a well-designed sampling plan, there is usually a gap between the intended and the achieved sample. For example, research using postal questionnaires often has a non-response rate of around one-third (Dillman, 1978). Non-responders usually differ considerably from responders, e.g. in terms of interest, motivation and educational level. Similarly, studies which recruit volunteers via advertisements may obtain an unrepresentative sample. Sometimes it is possible to estimate the nature of the sampling bias and partially control for it statistically when you analyse the data. For example, if respondents are older on average than non-respondents, you can look at the association of age with whatever variable you are studying, and possibly use partial correlations to remove its influence. However, as we discussed under the non-equivalent groups pretest–posttest design in Chapter 7, *post hoc* statistical adjustments can only partially compensate for a biased sample, because of unreliability of measurement and because you can never fully compensate for all possible variables on which bias may occur. Such *post hoc* analyses are often worth doing, but must be treated with caution.

Another serious drawback of the convenience sampling approach is that certain populations may be underrepresented. For example, Graham (1992) analysed the participants used in studies published in the major American Psychological Association journals. She concluded that all too often papers reported that "most of the subjects were white and middle class" and that psychological research has ignored black and ethnic participants.

When the size and composition of the target group is unknown at the outset, it is possible to use a sampling procedure known as "networking" or "snowballing" (Patton, 1990; Rossi & Freeman, 1993), which operates by asking each respondent to name one or two other people who fit the research criteria. Sampling continues up to the point where additional respondents provide little or no extra information. For example, Pistrang (1990) used this method to study the mental health needs of London's Chinese community. She wanted to interview community and health workers who were involved with the Chinese population in London's West End. Before the project started, it was not known precisely how many such workers there were or where they were to be found, but suitable interviewees were located via networking as the project progressed, up to a final total of 20. However, a potential problem with the snowballing procedure is that the initial respondents might direct you to other like-minded people who share their viewpoint, and thus the researcher needs to be aware of possible biases in the achieved sample.

Sample Size

From the point of view of inferential statistics, the obvious rule of thumb is that the larger the sample is, the better, since you are then more able to separate out the variance associated with the effects you are interested in from the variance due to errors of sampling and measurement. In other words, with a large sample you are more able to separate the signal from the noise. However, as Cohen (1990) has pointed out, a sample can be too large in the sense that it exceeds the requirements for statistical power (see below), thus involving a waste of research effort, and it is also likely to identify trivially small effects. If you are fortunate enough to be well funded, a better strategy may be to carry out several smaller studies rather than one large one.

The attainable sample size may also depend on practical issues, such as recruitment difficulties, time constraints, money or the rarity of the condition studied.

Statistical power analysis

The main way of estimating the appropriate sample size is known as "statistical power analysis" (Cohen, 1988, 1990, 1992; Kraemer & Thiemann, 1987; Singer, Lovie & Lovie, 1986). In a nutshell, the statistical power of a study is the likelihood that it will detect an effect that is actually present, e.g. an actual difference in effectiveness between two treatments. A low-power study will have a poor chance of detecting such effects; a high-power study will have a good chance. Many previous studies in clinical and counselling psychology have simply not been powerful enough and thus may have overlooked the presence of important effects (Cohen, 1990; Kazdin & Bass, 1989).

In any study, there are four related parameters. For any given statistical test, if you know any three of them, you can find the other.

1. The *sample size* (N) is usually what you want to determine, but if you know it in advance, it facilitates the calculation of the other parameters.

2. *Alpha* (α) is the probability of detecting an effect when in fact none exists (this is called a Type I error or false positive). In most psychological research, alpha is set by arbitrary convention at $< .05$, but a more lenient value of $< .10$ is sometimes used for exploratory research or defining non-significant trends. On the other hand, more stringent values (e.g. .01 or .001) may be used to increase the confidence in one's findings or to control for the effects of conducting multiple tests of statistical significance.

3. *Beta* (β) is the probability of missing an effect which is in fact present (this is called a Type II error or false negative). Statistical power is defined as 1 minus beta ($1 - \beta$): it is the probability of detecting an effect that is really there. Cohen (1988, 1992) recommends .80 as the standard level for power. If you were

interested in rigorously testing a null hypothesis, a power of .95 would be recommended, as it is equivalent in stringency to the alpha $< .05$ standard. Conversely, it would be inadvisable to design a study whose power was less than .50; you should always have at least a 50–50 chance of finding an effect that is present.

4. *Effect size* is the key concept in power analysis. It is a measure of the strength of the underlying relationship in which you are interested. Effect sizes are usually talked about in terms of small, medium and large effects. A large effect can be thought of as one which is large enough to see with the naked eye—that is, without statistical analysis. The way the effect size is calculated depends on the type of statistical methods used in the study (e.g. chi-square, t-test, correlation or analysis of variance). This is reviewed by Cohen (1988, 1992), who presents standards for what amounts to a small, a medium and a large effect with each type of statistical test. For example, in correlational studies, a Pearson correlation coefficient of .10 is considered to be a small effect, .30 a medium effect and .50 a large effect. Clinical and counselling psychology researchers usually deal with medium effect sizes, though small effects may be of interest in epidemiological research. Note that effect size is not the same as clinical significance (see Chapter 11); an effect may be large but trivial, if the variable which shows the effect is trivial (e.g. teaching counsellors to say "uh-huh" more frequently).

If you establish your effect size and select your alpha and beta levels, you can then calculate the required sample size. This is known as a statistical power calculation. It is always worth doing such a calculation before finalising your research design. Cohen (1988) and Kraemer and Thiemann (1987) provide the tables for different designs, and Cohen (1992) gives a brief outline of the central concepts and a table to calculate sample sizes for a power of .80, the most commonly adopted value. For example, in a design which compares two groups using a t-test, with medium effect sizes and an alpha of .05, a sample of 32 per group is needed to attain a power of .50, and a sample of 64 per group is needed to attain a power of .80. Studies with many variables (e.g. factor analytic studies of long inventories) or many subgroups (e.g. norming a psychological test on different subpopulations) require larger samples. In fact, the sample size requirements for certain types of research, e.g. comparative therapy and counselling outcome research, are so large that we recommend that you only conduct such studies if you have adequate funding and staffing to do so.

Alternative Approaches to Sampling and Generalisability

Qualitative and case study research typically uses smaller samples than traditional quantitative research, sometimes as little as a single case or significant event. Unsurprisingly, the most common criticism of such research is that you cannot generalise the results. In this section, we will describe some alternatives to the traditional approach to sampling and generalisability.

Generalisability through replication

A rational (as opposed to a statistical) approach to generalisability and sampling can be found in the behavioural $N=1$ tradition (see Chapter 8), in which research is carried out one case at a time, manipulating variables and measuring effects until you achieve an understanding of the causal relationships involved. The relevant characteristics of the case, including any background and situational variables which appear to be important, are carefully described.

In this approach, you then attempt to replicate the first case study by finding a case as similar as possible to the first case (this is referred to as direct replication: see Sidman, 1960). If you obtain different results (i.e. there is a failure to replicate), you try to understand what made this case different from the first, and then try to find a case which matches the first (or second) on this variable. If the same results are obtained, you next begin to vary apparently relevant features of the case in order to establish the limits of generalisability in a rational manner (this is referred to as systematic replication). Replications establish the breadth or range of generalisability, while failures to replicate establish the limits of generality, just as a control group would in traditional research; the two complement each other. Thus, as Cook and Campbell (1979) note, external validity is better served by a number of small studies with specified samples than by a single large study. Cronbach (1975) refers to this approach as "locally intensive observation" (see Chapter 8).

Falsificationist approach

If you work within a falsificationist framework, based on Popper's ideas (see Chapter 2), you are not concerned with representativeness, since you are looking not to generalise but for counter-examples, which could even consist of a single case (Dukes, 1965; Eysenck, 1975; Meehl, 1978). If your theory predicts that unsupported apples will fall to the ground, then a single levitating apple will falsify it. Similarly within clinical neuropsychology, a single example of a patient with a certain pattern of abilities may invalidate a proposed model of mental structure (Shallice, 1988). In these instances, qualitative or quantitative descriptive research which establishes the existence of the counter-example is sufficient.

Theoretical sampling in descriptive qualitative research

Although phenomenological and qualitative in nature, the grounded theory approach to sampling (Glaser & Strauss, 1967; Rennie, Phillips & Quartaro, 1988; Strauss & Corbin, 1990) is similar to the replication sampling approach of the early behavioural single-case researchers. The main difference is that the behaviourists are trying to establish control over behaviours, while the grounded theorists are trying to develop a rich description. The phrase "grounded theory" refers to the fact that the theory emerges from and remains firmly based in the data.

In grounded theory, generalisability is established through an approach referred to as theoretical sampling, in which the researcher's emerging theory determines the sampling. You begin by selecting a typical instance of the phenomenon under study (a small pilot sample of 5–10 protocols might have been collected beforehand in order to determine what is most typical). This initial protocol is analysed before going on to collect additional data. The second (and usually the third) protocol should also be fairly typical and apparently similar to the first. As you analyse these successive protocols, you note what new aspects of the phenomenon appear. After a relatively small number of protocols has been analysed (sometimes as few as three) you begin to experience diminishing returns, in that no new variations or features of the phenomenon are appearing. This is referred to as saturation.

After this, you begin to sample different types of protocols on the basis of variables which may make a difference. Optimally, this is based on your emerging theory, but demographic variables such as age, gender or severity can be used early on in the absence of a better alternative. Within each variation, you replicate until saturation begins. Finally, you sample a few instances that you think will be quite different (i.e. sampling for heterogeneity); this is important for establishing the limits of your results, and serves the comparative function of a control group in traditional research. Final saturation occurs when: (1) no relevant new information emerges; (2) category development is dense or rich (including a range of aspects and variations); and (3) relations among categories are well established and validated by their recurrence.

The sample size needed in theoretical sampling cannot be determined in advance. However, for very rich protocols (e.g. based on several hours of interviewing), clearly defined areas and careful sampling, saturation can be obtained with samples of 5 to 10. On the other hand, thin protocols (e.g. ten-minute interviews or written questionnaire data) or a broad or ill-defined area (e.g. criminal victimisation) both necessitate a larger total sample (e.g. as many as 20 to 50). Interestingly, if one is interested in qualitative themes which occur in all or almost all protocols, probability theory suggests that samples in the 5 to 10 range are adequate (Elliott, 1989c).

Generalisability in phenomenological research

Finally, in the Duquesne or reflective–empirical form of phenomenological research (Giorgi, 1975; Wertz, 1985) generalisability is a function of both sampling and a special mode of analysis, in which the researcher attempts to identify the general structure of the phenomenon under study. This research is definitional in nature, seeking to define the general constituents which make the phenomenon what it is and not something else.

Phenomenological researchers attempt to study diverse cases. Each individual protocol is examined for what may be general versus specific in relation to other instances of the phenomenon. Multiple protocols are then compared for similarities (indicators of general features) and differences (suggesting unique features or important variations). Finally, the researcher uses the method of imaginative variation to get at what is essential about the phenomenon being studied, taking each of the similarities and imagining what the phenomenon would be like if the feature were absent. For example, Wertz (1985), in a study of people who had been criminally victimised, found that the loss of an everyday sense of safety and helpful community was an essential element of the experience.

Summary

The central point we are attempting to convey in this section is that researchers need to think carefully about to whom the conclusions of their study can apply and how they are going to support the strength of those conclusions. All too often, clinical and counselling psychology researchers seem to neglect sampling and generalisability issues. Unfortunately, there is a long tradition of clinicians making overconfident generalisations on the basis of observations on the biased sample of clients who have appeared in their consulting rooms. Freud's case histories were partly responsible for this, as modesty in drawing inferences was not one of Freud's characteristics. Neurotic Victorian women seeking psychoanalysis are not a good foundation on which to base general theories about the human condition; or, more precisely, it is possible to form one's theories with such a client group, but they must be replicated in other ways if they are to have any credibility. Clinicians and counsellors often seem unaware of the evidence from studies of psychological help-seeking that people who seek formal help for their psychological problems are in a distinct minority (e.g. Barker et al., 1990; Veroff, Kulka & Douvan, 1981). Thus clinical researchers need to develop more humility about the limits of application of their findings.

True random sampling, in the sense of drawing participants randomly from a large population of potential participants, is rarely performed in clinical and counselling psychology research. At best, convenience sampling is used—that is, whoever can be obtained at the time of the study (e.g. all the participants who can be recruited in a given time period). Researchers need to take this into account when analysing the data and making generalisations.

Having dealt with sampling issues, we will now examine the other major topic area that is raised by working with the participants, that is, ethics.

ETHICAL ISSUES

Ethical principles are concerned with protecting the rights, dignity and welfare of research participants. Interest in the ethics of psychological research grew out of outrage at earlier abuses, including medical research in Nazi concentration camps during World War II and early stress induction research by psychologists. These concerns were further fuelled by the widespread use of deception in the social psychological research of the 1950s and early 1960s, which shaped the public attitude of psychologists as scientific deceivers. The civil rights movement and populism of the 1960s and 1970s resulted in a greater sensitivity to ethics on the part of psychologists (Imber *et al.*, 1986; Korchin & Cowan, 1982). Finally, especially in the United States, concerns about litigation and the general trend toward increased bureaucratisation and governmental control of research led in the 1970s and 1980s to government-mandated practices for the review of research involving human participants.

Previous chapters have touched on some ethical issues associated with particular research methods or designs, such as covert observation or no-treatment control groups. Here we will examine some central principles common to all psychological research. Following Korchin and Cowan (1982), we group them under the headings of: (1) informed consent, (2) minimisation of potential harm/deprivation of benefit and (3) confidentiality and protection of privacy.

However, before examining these principles, some general points need to be made. First, the researcher is under an obligation to explore and seek others' advice and judgements about the specific ethical issues involved in his or her study. Second, as Korchin and Cowan (1982) noted, validity and ethics should not be seen as separate issues. Instead, unethical practice reduces the external validity of the research, because it results in research procedures that cannot be translated into practice. Conversely, poorly designed research reduces the ethical standing of the research, because in such situations there are usually only minimal scientific or social benefits possible to counterbalance the possible risks of participation in the research. Finally, it is worth noting that we are operating in the domain of value judgements, in which one needs to balance negative effects (usually accruing to the participant) with positive effects (usually accruing to society in general). Sometimes there are conflicting ethical considerations, and difficult choices need to be made for which there are no clear-cut answers.

Informed consent

Informed consent refers to disclosure by the researcher, before the study, of what will happen during the study and of any other information that might affect the person's decision to participate. This enables prospective participants to make a free and informed decision about whether or not to enter the study. Thus informed consent involves both full information and freedom of choice.

Full information

Full information refers to the principle of telling prospective participants everything they need to know in order to make a rational decision about whether to take part in the study. An important corollary is that the participant should be able to understand the information provided (i.e. that it should not be written in overly technical or bureaucratic prose or in a language in which the participant is not fluent).

Problems arise when the person's understanding of the issues is limited. Informed consent becomes difficult with children or adults who are not fully competent to make their own decisions (Korchin & Cowan, 1982), or even with well-informed and educated adults in complicated clinical trials in medicine (Thornton, 1992). For example, if the child is less than 7, parental permission plus the child's verbal agreement is usually required. If the child is between

7 and 17, then his or her written assent is usually required in addition to parental permission. Similarly, with adults with severe dysfunctions (e.g. people with severe learning disabilities or people who are psychotic), then sensitivity and clinical skills are required and the level of readability and comprehensibility of the description is important.

A second issue is the role of deception in psychological research. Although it is more common in social than in clinical or counselling psychology, there are some well-known examples of deception, e.g. Rosenhan's (1973) "pseudopatient" study in which participant observers faked a psychotic symptom in order to gain admission to a mental hospital as a patient. There is also the less dramatic issue of deception by omission: good scientific practice dictates that participants should not be aware of the hypotheses under investigation, since this knowledge may cause them to alter their behaviour. Thus deception is a matter of degree, ranging from relatively trivial instances of withholding information about specific hypotheses or naturalistic observation of public behaviour, to more serious cases of lying to the participants. Deception is an especially serious problem when the study uses fictional environments or contrived situations (e.g. in good samaritan studies when a serious crime or accident is feigned), or when double deception (i.e. false debriefing) is used.

At a minimum, a full debriefing is needed at the end of any study in which deception is used, in order to provide complete information, including the rationale for the deception, and to answer all questions about the study. However, debriefing cannot always be relied on to undo the effects of the deception, because this may cause greater pain when the participants learn that they have been deceived. For this reason, Korchin and Cowan (1982) recommend that alternative methods should be used wherever possible, including obtaining the person's consent to be uninformed, seeking feedback from surrogate participants who are similar to proposed participants, role playing and simulation research, and naturalistic, descriptive research.

Freedom of choice

Freedom of choice requires that the participant's consent be voluntary, without direct or indirect pressures to take part. There should be no coercion, explicit or implicit. Thus the researcher must foster the possible participant's autonomy and self-determination and should evaluate implicit situational or personal factors which may limit freedom.

There is often a considerable power imbalance between the researcher and the potential participant. In this case, the problem of making sure that there is no implicit coercion becomes acute. This is often an issue in clinical settings, where a therapist or doctor wishes to conduct research with his or her patients, who may fear that refusal will prejudice their treatment. It is also an issue with captive populations, e.g. in-patients, prisoners or students. Such power imbalances inevitably limit freedom. It is a matter for concern that these populations tend to be overused by psychologists.

Informed consent form

In practice, the study is described and the participant's consent is recorded by means of an informed consent form. Although specific requirements vary (depending on the particular study and the setting in which it is conducted), at a minimum this should contain:

- a description of the study's procedures;

- an explanation of its risks and potential benefits;

- an offer by the researchers to answer questions at any time;

- the statement that participants may withdraw their consent at any time during the study without prejudice, especially without prejudice to their present or future treatment;

- a space at the end of the form for the potential participant to sign in acknowledgement that he or she understands what the study involves.

The informed consent form is given to participants to read and sign after the study is initially described to them and after they have had a chance to ask any questions about it, but before the study proper begins. It is good practice to give participants a duplicate copy of the informed consent form to retain for their records.

Harms and Benefits

In general, research should not harm the participants. However, some people may freely consent to suffer harm for the greater good of humanity, e.g. in testing new medical procedures. There is a trade-off between any harm caused to the participants and the potential gain to humanity from the knowledge acquired.

In psychological research, harm is most likely to come from such things as stirring up painful feelings or memories, threats to one's self-image and embarrassment. Two extreme examples are Milgram's (1964) obedience studies, in which participants believed themselves to be giving dangerous electric shocks to other participants, and Zimbardo's (1973) prison simulation, in which college students role-playing prison guards brutalised other participants who were role-playing prisoners. In addition to psychological risk to the individual, there is also the possibility of social risk, e.g. to members of ethnic or cultural groups who may be harmed by the findings of studies examining group differences (Scarr, 1988).

As part of debriefing the participants after the data collection, you should ask whether they have experienced any upset or psychological problems during the study. Furthermore, if the respondent becomes highly upset during the study itself, you may need to terminate, or at least suspend, data collection. Your clinical and counselling skills become useful here, both in detecting the presence of distress and also in being able to respond to it appropriately. However, in some cases participants may need to be referred to sources of help outside the study, for example if an interview about psychological trauma stirs up painful memories, or if a study of marital interaction produces considerable conflict in the couple. Occasionally, people may volunteer for psychological studies in order to find a way of getting help for their difficulties.

Another aspect of harm is withholding of benefit. For example, participants in the no-treatment or placebo control conditions of a randomised clinical trial are deprived of a potentially effective treatment (see Chapter 7). This can be partially compensated for by giving the beneficial treatment later on in the study (i.e. employing a wait-list control procedure). The researcher must balance the need for scientific knowledge about the efficacy of a treatment against the likely consequences for the individual participants of being deprived of treatment.

Privacy and Confidentiality

Invasion of privacy and loss of confidentiality are special cases of harm. Privacy refers to the person's right to not provide information to the researcher, while confidentiality refers to the person's right (and the researcher's corresponding obligation) to withhold information from third parties.

In a trivial sense, all psychological research invades privacy, since otherwise it would not be finding out anything new. However, the ethical issue of privacy is concerned with the intrusiveness of research. Different people have different personal boundaries: some do not mind disclosing intimate information about themselves, while others want to maintain a tight control on what is known about them. The researcher needs to be aware of each participant's limits on disclosing information and respect their right to withhold certain information.

Types of confidentiality protection include anonymity, in which no identification is possible, and the more usual situation of protecting the participant's identity through secure research codes which are separated from the data itself. Participants are likely to be more open and to provide better data if they feel assured of confidentiality safeguards. Finally, it is important to keep in mind that no confidentiality guarantee is absolute, in that research records are always vulnerable to theft or legal subpoena.

Ideally, the informed consent form should specify who will have access to the data and the findings. (As an aside, the common phrase "strict confidentiality" on an informed consent form is redundant, since something is either confidential or it is not.) When audiotapes or videotapes are made, it should be clear who will hold them, for what purposes, and for how long; it is good practice to have a separate informed consent form to cover consent to make and retain recordings. When case material is written up, the participants' personal details should be altered so that they are unrecognisable (this sometimes requires creativity).

The issue of confidentiality becomes increasingly critical as the information becomes more sensitive or potentially damaging, should it become known to others. The kinds of danger from potential breaches of confidentiality include embarrassment, loss of employment, legal action, labelling and social stigma. In these situations, the researcher should give details on the informed consent form about the kinds of information that the participants will be asked to provide.

Ethics Self-study Exercise

We recommend that the researcher review his or her study in order to appraise its risks and benefits (Davison & Stuart, 1975). This self-appraisal begins by asking, "What risks are possible?", "How serious are they?", "How likely are they?"

The risk estimates typically increase when new procedures (i.e. new measurement or intervention methods) are employed, as opposed to established, tested procedures. Another important situational factor is the degree of coercion. The researcher should ask, "What obvious or implicit pressures are operating on prospective participants, which may prevent them from refusing to take part?" These may include the need for psychological or medical treatment, to impress legal authorities, or for release from prisoner or patient status.

Having evaluated the study's risks, the researcher should then ask, "What benefits are likely?", "For whom?", "How realistic are they?" Some benefits may accrue directly to the participant, including help with problems, self-knowledge or growth, general education, and increased self-esteem or altruism; other benefits are more general, such as the knowledge gained and the increased potential for helping others.

In general, greater potential risks, lesser benefits, unknown procedures and coercive situations call for stronger safeguards for informed consent and participant safety. These safeguards include greater disclosure of risks; careful screening and exclusion of at-risk participants (e.g. borderline personality disorder in short-term expressive therapy); supervision and monitoring of the participant's condition during the course of the study; and the use of contingency plans for removing participants from the study and finding appropriate treatment for research-induced problems. Finally, Davison and Stuart (1975) argue that there are some situations in which it is impossible to conduct ethical research, e.g. prisons can be said to be inherently coercive to such an extent that the participant's consent is compromised.

In evaluating the risk–benefit ratio, be aware of the dangers of self-deception: there is a tendency to rationalise and underestimate research risks while overestimating benefits, under implicit assumptions such as "the ends justify the means" and "what is good for me must be good for psychology". You will ultimately have an easier conscience if you follow the precept that "people are more important than data".

Ethics Committees

You cannot do psychological research without coming into contact with the committee delegated by your university, hospital or other agency to review and approve (or disapprove) the ethical treatment of human participants in research (Bruce, 1990; Ceci, Peters & Plotkin, 1985; Korchin & Cowan, 1982; National Health Service Management Executive, 1991). These committees are known as ethical committees in the UK and institutional review boards (IRBs) in the USA. The purposes of this review process are to protect the participants in the research, and also to protect the institution from legal reprisals for ethical lapses and harm done to research participants. An additional purpose is to comply with the regulations of grant-giving institutions.

Ethics committees are typically made up of academics, drawn from a range of disciplines, or medical doctors. Many committee members may be unfamiliar with psychological research. In the USA, their make-up is dictated federally, including a balance of gender and scientific disciplines and the inclusion of lay persons from the community and physicians. This range of backgrounds usually provides a breadth of perspectives to evaluate the ethical appropriateness of the research. However, occasionally ethics committees appear to exceed their brief and to make decisions on political rather than ethical grounds (Ceci, Peters & Plotkin, 1985).

For example, we knew of one project, intended to examine how well informed psychiatric patients were about the side effects of their psychotropic medication, which was refused ethical permission. It seemed that this was not because the project was unethical, but rather because certain committee members felt threatened by what the results might say about the state of professional practice.

Committees can sometimes take months to process an application, so it is wise to apply early, especially if your research is being done to a tight deadline (this particularly applies to student projects). However, there is a dilemma here, since if you apply for ethical approval early in the planning stage, before your protocol is finalised, your application may look less polished and your study may also change somewhat after it has been approved. If your research is still in the planning stage, you can attach a covering letter saying that the study is being developed but you would like to apply for provisional approval of the draft protocol.

There are often three levels of review: exempt, expedited and full review.

Exempt status. A study may pose such minimal risks as to be exempt from regular review. Such research includes:

- surveys using interviews or questionnaires, where the participants are not identifiable or are not asked to reveal sensitive information of a personal or potentially damaging nature;

- research on established educational practices, where the participants are not at risk and are not identifiable;

- research using existing archival or public data, where the participants cannot be identified;

- overt observation of public behaviour, under the same conditions of confidentiality and unintrusiveness.

The catch with exempted review status is that you are not allowed to make this decision yourself (because of possibly vested interests). Thus there is usually some form of screening required to determine whether a study should be exempted or not. A typical procedure for doing this is to consult with the ethics committee chair or one's departmental review committee.

Expedited review. The next level of review is expedited, a fast-track review process only for low-risk studies. Examples include the use of archival data where a particular use of the data has not previously been consented to; and non-stress-inducing behavioural research without manipulation of participants' behaviour or emotions. In expedited review the researcher still submits forms to the committee, which may subject the study to limited review by a subcommittee (e.g. the chair plus one other committee member).

Full review. The third level is full review, which applies to everything that does not fit the exempt or expedited criteria, to all government grants, and to all research with people who are not competent to give informed consent. Sometimes the researcher may be requested to meet with the committee to answer specific questions about the study.

Some research practices, such as deception and covert observation, raise red flags and require special consideration. These practices have a number of potential costs (Korchin & Cowan, 1982), including the fact that they tend to undermine trust in psychology; they may change people's behaviour (e.g. decreased bystander intervention in emergencies because people now think it might be an experiment); and their artificiality may yield distorted findings of low external validity. Finally, the need for comprehensive scrutiny also becomes more acute if you are working in a socially sensitive area (Sieber & Stanley, 1988) such as child sexual abuse.

FURTHER READING

More detail on sampling is given in Sudman's (1976) book *Applied Sampling*, which covers the issues in a non-technical way; Cochran (1977) provides the statistical background. Cohen (1990) gives a good overview of the issues in statistical power analysis and Cohen (1992) provides a "primer" covering the most commonly used cases. Alternative views of sampling and generalisation are covered in Patton (1990), Sidman (1960), Strauss and Corbin (1990) and Taylor and Bogdan (1984).

Researchers should familiarise themselves with the relevant set of ethical principles (e.g. American Psychological Association, 1992; British Psychological Society, 1990). Korchin and Cowan's (1982) chapter gives a full discussion of ethical issues in the clinical context; we have drawn on it extensively for the present chapter. Imber et al. (1986) focus on the issues as applied to psychotherapy outcome research.

+ In kendall,

phdacopy ps 264 & ps262. ps 266
ps271

CHAPTER 10 Evaluation research

In everyday parlance, evaluation means judging the worth of something. Good therapists do this informally: they build up a personal knowledge base of which interventions work best with whom. Clinical and counselling psychology training, in particular, encourages a reflective, self-critical attitude towards one's work: psychologists are taught to evaluate their own practice themselves. Here we will use the term evaluation in a more formal sense, to denote applied research into the implementation and effectiveness of clinical services. Much of the early evaluation work was done in the USA in an educational context, where it is known as program evaluation (Rossi & Freeman, 1993). It arose as a way of monitoring the federal money spent on large-scale social programmes in the 1960s, such as Head Start, a large pre-school educational intervention programme (Levine & Perkins, 1987).

This chapter departs from our chronological, research process framework. We have previously concentrated on fundamental issues in research methods, which can be applied across different content areas of psychological research. This chapter draws on ideas from the groundwork, measurement and design chapters, and applies them to the task of studying specific services in specific settings. Evaluation is a messy area in which sociopolitical and organisational issues are often as prominent as scientific ones (Cowen, 1978; Weiss, 1972). The design compromises that we discussed in Chapter 7 become more acute here: there is often a choice between collecting inadequate data and collecting no data at all. We are devoting a separate chapter to evaluation because there is a large literature on evaluation and related topics which it is important to address, and also because we anticipate that many readers will never conduct basic research, but may well be involved in evaluation. We argue that evaluation should be a routine part of applied psychology: much clinical and counselling work is based on custom and practice rather than any formal knowledge base, and evaluating it is a way of seeing whether or not it lives up to its claimed benefits.

The two central questions of evaluation can be simply stated: "What are you trying to do?" and "How will you know if you've done it?" The methods of evaluation research aim to answer these two questions. This chapter looks at the practical issues in incorporating evaluation into working clinical and counselling services. Before that, we will examine some of evaluation research's basic concepts and specialised vocabulary.

The Nature of Evaluation

There is a long-standing debate over whether evaluation is an art or a science. On the one hand, Campbell and his collaborators have argued for the use of rigorous research methods in evaluation (e.g. Cook & Campbell, 1979). On the other hand, Cronbach has argued that evaluation is an art, and that it should be tailored to the specific circumstances of the programme being evaluated (Cronbach, 1982). The issue is whether general principles of evaluation can be laid down, or whether the selection of methods must largely be left to the expertise of the practitioner in the specific setting. We stand in between these two positions, although leaning more to Campbell's, but within a broader definition of science. In any case, we see evaluation as being as systematic an endeavour as one can manage within practical and organisational constraints.

As we discussed in Chapter 2, the pure–applied research distinction is better regarded as a continuum than a dichotomy. Evaluation, at the applied end of the continuum, differs from pure research in several ways (Milne, 1987; Watts, 1984; Weiss, 1972):

- Its primary aim is to assist decision making, rather than to add to an existing body of knowledge. Thus it tends to be less concerned with theory and more with solving a particular setting's operational problems.

- It is done on behalf of a decision maker, often a manager, who may be distinct from the evaluator.

- It takes place in a complex "action setting" (Weiss, 1972), as opposed to the more controlled academic research environment.

- It is intended for immediate use and is usually done under considerable time pressure.

- It is often written up for purely local consumption, rather than for wider dissemination in professional journals. This may be partly because it may not meet exacting scientific standards and partly because the time and effort needed to write up the findings for publication may be beyond the evaluator's resources. Also, sometimes evaluators are unable to publish their findings because the people who commissioned the study do not want its results to be known by their commercial competitors.

Types of Evaluation

Scriven (1972) classified evaluations into formative and summative evaluation. A formative evaluation is one which feeds back its results continually to influence the service as it is developing (or forming itself). A summative evaluation provides a summary; it is done on a larger scale and its results are not delivered until the end of the evaluation period, which may be many months or years after the evaluation was commissioned. Formative evaluations are obviously more appropriate for new services; summative evaluations for well-established ones.

Donabedian (1980), a key figure in the quality assessment literature, distinguished three different foci of evaluation: structure refers to the resources that are available for a service, such as staff, buildings and psychological tests; process refers to the activities that constitute the service delivery—in psychology these are essentially a series of specialised conversations or assessment procedures; outcome is how the service affects the clients, e.g. how they change psychologically as a result. The parallel concepts of input, activities and output, which originated in economics, are also sometimes used (Fenton Lewis & Modle, 1982). The present chapter mostly concentrates on process evaluation: evaluation of structure is psychologically uninteresting (except from an organisational development point of view) and outcome evaluation overlaps considerably with our previous discussion of design.

The variables to be examined can be conceptualised using Maxwell's (1984) widely quoted list of six criteria for quality assessment: access to services, relevance to need (for the whole community), effectiveness (for individual patients), equity (fairness), social acceptability, and efficiency/economy. For example, Parry (1992) uses this framework to address how psychotherapy services might be evaluated.

Evaluation, Audit and Quality Assurance

Two areas closely related to evaluation, audit and quality assurance, have recently come into prominence. Audit and quality assurance both overlap with evaluation, but as they tend to be more narrowly focused we will consider them here as aspects of evaluation research.

The term "audit" has recently come into vogue in the UK (Cape, 1991; Crombie et al., 1993; Department of Health, 1989; Firth-Cozens, 1993; Parry, 1992), although it has a history stretching back to the beginning of the twentieth century (Lembcke, 1967; Young, 1982). Audit is a loosely defined term that refers to an intensive examination of one or more aspects of a service. For example, an out-patient psychotherapy service might audit the ethnic background of its referrals. As in this example, audits can be specific, or they can be more wide ranging. Recent definitions of audit have tended to emphasise comparison against an agreed standard (Crombie et al., 1993; Firth-Cozens, 1993). For example, an audit of waiting times in an out-patient service might involve the standard that all clients should receive an appointment within six weeks of referral. Under this stricter definition, simply monitoring practice prior to a standard having been set, or developing a standard itself, are important precursors to audit, but not the audit proper. Audit may be described as medical audit, to indicate that it is being performed by doctors, or clinical audit, if it is done by a multi-professional team.

Both audit and evaluation are closely linked to quality assurance, which emphasises setting up procedures to ensure that the standard of a service's work remains consistently high (Cape, 1991; Clifford *et al.*, 1989; Green & Attkisson, 1984; Young, 1982). Methods for quality assurance could include peer review or systematic involvement of service users in monitoring delivery.

Audit and evaluation are retrospective, looking at the service after it has happened, although the results will naturally be fed back to help improve the service. This process of evaluating, feeding back, making changes in the service and evaluating again is referred to as an audit or quality cycle (Crombie *et al.*, 1993; Firth-Cozens, 1993). Quality assurance, on the other hand, is essentially prospective, to make sure that no problems occur in the service, although it is also retrospective in the sense of identifying problems and making sure that they do not happen again. To take an example from manufacturing (where much of this language originated), evaluation (or auditing, or quality inspections) will count the number of flies in the baked beans; quality assurance will try to stop them getting in there in the first place.

The Socio-political Context

It is vital never to underestimate the sense of threat that accompanies evaluation. Even people who feel largely positive about it will often be worried or irritated by it; other people may just pay lip-service to enlightened attitudes about evaluation, but ultimately be defensive and obstructive. Some of the most important concerns are as follows:

- An oppressive sense of being continually scrutinised, that can feel like "Big Brother is watching you".

- Resentment at having to take the time to provide the data for evaluation, since it leaves less time for client contact.

- Fear that the results of evaluation may provide ammunition for managers or other colleagues to attack the quality or quantity of work being done.

- Annoyance that the criteria used in evaluations do not capture the important aspects of a service's work. Evaluations may just focus on quantitative measures that are easy to collect, such as numbers of clients seen, rather than the more valid but less tangible indicators of quality.

These are important objections. Even if you do not feel them strongly yourself, they will undoubtedly be felt, if not voiced, by a significant proportion of your colleagues. As we discussed in Chapter 3, this is an area where psychologists can use their skills to understand and possibly reduce the sense of threat. Clinical and counselling psychologists typically have had much better training in this than other professionals involved in evaluation.

We have been tacitly assuming that you are evaluating a service which you yourself partly deliver: this is often called an in-house evaluation. An alternative possibility is to use an external evaluation consultant. External consultants are usually more objective, since they are less emotionally attached to the service and more able to weigh it up dispassionately. On the other hand, external evaluators are usually more threatening, less knowledgeable about the service and more expensive. For the rest of the chapter, we will assume that you are conducting an in-house evaluation, since that is the more common situation. However, sometimes psychologists are employed as external consultants to evaluate other services. External evaluations cover the same ground as in-house evaluations, but in addition they require the evaluator to possess specialised consultancy skills.

Our own view is that, despite its potential difficulties, evaluation of the services they deliver needs to become a routine component of psychologists' work, and that evaluation can be made more relevant if conducted by the psychologists themselves. The mental health field, in particular, is awash with programmes and interventions that are very poorly monitored. No one knows what their effects are, and there is often at best a lack of interest in, and at worst a contempt for, the views of the clients. Furthermore, the current climate of accountability in the USA and the UK emphasises evaluation, audit and quality assurance (Crombie *et al.*, 1993; Department of Health, 1989; Iglehart, 1992; Parry, 1992; Zimet, 1989). So the issue is not whether to evaluate, but how. We believe that it is better to take control of evaluation yourself, rather than have it imposed on you.

The various stakeholders (evaluation jargon for someone who has an interest) in the service will each have different reasons for wanting the evaluation done. These reasons are not necessarily mutually incompatible, but each stakeholder will attach their own weighting to each one. For example:

- *People funding a service* (e.g. managers or grant-giving bodies) may want to know whether it is doing what it is supposed to be doing, and that it is using its resources effectively.

- *Clinicians* may want to test the effectiveness of an intervention or to compare it to other interventions. They may also want to know if their time is being used efficiently.

- *Service planners* may want to justify the development or continuation of a service, or to improve its delivery.

- *Service users* may be concerned about the accessibility, convenience or effectiveness of the service.

- *Community leaders* may want to know if the service is reaching its intended target population.

Aside from these overtly expressed, rational reasons, there may also be some less legitimate, covert reasons for evaluating (Weiss, 1972). For example, evaluation may be used to delay making a decision, or as an empty public relations exercise, or as a way of generating information that can be used to justify closing down an awkward service. Evaluation is a messy political arena, in which some people do nasty things for nasty reasons, but rarely admit that they are doing so.

The next section examines the preparatory thinking that is needed to set up an evaluation. Then we will look at ways of monitoring service delivery, and finally touch on evaluation of impact and effectiveness.

PREPARATION FOR EVALUATING A SERVICE

As we stated at the beginning of the chapter, the first question to address in evaluating a service is, "What is the service trying to do?" This is usually closely followed by the subsidiary question, "Why is the service trying to do that?" Before the evaluation proper can proceed, these questions must be addressed. We will adopt Rossi and Freeman's (1993) framework, which consists of six steps, which we will cover in turn:

1. Setting down the aims and objectives.

2. Specifying the impact model.

3. Specifying the target population.

4. Estimating the extent of the target problem in the target population.

5. Assessing the need for the service.

6. Specifying the delivery system design.

They are all easier to do when you are setting up a new service, as building in evaluation can be helpful in defining the service's goals and procedures. Thinking about how it is going to be evaluated helps you to become clearer about what it is trying to achieve, and vice versa. However, these preparatory steps are also useful if you are evaluating an existing service.

Aims and Objectives

Aims and objectives are the *sine qua non* of evaluation, especially for new services. They are a concrete expression of what the service is for. Without knowing what the service is trying to do, the evaluator has no benchmarks to measure its operation against. Aims are global statements of the desired outcomes of the service, expressed in a general, often rather idealised way. For example, "The service aims to reduce depression in mothers of young children." Objectives are specific actions, ideally occurring within a given period of time, which detail what the service is actually going to do to achieve its aims and which give specific targets to indicate whether or not the aims have been met. The objectives should be clear, simple and, if possible, measurable, so that there will be no ambiguity about whether each one has been reached. For example, "The service plans to set up three self-help groups for mothers of children under two years of age in the London borough of Camden by the end of the current financial year."

The exercise of specifying aims and objectives helps to clarify the goals of a service. Debating them within a clinical team usually results in the individual team members understanding each other's values better. Furthermore, without aims and objectives team members may not know what they are supposed to be doing or may even be pulling in different directions or undermining each other. For example, in an HIV service, some members may emphasise prevention, others counselling, some individual work, others work with couples, yet others research. While there is clearly healthiness in this diversity, the team also needs a sense of direction so that its energies are not spread too thinly.

The Impact Model

The impact model specifies the theoretical or empirical basis for each of the activities that the service is undertaking (Rossi & Freeman, 1993). It may never be formally specified, but thinking about each of its three components helps you to plan an effective service. These components are:

1. The *causal hypothesis* describes what causes or maintains the target problem(s) that the service is seeking to modify.

2. The *intervention hypothesis* specifies how the proposed intervention will affect that causal determinant.

3. The *action hypothesis* specifies that the intervention will in fact reduce the target problem(s).

For instance, in our maternal depression example, the causal hypothesis is that depression in mothers of young children is partly caused by a lack of social support; the intervention hypothesis is that a self-help group will increase social support; the action hypothesis is that the self-help group will decrease maternal depression. The three parts of the impact model can be depicted as follows:

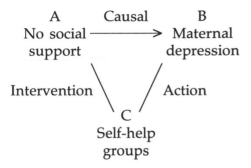

Sometimes, however, it may not be possible or necessary to address the cause of the problem directly. For instance, with adult survivors of child sexual abuse we cannot alter the cause, because it occurred years ago. Furthermore, addressing the cause may not be the best strategy for alleviating the target problems: etiology does not necessarily determine treatment. The point of specifying the impact model is simply to make the rationale for the service's actions as explicit as possible.

The Target Population

Having specified the impact model, the next step is to identify the targets, direct and indirect, for the intervention. Direct targets are those people on whom the intervention is specifically focused, e.g. mothers of children under two. It is important to define the unit of analysis, which could be individuals, families or groups. Indirect targets are those people who may benefit indirectly from the service, e.g. the families of the above women. Including the indirect targets gives a full picture of the impact of the service. Ideally, the targets should be specified in the aims and objectives of the service.

Target boundaries should be clearly defined using both inclusion and exclusion criteria, e.g. a specified geographical catchment area, and demographic and clinical characteristics of the client group. When specifying the criteria, try to strike a balance between definitions that are too broad/overinclusive and those that are too restrictive/underinclusive. The following model, taken from a local drop-in service, is a good example of a target description:

> To be in the Target Group, a person has to be: aged over 16 years; be living, staying or sleeping out in the South Camden sector of Bloomsbury Health District; have severe and enduring mental health problems; have positive or negative symptoms of psychotic illness; have had previous contact with mental health services; not be actively involved with other services; be experiencing severe social problems. People who meet these criteria but whose primary problem is due to the abuse of alcohol or drugs do not come into the Target Group.
>
> (Compass Project, 1989)

Estimating the Extent of the Target Problem in the Target Population

When planning a service, it is naturally important to estimate the extent of the target problem in the target population. Three epidemiological concepts are useful here. Incidence is the number of new cases during a specified time period, e.g. the one-year incidence of flu. Prevalence is the number of existing cases, either at a specified time ("point prevalence"), or during a time interval. For example, Pantelis, Taylor and Campbell's (1988) point prevalence study attempted a census of all individuals diagnosed as suffering from schizophrenia in the South Camden sector of London on a specific day. The Epidemiological Catchment Area study (Regier *et al.*, 1988) assessed the one-month prevalence rate of serious psychological disorders in five US cities. Incidence and prevalence are related to each other by the duration of the illness: higher incidence or a longer duration will both increase the prevalence. Incidence is a more useful measure for illnesses of short duration, e.g. flu; prevalence is more useful for those of longer duration, e.g. Alzheimer's disease.

With psychological problems it is not always clear whether to measure the extent of the target problem in terms of incidence or prevalence. For example, in providing services for dealing with cases of child abuse, do you want to measure the number of new cases per month (incidence), or the total number of cases on the social services list (prevalence)? The issue is whether you are concerned with detecting and treating new cases as they appear or with knowing the number of existing cases in a population, whatever the time of origin.

The third concept, population at risk, is the subset of the general population that is more at risk of contracting a disease, e.g. intravenous drug users are a population at risk of HIV infection. It is particularly helpful to consider this target group for preventive projects.

There are several methods for estimating the extent of the target problem (McKillip, 1987). There is a trade-off between their validity on the one hand and their complexity and cost on the other.

1. *Surveys and censuses* can be done in order to get the respondents' direct estimates of the size and severity of a problem. They generally yield the most valid data, especially if they include structured interview measures (Robins *et al.*, 1981), but they are time consuming and expensive.

2. *Rates under treatment*. The size of the target problem in the target population can sometimes be estimated by looking at the rates under treatment in similar communities (if they exist). The number of people who seek treatment is usually a small fraction of the actual number of cases, but there may be ways of estimating the size of the untreated population, based on previous studies. For example, Weissman (1987) estimated that only one in six people suffering from severe depression was receiving formal treatment.

3. *Indicators*. This method uses statistical techniques, such as linear regression, to predict the size of the target problem from non-clinical criteria. For example, one indicator of the number of heroin addicts in a community is the number of arrests for sale or possession of the drug (Hartnoll *et al.*, 1985).

4. *Key informants*. The researcher can use "networking" or "snowballing" sampling methods (see Chapter 9) to find knowledgeable people who might be able to help estimate the extent of the target problem. This is a simple and inexpensive method. In our experience, 20 or 30 respondents are usually sufficient. The advantage is that it develops the support of influential workers in the community; the drawback is the

possible bias of the individuals surveyed. Qualitative and/or quantitative interviewing methods can be used.

Needs Assessment

Assessing the extent of the target problem in the target population is the first step in planning a service, as it gives an indication of what the volume of demand is likely to be. However, it is easy to assume that everyone suffering from the target problem needs or desires the service, which is not necessarily true. Needs assessments collect data that are more relevant to the service's operation: it is the healthcare equivalent of market research. In the British National Health Service, District Health Authorities have an explicit responsibility to assess the healthcare needs of their local populations.

The concept of need is often used in a technical sense, defined as a problem for which there is a potentially effective intervention (Brewin *et al.*, 1987; McKillip, 1987; Stevens & Gabbay, 1991). Under this definition need is thus determined by professionals, rather than by the users themselves. On the other hand, "demand" is defined as what people ask for and "supply" is what is provided. Stevens and Gabbay (1991), in an article nicely entitled "Needs assessment needs assessment", discuss the relationship between need, demand and supply. They depict this relationship in the Venn diagram shown in Figure 10.1.

The Venn diagram helps to conceptualise and label the other areas, e.g. need that is not supplied (areas 1 and 4) is called "unmet need", and need that is supplied (areas 6 and 7) is called "met need".

Needs and demands can be assessed using the same methods as described above for assessing the extent of the target problem. Such studies are not always popular with health service managers, as they imply the expenditure of further resources to satisfy whatever unmet needs are identified.

Delivery System Design

With new services, the foregoing are the preliminary steps in establishing the likely need and demand. The final step is to design

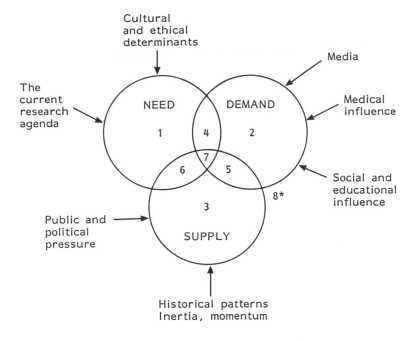

Figure 10.1 Need, demand and supply: influence and overlaps. Crown copyright. Reproduced from Stevens & Gabbay (1991) with the permission of the Controller of Her Majesty's Stationery Office

the service itself. The delivery system design, which is ideally set out in the form of an operational policy document (Øvretveit, 1986), specifies how the clinical team will go about delivering the service. It includes the organisational arrangements, such as procedures and activities, and structural aspects such as the physical setting, staff and materials that are needed to provide the service. The discussion needed to produce an operational policy document, and the existence of the document itself, may help to anticipate some common problems in newly established clinical teams.

Having set down an operational policy, the team can use role-plays or simulations to see whether things will work smoothly in practice (e.g. what exactly will happen when a client walks in the door or when someone makes a telephone referral). Larger-scale services may use operational research methods (a set of scientifically based procedures to aid decision making) to see if the services are planned in an optimal way (see e.g. Rosenhead, 1989), for example whether the staffing levels at different sites are appropriate for the anticipated workloads. This is a type of formative evaluation.

MONITORING SERVICE DELIVERY

Having gone through the above preparatory steps, the evaluation now focuses on what kind of service is being delivered: in Donabedian's (1980) terminology, the process of the service. Monitoring service delivery means asking "Who does what to whom?" It also addresses such questions as, "Is this service being delivered in the best possible way?" and "Is it accessible to its consumers?" (Maxwell, 1984). This differs from evaluating the outcome of the service, which we will cover in the next section.

Rossi and Freeman (1993) distinguish two main targets of monitoring: coverage and implementation. Monitoring coverage asks the question, "Who is getting the service?", i.e. is it reaching the appropriate target population? Monitoring implementation asks, "What service is being given?" Is the service's delivery consistent with its design specifications, i.e. is it delivering what it is supposed to be delivering? In addition, there is financial monitoring (to make sure that the funds are being properly used) and legal monitoring, to make sure that the service operates within the relevant laws (e.g. equal opportunities, health and safety). As the latter two kinds of monitoring are specialised activities, being the province of accountants and lawyers respectively, we will not cover them here.

Coverage and Bias

Two key concepts in monitoring are coverage and bias. Coverage is defined as the extent to which the service reaches its targets: is it reaching everyone it intended to, or just a certain subgroup of the target population. Bias is the degree to which subgroups of the target population participate differentially, i.e. the degree to which some subgroups are more thoroughly covered than others. Bias can arise from several factors:

- Self-selection, e.g. if only the more motivated clients come to a drop-in service.

- Programme/service actions, e.g. if staff favour some clients at the expense of others. In particular, there may be "creaming": that is, a bias towards the more advantaged subgroups of the target population. For instance, Community Mental Health Centres in the USA ended up seeing a large proportion of better functioning people who were easier to work with, and tended to neglect older clients and clients with long-term needs (Orford, 1992). Other examples of programme bias are where services do not adequately cater for the needs of physically disabled clients or of certain ethnic groups (possibly because of unconscious racism).

- Unforeseen influences, such as where the service is located, e.g. if it is somewhere that is difficult to get to by public transport (strictly speaking, this is an aspect of structure rather than process). These factors may be again reflect unconscious programme bias.

Undercoverage occurs when there are some people in the target population with unmet needs. This is often a problem in face-to-face psychology services, as there are often many people in the community who need the service but do not get it (Hawks, 1981). Overcoverage occurs when some inappropriate targets are served. For example, in health promotion campaigns, e.g. to reduce smoking or to promote safer sex, material may inevitably be directed at some people outside the target population. This is usually not a great problem.

Assessing coverage

Several methods can be used to assess coverage:

- *Service records* are the most obvious and commonly used method. Most psychology services keep records of basic client characteristics. These are often held in computerised form on a database, which makes it much easier to conduct statistical analyses. Thus the coverage can be monitored according to demographic characteristics, e.g. client gender, age or ethnicity, and possibly also according to clinical characteristics such as presenting problem or the source of referral.

- *Surveys* can be used when services are not targeted at selected, narrowly defined groups of individuals, but at an entire community. They are more appropriate for preventive health education or health promotion services. For instance, Barker, Pistrang, Shapiro and Shaw (1993) assessed the coverage of a BBC television series on preventive mental health. Although it was accessible to a national audience, the series was primarily aimed at certain subgroups of the population, that is, those people who were experiencing psychological problems themselves or who had a friend or relative who was. A national survey was used to estimate the nature of the viewing audience and their reactions to the series.

- *Analysis of dropouts* can be used to assess bias, by comparing people who participate fully in the service with those who drop out before the end. A high drop-out rate indicates that something is wrong with the service. It may reflect client dissatisfaction, or conditions in the community that prevent full participation (e.g. lack of transport). Data on drop-outs can come from service records or from surveys designed to find non-participants. Such data help identify subgroups of the target population that are not receiving the service. It may be possible to ask them about any dissatisfactions with the service and then to use their opinions to help design a different intervention more suited to their needs.

An index of coverage efficiency

If you need to specify precisely the accuracy of coverage, the following numerical index can be used (Rossi & Freeman, 1993):

$$100 \times \left(\frac{\text{Number served in target pop.}}{\text{total number in target pop.}} - \frac{\text{number not in target pop.}}{\text{total number served}} \right)$$

This will take a value of $+100$ when the actual number served is equal to the designated target population, with no inappropriate targets. It takes a value of -100 if only inappropriate targets are served, and an intermediate value when there is a mixture of appropriate and inappropriate targets. For example, with a target population estimated at 2000, assume that you actually serve 1000, of which 800 are appropriate. Then the efficiency index would be $100 \times (800/2000 - 200/1000) = +20$.

The formula provides a means of estimating the trade-offs in a service including appropriate and inappropriate targets. A manager confronted with an index of -40 might impose additional selection criteria to eliminate some of the inappropriate targets, and extra recruitment to secure replacements. Another option would be to expand the programme to include more appropriate targets, i.e. keep the same number of inappropriate targets but increase the total number served.

Implementation

Monitoring service coverage focuses on which clients the service is reaching; monitoring service implementation or delivery focuses on what kind of service the clients are getting. It can look at both descriptive aspects, to label what components of service they receive, and quality aspects, to describe how well the service is given. Implementation can be assessed by:

- *Observation* (qualitative or quantitative) in the clinical setting.
- *Service records*, e.g. in antenatal care, to ensure that the right number of visits were made and the correct things done at each one. Standard clinical records can be augmented by asking clinicians to complete a checklist of activities. They can be given a standard form to tick off each procedure as it is completed, e.g. in HIV pre- and posttest counselling, or an audit team can review the casenote files at regular intervals to make sure that they are complete and that proper procedures are being followed.
- *Management information systems* and case registers (computerised databases) can keep track of each client's visit to a service and the types of service they received and produce regular reports on the data.
- *Service user surveys* may be desirable when it is not possible to obtain user data routinely as part of service activities, or when

the size of the target group is large and it is more efficient to do a sample survey than to obtain data on all participants. You can ask the clients about what kind of service was actually given to them. A natural step if you are doing this is also to ask them about their satisfaction with the service and what its impact was, which leads into the next area, outcome evaluation.

OUTCOME EVALUATION

Outcome evaluation examines the impact of the service on the client. It asks the central question, "Do clients benefit from this service?" Benefits may be manifest in the form of an improvement in the target problem (called "health gain" in the current jargon) or in the form of changes in attitude about the problem, so that it becomes less problematic.

Assessing outcome involves applying the research methods that we have discussed in previous chapters, in so far as that can be done within the constraints of the setting. The first step is to choose measures that capture the key objectives of the service (e.g. a service aimed at helping depressed adults might use the Beck Depression Inventory). Secondly, select a research design that will assess any changes in those measures and if possible enable such changes to be attributed to the service itself rather than to other variables (Cook & Campbell, 1979; see also Chapter 7). Of course, in many services this is a counsel of perfection, and the evaluator may have to be content with drawing inferences from less than adequate designs or measures.

Naturalistic field research of this sort is often imperfect from a scientific point of view. The issue here, however, is whether it is good enough to draw plausible conclusions to aid practical decisions. Managers are often more convinced by research conducted in their own service, even if it is scientifically flawed, than by a methodologically sound piece of research published in a reputable scientific journal, which was conducted in another setting by other investigators (Watts, 1984).

Client satisfaction surveys

One good example of a scientifically problematic, but professionally valuable, area of study is client satisfaction research (Lebow, 1982). Clients' views of the service they have received are usually assessed via standardised self-report instruments, e.g. the Client Satisfaction Questionnaire (CSQ: Larsen *et al.*, 1979), which can be adapted to most services.

Clients' views are often minimised or dismissed by professionals, usually on two grounds. Firstly, they consider that the client's view is invalid, possibly because of psychological problems or because of transference aspects of the therapeutic relationship ("What's the point, clients don't know anything about therapy, their viewpoint is biased") or because of positive response sets ("Everyone will just say it's a good service"). Secondly, client satisfaction surveys mainly use a one-group posttest-only design, which has many internal validity threats (Cook & Campbell, 1979; see also Chapter 7). Biases and design problems are hard to overcome in client satisfaction research, but it seems wrong to use their existence to dismiss the whole enterprise out of hand (Lebow, 1982). Professionals' views of the effectiveness of the services they deliver are also biased; service evaluation ideally needs to take both perspectives into account. Positive response sets in clients' reports can be avoided to some extent by asking clients explicitly to list any problems with or complaints about the service (Parry, 1992), and threats to internal validity can be taken into account when interpreting the findings.

Cost effectiveness

A final issue to consider is cost-effectiveness evaluation (Krupnik & Pincus, 1992; Mangen, 1988). This compares the service's costs with its outcomes, in order to ensure that its funds are being well used. In economic terms, it compares inputs to outputs. This kind of evaluation has become more prominent in the UK and the USA, as purchasers of healthcare services (in the UK health authorities, in the USA health maintenance organisations or insurance companies) must decide what to spend their limited resources on. Their decisions will be based on which services they think will give the greatest outcome per unit of resource employed.

There are clearly problems in measuring both input and output. At the input end, costing must take into account both direct costs, principally psychologists' contact time, and overheads, such as the cost of buildings, equipment and support staff. Cape, Pilling & Barker (1993) present a method of cost allocation, based on a survey of the relative proportion of psychologists' workloads spent in various components of their role, such as face-to-face client contact, service development and supervision.

The output end of the calculation is more problematic, since there is no universally agreed measure of effectiveness or of benefit. Different healthcare services (e.g. heart surgery compared to psychiatric in-patient treatment) use different criteria to measure outcome. One solution, derived from health economics, is to combine quality of life and life expectancy into quality adjusted life years, or "QALYs". Thus an outcome of a treatment, say an operation for cancer, may give a person a high-quality life for a short time or a medium-quality life for a longer time. These outcomes would be considered equivalent in terms of QALYs. Such an approach, although it fulfils the economists' goal of giving a single index on which to base resource allocation, clearly makes a number of problematic assumptions (Cox et al., 1992).

Another approach is to attempt to measure the burden of illness or psychological disorder in terms of lost productivity, increased social services expenditure and increased use of medical services (e.g. general practitioner consultations, visits to accident and emergency departments or hospitalisation). Then the outcome of a psychological intervention can be partly assessed by the savings made in terms of increased productivity and reduced social services and healthcare expenditure—often referred to as "cost offset"—which may represent a substantial financial return in relation to the expenditure on the psychological intervention (Krupnik & Pincus, 1992).

A simpler form of cost-effectiveness analysis, and one with direct relevance to practitioners, is to compare practitioner input, measured in terms of number of sessions, with output in terms of client improvement. Counsellors and therapists must ask themselves, implicity or explicitly, whether it is better to give one client twenty sessions or two clients ten sessions (or ten clients two sessions). Cost-effectiveness evaluation attempts to make the basis of such decisions explicit. Howard *et al.*'s (1986) analysis of dose–response relationships in psychotherapy falls under this heading. They used the statistical technique of probit analysis on a data set drawn from 15 published studies to estimate the improvement rate of clients after a given number of sessions. They estimated, for example, that 53% of clients had improved by 8 sessions and that 74% of clients had improved by 26 sessions. However, to be a true cost-effectiveness analysis the input must then be expressed in monetary terms: that it costs so many pounds or dollars to produce such and such an outcome.

FURTHER READING

Rossi and Freeman's (1993) text, which we have drawn on extensively here, gives a comprehensive framework for program evaluation. Sage has published a nine-volume, step-by-step cookbook, the *Program Evaluation Kit* (Herman, 1988). Weiss (1972), one of the founders of the evaluation movement, has an excellent discussion of the rational and irrational feelings about evaluation. Cape (1991) and Parry (1992) review the audit and quality assurance literature as applied to clinical psychology.

CHAPTER 11 Analysis, interpretation and dissemination

Having collected the data, the final stage of the research process consists of making sense of it, first for yourself, then for a wider audience. This stage can itself be broken down into three components: analysis, interpretation and dissemination. Analysis means establishing what the findings are and how they answer the research questions, interpretation means understanding the findings in terms of their broader implications, and dissemination means communicating both the findings and your understanding of them to other people. Analysis is typically reported in the Results section of a research paper; interpretation is reported in the Discussion section. As always, the components overlap and intermingle: an interpretation of the findings might suggest a further analysis of the data, or presenting the study at a conference might lead to new ideas about its interpretation. However, for simplicity, we will cover the three components as though they were distinct and sequential.

ANALYSIS

The goal of the analysis is simple: to use the data to answer each of the research questions. We will cover the quantitative and qualitative cases separately, although the preliminary steps in both approaches follow a parallel sequence. Many techniques of data analysis, both qualitative and quantitative, involve specialised methods which are beyond our present scope. They are covered in the standard texts on statistics (e.g. Howell, 1992; Siegel & Castellan, 1988; Winer, 1971) and on qualitative methods (e.g. Patton 1990; Strauss & Corbin, 1990; Taylor & Bogdan, 1984).

Quantitative Data Analysis

As we discussed in Chapter 7, there are an enormous number of possible research designs, which can be broadly classified into descriptive, correlational and experimental. The complexity of the research design and the nature of the research questions will determine the complexity of the analysis. For some designs, the analysis might need to use solely descriptive statistics, such as means or frequencies, whereas others may require complex multivariate analyses. Depending on the type of research questions, the analysis may be either exploratory (or discovery-oriented), which is aimed at finding patterns in the data, or confirmatory (or hypothesis testing), which is aimed at testing prestated hypotheses (see Chapter 3). In other words, exploratory data analysis is inductive, whereas confirmatory analysis is deductive (Tukey, 1977).

Regardless of the type of analysis, there is a sequence of preparatory steps to go through before formal analyses or hypothesis-testing can be carried out. These are data entry, data checking, data reduction and data exploration. We will cover each in turn.

Data entry

The first step is to enter the data into a computer. Before this can be done, the variables must be named and defined so that the computer knows which data correspond to which variables, and also so that it is able to recognise missing data which may then be omitted from subsequent analyses. One convenient way to define variables and enter data is via the SPSS Data Entry program (Norusis/SPSS, 1990), which uses a spreadsheet format.

When using a scale composed of multiple items, it is usually better to enter all of the raw item scores rather than just the total scale score. This enables you to analyse the scale's reliability and factor structure, and to use the computer to calculate the total score. Any reverse-scored items will need to be recoded so that their values are consistent with the rest of the items in the scale. This can be done manually before the data are entered, but it is usually simpler and more reliable to use the computer to perform the recoding.

Data checking

Data entry errors can arise either from transcription and typing mistakes, or from wrong instructions being given to the computer. It is important to control for both possibilities. In order to ensure that the data have been entered correctly, it is a good idea to proofread the entries by asking someone to read them back aloud from a printout and checking them against the original source. Rosenthal (1978) estimated that, on average, about 1% of data points are wrongly entered. Sometimes computer scan sheets can be used in order to eliminate typing errors, but these also need to be checked to ensure that they have been filled in properly.

To check that the data are being read correctly by the computer, some simple descriptive analyses can be performed. These also provide the basic descriptive statistics that you will probably need for the Results section of your research report. For nominal scale data, frequency analyses can be used; for interval scale data, summary descriptive statistics, such as the mean, the standard deviation, minimum and maximum values, and the number of valid observations. The SPSS Descriptives command (Norusis/SPSS, 1990) is a simple way to do this. Such analyses help you to check that missing values are being handled properly and that there are no out-of-range (i.e. impossible) values. Discrepancies in standard deviations (i.e. ones much smaller or larger than other variables of the same type) often indicate problems with unreliability or restricted ranges, which may suggest the elimination of items or measures before further analyses are carried out.

Data reduction

Data reduction consists of condensing the data, so that it is more manageable and easier to analyse. One obvious approach consists of simply dropping some of the variables from the data set. Researchers are often overambitious in the initial stages of the project and then they realise at the start of the analysis that they have more variables than they know what to do with. Such planning errors can often be corrected by eliminating variables from the analyses, thus reducing the size of the data set. It is better to focus your energy on thoroughly analysing a few important variables, rather than struggling to analyse everything that you optimistically included because you thought it might be interesting to look at.

Once the basic variables have been decided on, the data set can be reduced by summing or averaging the items of any multi-item scales to provide a total score or subscale scores (e.g. by using the SPSS Compute command). With a new scale, it is important first to conduct an item analysis, as the averaging process assumes that the items are parallel (see Chapters 4 and 5). Item analysis will identify bad items, that is, items which do not hang together with the rest of the scale, and will also show whether the scale as a whole has a high enough internal consistency to warrant its use as a homogeneous measure. Once these analyses are done, the raw item scores can be dropped from the data set.

A third method of data reduction is factor analysis (Gorsuch, 1974; Harman, 1976; Tinsley & Tinsley, 1987), a multivariate statistical technique that is designed to determine the structure of a set of variables. It is often used as a step in measure development research (see Chapter 5), to investigate the number of underlying dimensions of a new measure or set of measures. Factor analysis can also be used when the researcher wants to represent most of the information in a large number of variables by the scores on a small number of independent factors.

Item analyses tend to be regarded as preparatory analyses and are usually reported in the Method section of the research paper, whereas factor analyses tend to be regarded as proper analyses in their own right and are usually reported in the Results section.

Data exploration

The final preparatory step is to get a feel for the patterns of your data. Even if you are working within a hypothesis-testing framework, it is still a good idea to look at the data from other angles to see what else they can teach you, if only to generate ideas for future studies. Scientific advances often come from unexpected findings, which purely confirmatory procedures may fail to pick up (Merbaum & Lowe, 1982). It is worth trying to develop a playful attitude to the analysis, looking at things from different angles, so that you end up feeling that you know the data inside out.

In the last 20 years, several statistical techniques have been developed to assist this process. Tukey's (1977) *Exploratory data analysis* (often abbreviated to EDA) is the standard reference volume: briefer accounts are given by Jackson (1989) and Lovie and Lovie (1991). EDA methods emphasise graphical displays of data and, in line with its spirit of taking a more playful stance towards the data, they often have appealing names, such as stem and leaf plots or box and whisker plots.

A first set of analyses involves looking at the frequency distributions of each of the variables. This will enable you to check, for example, whether or not the variables are approximately normally distributed, whether there is any systematic pattern to the missing data and whether there are any outlying observations that will distort the subsequent analyses. For some descriptive studies, e.g. opinion surveys or consumer satisfaction research, knowledge of the frequency distributions may be all that is required to answer the research questions.

A second set of preliminary analyses involves exploratory correlations, particularly between all the independent variable measures and between all the dependent variable measures. Such analyses usually reveal patterns in the data that help you to understand subsequent results. For example, if one criterion measure performs differently from the others, it is useful to have studied its patterns of correlations with the other variables. Similarly, repeated confirmation of hypotheses is less impressive if the variables in question are strongly interrelated, suggesting that they are different measures of the same construct.

There is a dilemma between, on the one hand, the desire to get the maximum mileage out of the data by conducting many analyses and, on the other hand, the need to avoid the common error of overanalysing the data, of trying to relate everything to everything else. As we discussed above, you need to be ruthless in deciding which are the most important variables that you want to focus on and then omitting the rest.

Answering the research questions

If the research is discovery oriented or the research questions are very broad, most of the analyses may not be precisely planned in advance; instead they will follow interesting leads from the data. If, on the other hand, the research is being conducted within a hypothesis-testing framework, there will be specific analyses corresponding to each of the hypotheses. In either case, the selection of statistical tests that are appropriate to your research questions and design lies outside our present scope. You will need to draw on your own statistical expertise and reference books. However, do not be reticent about seeking advice from psychologist colleagues or from statisticians: even experienced researchers often need help for more complicated analyses (although statisticians usually prefer to be consulted before the data are collected, so that they can have some input into the design).

Qualitative Data Analysis

Much has been written recently about qualitative data analysis. Some key references include Strauss and Corbin's (1990) description of the Grounded Theory approach; Giorgi's (1975, 1985) and Wertz's (1985) presentations of the Duquesne phenomenological approach; Potter and Wetherell's (1987) book on discourse analysis, as well as some more general descriptions (e.g. Dey, 1993; Henwood & Pidgeon, 1992; Patton, 1990; Taylor & Bogdan, 1984). Here we will describe methods common to most approaches, but we will lean towards the more systematic methods favoured by Grounded Theory and the Duquesne School, as these seem to have a greater appeal to psychologists than the less structured methods. However, flexibility is required in all phases of qualitative research, including analysis. It is important to adapt the analytic method to the data, research question, and your own cognitive style and talents.

Strategies in qualitative data analysis

Regardless of one's general approach to qualitative research, there are three forms of qualitative data analysis: narrative presentation, interpretive case analysis and cross-case analysis.

Narrative presentation. The first approach is to organise the material chronologically into a story or narrative, usually an individual case study. The scientific task is the basic one of description. This approach is non-interpretive and minimally analytic: instead of searching for themes or patterns, the researchers restrict themselves to arranging the material into a story which is allowed to speak for itself. Such presentations are excellent for demonstrating the existence of a phenomenon. A good example is Bogdan and Taylor's (1976) study of "Ed Murphy" (reprinted in Taylor & Bogdan, 1984), which demonstrates the existence of perceptive self-awareness in a young man labelled as being "retarded".

Interpretive case analysis. Even when qualitative researchers focus on particular cases, however, they are usually interested in going beyond description to explanation or interpretation. They wish to explain the meanings, reasons, causes, themes, categories, rules, structures or patterns of what has been observed or described. Often, consistent with clinical and counselling psychologists' interest in understanding individuals, this analysis is carried out in the context of idiographic case studies. For example, in the Duquesne phenomenological approach (e.g. Giorgi, 1985; Wertz, 1985), the psychological structure of the individual's experience is interpreted (e.g. one woman's experience of attempted rape), before an attempt is made to understand the constituents or general structure of an experience (e.g. the transformation of the person's world through being criminally victimised). The analysis of individual cases within a larger cross-case analysis is referred to as an "embedded cases design" (Yin, 1989).

Cross-case analysis. The third general strategy looks across individuals in order to identify what is typical about the phenomenon being studied. Often the researcher attempts to identify the defining features of the phenomenon, i.e. those which make it what it is and not something different. For example, Wertz (1985) found that the experience of being criminally victimised was defined in part by a breach in the person's previously taken-for-granted world of safety and supportive community. Sometimes the researcher is interested in describing variations within the phenomenon, that is, repeated patterns which occur more than once, but not in a majority of instances (e.g. different types of criminal victimisation). Finally, after identifying defining features and variations, the researcher also tries to link them together, for example as sequentially ordered, as opposites or in hierarchical category–feature relationships. In the Duquesne phenomenological approach, the cross-analysis focuses on the nomothetic defining features of the experience and is carried out only after idiographic case analyses; in Grounded Theory research (e.g. Rennie, Phillips and Quartaro, 1988) this intermediate step is omitted and the analysis is focused throughout on identifying general descriptive themes and variations across individuals.

For example, McGlenn (1990) was able to identify common features of important "weeping events" in people's lives. Some of the features served to define the phenomenon (e.g. the sense of weeping as marking something of significance in the context of the person's life; the experience of physical and emotional release). Other features, however, were more descriptive of variations in the phenomenon (e.g. interrupted versus completed weeping) or of incidental features of the experience (e.g. the use of hydraulic metaphors).

Data preparation

As in quantitative analysis, the first step in qualitative analysis is to prepare the data. It must be assembled, transcribed, unitised, judged for relevance and reorganised before the analysis proper can begin.

Data assembly. In interview studies, gathering the data together is a straightforward matter of getting the material transcribed (although it is important to check the transcripts). However, in research using multiple perspectives and sources of information (e.g. Comprehensive Process Analysis: Elliott, 1989a) this process takes on greater importance as the different types of data must also be collated. Patton (1990) refers to the compendium of data on a case as a case record.

Data cleaning. The collected data are often cluttered with irrelevancies which can impede the analysis. These include errors, ambiguities, repeats, distractions and sidetracks, especially descriptions unrelated to the phenomenon under investigation. The researcher reviews the material, preparing a record which contains only relevant material. In the Duquesne phenomenological method (Giorgi, 1985; Wertz, 1985), this is referred to as the judgement of relevance; it hinges on determining whether or not each piece of information contributes to understanding the phenomenon.

Establishing units. It is difficult to analyse a protocol or case record all at once; furthermore, global analysis encourages the ignoring of data which do not fit one's expectations or emerging understanding. For this reason, researchers usually divide the protocol into units. The most common is the meaning unit, which consists of material on a single point in the informant's description (Wertz, 1985), e.g. "When I got out of my car, I looked back because I always get a fear over my shoulder." Their use is largely a practical strategy; their exact definition is not critical and may vary among researchers with different cognitive styles and among studies with different research objectives.

Reordering the data. The data are also likely to be disorganised, containing narrative defects, e.g. backtracks or repeated descriptions of similar material. Themes and categories will be much more apparent if the meaning units are regrouped. If the data are part of a narrative, this typically means putting the pieces into chronological order; otherwise, the material can be arranged into logical groupings. This process is partially encompassed by what Grounded Theorists call "axial coding", that is, the ordering of data within a general framework which organises the material without suggesting specific substantive themes. For example, in Comprehensive Process Analysis, information about a significant event in therapy is first sorted into three broad headings: Context, Process and Impacts (Elliott, 1989a).

Developing categories or themes. The central analytic process in the Grounded Theory approach is open coding: a categorisation which allows categories to emerge inductively. These categories cannot be fixed beforehand and, like categories in everyday life, they are not mutually exclusive; that is, a particular meaning unit may be assigned to a number of different categories. For example, the meaning unit above—"When I got out of my car, I looked back because I always get a fear over my shoulder"—may possibly be assigned to two categories, "normality" and "suspicion". An important aspect of open coding is developing labels for the emerging categories; these derive from numerous sources, including the informant's own words, the literature and metaphor. The researcher often attempts to invent a special set of terms to capture aspects of the phenomenon for which we do not have precise language (referred to as languaging). For example, in her analysis of weeping events, McGlenn (1990) developed the term "everydayness" to capture the quality of things seeming routine and ordinary before many of the weeping events. However, this approach runs the risk of developing an offputting jargon that can act as a barrier to communication of the findings.

The categories typically exist in relation to other categories, often in a hierarchical or outline structure, with more descriptive, lower-order categories functioning as properties, defining features, alternative forms or examples of higher-order, more abstract categories (Strauss & Corbin, 1990). For example, in the weeping moments study, McGlenn (1990) found a higher-order contextual theme of prior unawareness; this larger theme took a number of different forms, which McGlenn labelled as everydayness, undiscussability (implicit taboo on talking about something) and partial awareness/dawning (the state of knowing implicitly the existence of something painful, but avoiding its emergence into full conscious awareness).

Two methods are useful for developing categories or themes: psychological reflection and the constant comparative method. Wertz (1985) has described psychological reflection in terms similar to therapeutic empathy. In particular, he describes a process of "entering and dwelling", in which the analyst attempts to immerse him- or herself in the informant's world. The analyst tries to slow down the story and to dwell on its details and meanings, setting aside (bracketing) the assumption that he or she already understands what is being described. At the same time, the analyst tries to step back from the description, attending to meanings rather than matters of truth or falsity. Often this process incorporates a dialogue with the data, in which the analyst interrogates each unit, asking questions such as, "What is really meant here?", "What kind of thing is being described?" and "How does this relate to the phenomenon I'm trying to understand?" This method is interpretive in that it generates a deeper understanding by allowing the analyst to explicate the informant's implicit meanings and assumptions.

The constant comparative method is key to the Grounded Theory style of qualitative analysis (Glaser & Strauss, 1967; Strauss & Corbin, 1990). Here the analyst compares each meaning unit to the previous units and current set of categories. If the unit contains a similar idea to an existing category, it is added to that category and may help to clarify or elaborate it. If it differs from the previous units, it is noted as a possible new category. This process continues until saturation is reached; that is, until categories are no longer added or elaborated. As the analyst develops a set of open categories, their interrelationships become more apparent and further layers of higher-order categories often emerge. In a fully successful Grounded Theory, a core category eventually emerges. The core category is the most general label for the phenomenon, encompassing both its general features and its main variations: the headline of the story. For example, in Addison's (1989) study of the training of family practice physicians, the core category was "surviving".

Clarity and meanings of representations in qualitative research

Although the practices for evaluating qualitative research are not as well worked out as for quantitative research, the researcher nevertheless needs to evaluate the findings or representations of the data for their clarity and meaning. Specifically, it is important to consider whether the research questions (of definition, description or explanation) have been thoroughly and clearly answered. What remaining ambiguities are there? How could the analysis have been continued? What has been left out of the analysis? Do the analyses illuminate the phenomenon, or do they skate over its surface? Of course, this is ultimately a matter for the reader to decide (referred to as uncovering or phenomenological validity; see Chapter 4), but it makes good sense for the researchers to address these questions as well.

Moving from qualitative to quantitative analysis

Once a qualitative analysis has been carried out, it may be possible to develop a standardised quantitative measure of the phenomenon, which leads to substantial gains in the efficiency of data collection. For example, the categories or themes may be used as the basis for a content analysis measure, which can be applied to the same type of interview or field note data used in the qualitative analysis. Once raters have been trained in the use of the content analysis measure, they will be able to code the data much more efficiently. Even greater efficiency can be obtained by translating the analysis into a quantitative self-report measure, using the informants' own descriptions as a source of items.

INTERPRETATION

The analysis yields the basic findings of the study; the interpretation attempts to spell out their implications or broader meanings. Analysis, at least within the quantitative tradition, is often a mechanical exercise, which follows set rules and requires expertise rather than inspiration, whereas interpretation is often more intellectually demanding and requires imagination and insight into the psychological meaning of the phenomena. In qualitative research, the distinction between analysis and interpretation is not so clearly drawn; nevertheless, there is still room for taking a broader view of one's findings or representations of the data.

Interpretation consists of two main parts. The first part is to evaluate the strength, significance and validity of the results within the context of the study itself: are the results substantial or are they trivial? As part of this, the strengths and weaknesses of the study are assessed, to see whether it can really support the interpretations that you might try to bring to it. The second main part is to ask what are the implications of the findings in the larger scientific and professional context: how do they relate to existing research in the area, and what are their practical and professional implications? This is a broader conceptual task, aimed at bringing the results of the study to bear on the issues that initially inspired it.

Strength and Significance of the Findings

As we have said, the first step in evaluating findings is to assess their strength. The conceptual tools are mostly used for assessing the magnitudes of effects, and they were developed in the quantitative context. However, parallel ideas can also be used in the qualitative context. It is helpful here to return to Cook and Campbell's (1979) four validity types (see Chapter 7). We have already examined construct validity and internal validity; we will now look at the other two types, statistical conclusion validity and external validity, since they are particularly relevant to the interpretation phase.

Statistical conclusion validity

As we discussed above, quantitative data analysis will often demonstrate that two variables covary, i.e. they are associated with each other, for example that counsellor empathy is associated with client improvement. The assessment of statistical conclusion validity asks whether such conclusions about covariation are sound. It is a preliminary step before making causal inferences (which are covered under internal validity). Three questions need to be addressed (Cook & Campbell, 1979).

First, was the study sensitive enough to permit reasonable inferences about covariation? Greater sensitivity is obtained either by larger sample sizes or by reducing the amount of error, both of which give greater statistical power (see Chapter 9). Reducing error can be done both by selecting measures that are more reliable and by choosing a research design that controls for extraneous variation, for example by having a homogeneous sample (see Chapter 9) or by incorporating an individual difference variable as an extra factor in an experimental design (see Chapter 7).

Second, if the study was sensitive enough, do the variables in fact covary? Here the issue is whether the right statistical tests were performed. Did they meet the assumptions behind them (e.g. for a normal distribution)? Was an appropriate error rate set? How likely is it that the results were due to chance variations? "Fishing expeditions", that is, conducting a lot of tests in a large data set until something interesting turns up, will produce spuriously significant results. If you have to conduct multiple statistical tests, the alpha level (i.e. the critical value of p) at which the tests are performed needs to be made more stringent, or the statistical analysis can be conducted within a multivariate framework, which reduces the number of tests to be performed.

Third, if the variables do in fact covary, how strong is that covariation? This seemingly straightforward question opens up a number of difficult issues about how to measure the significance of the findings. There are three ways to do this, which we will examine in turn: statistical significance, effect sizes and clinical significance.

Statistical significance

It has long been argued that statistical significance in itself does not tell you much (D. Bakan, 1966; Barlow, Hayes & Nelson, 1984; Cohen, 1990; Lykken, 1968; Oakes, 1986). One issue is the arbitrariness of the conventional criterion of $p < .05$, in other words that a result has to have a probability of less than 1 in 20 of occurring by chance in order to be counted as being statistically significant. A result with a p of .049 is barely stronger that one with a p of .051, yet the first will be reported and the second will not. There is no logical reason why 1 in 20 was settled on, the convention could just as well have been 1 in 25 or 1 in 18.

A more serious issue is that, given a large enough sample size, any effect will become statistically significant, since no null hypothesis is ever exactly true (Meehl, 1978). Thus a result may be statistically significant but practically trivial. For example, in testing a new therapy for depression, a mean difference of two points on the Beck Depression Inventory between the experimental and control group may reach statistical significance with a large sample, but it will be clinically irrelevant if both groups remain severely depressed.

Effect sizes

One potential solution to this difficulty is to express the findings in terms of effect sizes (see our discussion of statistical power analysis in Chapter 9). There are a number of different effect size measures, depending on the statistical comparison being carried out. The basic principle is to create an index of the strength of the relationship between two variables that is independent of the sample size.

The calculations involved are best illustrated by considering a simplified one-group pretest–posttest comparison. In this case, the appropriate effect size measure is the difference in means between the pre- and the post-therapy scores divided by the standard deviation of the pre-therapy measure. For example, in the second Sheffield Psychotherapy study (Shapiro *et al.*, 1994), the Beck Depression Inventory (BDI) was given to clients before and after therapy. Let us consider one small part of the whole research design, the part which examined the effects of 16 sessions of cognitive-behavioural psychotherapy on severely depressed clients. The pre-therapy mean BDI score for this group of clients was 29.60, with a standard deviation of 7.38, and their post-therapy mean score was 11.58 (Shapiro *et al.*, 1994, p. 533). Then the measure of improvement, expressed as an effect size, is (29.60 – 11.58)/7.38. This comes to 2.44, which Cohen (1988) classifies as a large effect. Thus, using effect size measures, we can say that these severely depressed clients showed, on average, a substantial improvement in BDI scores over the course of the therapy.

Meta-analysis

Effect size measures have an important additional advantage: they make it possible to compare the strength of findings across different studies. Such comparisons are usually done using a method called meta-analysis. Meta-analysis is a study of studies and is a form of research in its own right. It is a sophisticated procedure which was pioneered by Smith and Glass (1977) in a seminal paper analysing psychotherapy outcome studies. It uses quantitative techniques to aggregate findings across studies and to look at what features of a study are associated with specific results (see e.g. Durlak & Lipsey, 1991). For example, in the psychotherapy outcome literature, you can examine whether studies that use a sample of volunteer, college student clients have a different pattern of results from studies that use a sample drawn from a clinical population who were actively seeking help for their difficulties (Shapiro & Shapiro, 1983).

The main advantage of meta-analysis over traditional qualitative or box score reviewing methods is that it is a more powerful way of aggregating the literature and of detecting trends across studies. However, it is still a controversial development, and has been criticised for giving too much weight to methodologically unsound studies. Despite these criticisms, it is a widely accepted method of reviewing large bodies of literature; meta-analytic reviews have been published in many areas of psychology where there is a large body of literature to be reviewed.

Although its general principles are not difficult to understand, conducting a meta-analysis is a technical business whose mechanics lie a long way beyond our present scope. Further details can be found in Durlak and Lipsey (1991) or Rosenthal (1991). The main point of relevance here is that in interpreting one's results, it is often useful to compare them meta-analytically with the findings from other similar studies in the literature. This involves calculating the effect size measures in your own study and comparing them with the corresponding effect sizes obtained in other studies, thus giving you an estimate of how your findings fit in with the rest of the literature.

Clinical significance

One problem with effect sizes is that they compare differences in mean scores against the standard deviations of the groups, rather than against any absolute standard. Although effect sizes are more meaningful than p-values, the presence of a large effect size still does not guarantee that a result is clinically significant: for example, in a two-group experimental design, a large effect could be due to small standard deviations in the experimental and control groups, rather than a substantial difference in the means themselves. A pre-post study of a psychological intervention could have a large effect size, but the clients may not feel much better after it. The search for a way of capturing which findings are clinically important and which are trivial has led to the development of indices of clinical significance, which are associated with the work of Jacobson and his colleagues (e.g. Jacobson, Follette & Revenstorf, 1984; Jacobson & Truax, 1991). Such indices are now being routinely incorporated into studies where clinical change is being assessed (e.g. Shapiro *et al.*, 1990).

Again, these ideas are best illustrated in the context of psychotherapy outcome research. Clinical significance essentially attempts to encapsulate quantitatively what is meant when we say that an intervention with an individual client was successful: that the client's level of functioning (in terms, say, of a depression, anxiety or self-esteem measure) must have substantially improved after the intervention. There are three different ways in which a successful outcome may be generally conceptualised (Jacobson & Truax, 1991):

1. That the client's post-intervention score has moved outside the range of the dysfunctional population on the measure in question. (Outside the range is usually defined as more than two standard deviations away from the mean of the dysfunctional population.)

2. That the client's post-intervention score represents a return to normal functioning, that is, it has moved inside the range of the functional population. (Inside the range is usually defined as being within two standard deviations of the mean of the functional population.)

3. That the client's post-intervention score is more likely to be in the functional than the dysfunctional population. (This is usually defined as being closer to the mean of the functional population than the dysfunctional population.)

These three alternative criteria for clinical significance are illustrated in Figure 11.1, which locates the cut-off points for each of the three possible criteria on the distributions of the dysfunctional and functional groups. Which of the three criteria to adopt in any given study depends on which of the three ways best fits your conceptualisation of a significant outcome of the intervention that you are researching.

Limitations of the Study

Having assessed the strength and significance of the findings, you next need to look at the other side of the coin and assess the weaknesses and limitations of the study. (In qualitative research this process is called discounting.) Are there any problems with

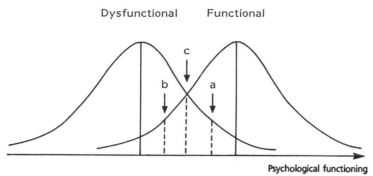

Dysfunctional   Functional

Psychological functioning

a. The area to the right of this line depicts the scores corresponding to criterion 1.
b. The area to the right of this line depicts the scores corresponding to criterion 2.
c. This line represents the mid-point between the means of the dysfunctional and the functional groups.

Figure 11.1   Three criteria for clinical significance. From Jacobsen & Truax (1991). Copyright 1991 the American Psychological Association. Adapted by permission

the study that might have influenced the results? You owe it yourself and to your readers to make these explicit. The physicist Richard Feynman forcefully expresses his belief in this aspect of scientific honesty:

> It's a kind of scientific integrity, a principle of scientific thought that corresponds to a kind of utter honesty—a kind of leaning over backwards. For example, if you're doing an experiment, you should report everything that you think might make it invalid—not only what you think is right about it: other causes that could possibly explain your results . . . Details that could throw doubts upon your interpretation must be given, if you know them. You must do the best you can—if you know anything at all wrong, or possibly wrong—to explain it.
>
> (Feynman, 1985, p. 341)

It is useful here to return to Cook and Campbell's (1979) concept of internal validity (see Chapter 7). Are there any possible third variables that might account for your findings equally well? In what other ways could your findings be explained, in addition to the variables that your research has focused on? For example, could the positive gains from a new intervention be simply due to the increased attention from the counsellor, rather than the specific intervention itself?

External Validity

Having assessed the strength, significance and validity of the findings within the context of the study itself, the second step in the interpretation phase is to ask to what extent they can be generalised beyond the immediate context of the study. This is the external (or ecological) validity question (Cook & Campbell, 1979), which asks about the representativeness of the study: its range of application across persons, settings and times. Any peculiarities of the sample, procedures, setting or timing will reduce the external validity of the study. Construct validity (see Chapter 4) can also be considered as an aspect of external validity, since it assesses generalisability across different measures.

A dilemma for researchers is that the demands of external validity and those of statistical conclusion validity often conflict. For example, one way to reduce error, and therefore to increase the statistical conclusion validity of the study, is to draw the sample from a homogeneous population. However, this will make the study less representative and thus lower its external validity. As frequently happens with decisions in research, there is no clear-cut answer here.

Replication

The best way to increase external validity is via replication. The more that you can reproduce the initial findings under diverse conditions, the more convincing they will become. Lykken (1968), drawing from Sidman (1960), distinguished three types of replication:

1. *Literal replication* is an exact duplication of the study conducted by the original researchers using identical procedures.

2. *Operational replication* is carried out by other researchers, using the methods published by the authors of the original study.

3. *Constructive or systematic replication* replicates the basic idea of the study, but uses different methods, for example a different population or alternative measures of the same constructs.

If the results of a study hold up under several constructive replications, we can have confidence in its external validity.

Research programmes often begin with laboratory studies which have a low external validity, since it may be a good idea to start out by a simple test of one's theories in such a setting, rather than in an expensive and time-consuming field study. For example, early behaviour therapy studies used college student volunteers who had spider phobias for which they had not sought help. However, if the first laboratory or analogue studies prove to be successful, the researcher then needs to conduct more ecologically valid studies to give the findings credibility.

Implications: Understanding the Meaning of the Findings

The final step is to understand what the findings mean, from the point of view of theory, method and practice. A central part of this task is to relate the findings back to the research, theory or conceptual model on which the study was based. How do the data answer the research questions? Do they support or contradict the theoretical model on which the study was based? How do you explain any discrepancies between your expectations and the findings?

"The facts are friendly"

Although it is much easier said than done, it is worth reminding yourself to approach this task with an open mind. Try not to be defensive or dogmatic about your theories, but allow the data to speak for themselves. Carl Rogers used to say "the facts are always friendly" (Kirschenbaum, 1979, p. 205); in other words, do not fight the results, even if they cause you discomfort. The opposite extreme to the attitude of openness is to deny the validity of the results if they conflict with your preconceived ideas: rather than adjusting your theories, you adjust reality instead. Research will often force us to rethink our ideas, which can be a painful process.

The old debate about the effectiveness of psychodynamic versus behavioural psychotherapy provides a classic example of arguing from preconceived positions rather than assimilating the data. Researchers and clinicians often uncritically accepted the validity of studies which supported their theoretical stance (either pro- or anti-behavioural methods), while attacking flaws in studies that contradicted them (Shapiro & Shapiro, 1977). Many similar examples can be found in other areas of the psychological and scientific literature. Much rarer are instances of researchers who have publicly changed their position as a result of their own or other people's findings.

Alternative explanations

Having related the findings back to the literature, you may wish to speculate more imaginatively about what they mean. Speculation is quite acceptable if labelled as such: that is, if you warn your readers that you are not claiming that your speculations are securely grounded in the evidence.

Also, much as you examined the weaknesses of the findings, you need to examine the weaknesses of your chosen theoretical explanation. Could the findings be explained in other ways than in terms of your pet theory? Are they compatible with other frameworks than your own? How would a psychoanalyst, a Gestalt therapist or a biologically oriented psychiatrist view them?

The next study

As we discussed in Chapters 1 and 2, research is often a circular process, in that the data may only partially answer the research questions. Often the study reveals, with the benefit of hindsight, that the research questions could have been better formulated, or that there were measurement or design weaknesses, or perhaps that the method shows promise and could be expanded or applied more broadly. Thus the study may lead naturally on to a plan for future research in the area.

Professional implications

Finally, in clinical and counselling research it is important to consider what implications your findings have for professional practice. What would you suggest practitioners do, or not do, differently on the basis of your study? For example, McGlenn's (1990) qualitative work on weeping suggests that the therapist maintain a non-intrusive but supportive presence while the client is crying and that they be attuned to important meanings which may have been accessed as a result of the weeping episode. As a second example, the finding of the second Sheffield Psychotherapy study (Shapiro *et al.*, 1994) that severely depressed clients showed substantially greater improvement after 16 sessions as opposed to 8 sessions, suggests that very brief therapy is not to be recommended for this client group. Consideration of the professional implications of the study leads naturally on to the next section, dissemination, which considers how the findings and their implications will be made known to people who might use them.

DISSEMINATION

Research is basically a public activity. On rare occasions you may be doing it for yourself alone, but normally your goal is to communicate your findings to others. Usually this involves a written report or published article, but it may also involve presentation in the research setting, at conferences or for policy makers in government departments.

Writing Up

Writing up the project can seem a mountainous task. It is easier if you start the process early on and think of the write-up as accumulating progressively by a series of successive approximations over the course of the project. It is worth starting to plan the report and write a first draft of the Introduction and Method sections while you are collecting your data.

Having said that, many of us resist writing up, for various reasons. For some people, putting pen to paper is the hardest step of all. It is arduous and intellectually demanding, since it forces you to present your ideas in a clear and watertight way. Fear of criticism—one's own or others'—can lead to procrastination (Parry, 1989). Also, the workload and the emotional stresses of many clinical and counselling jobs can make it hard to find the time for writing.

Good research reports are usually simple. They tell the story of the research project, sticking to the main themes without bogging the reader down in irrelevant detail. It is worth continually bearing in mind the one or two key questions that guided the investigation (or at least the part of it that you are writing up) and to structure your report around those themes. This is often hard to do at the end of a study, because you have often lost perspective on what is important and cannot see the wood for the trees. Try to step back and distance yourself from your study (this is not easy if you have just spent months fretting over it), attempting to see it through the eyes of a general, informed reader, as though it were done by someone else. Get criticism from trusted colleagues. Presentations at seminars or conferences are often a good way of shaping up your work and getting other people's reactions to it.

Writing style

Not only should you try to tell a simple and clear story, but also try to tell it in simple and clear prose. Journal articles in psychology, and in the social sciences generally, are notorious for using incomprehensible jargon or overelaborate sentence constructions. Much psychology writing is impenetrable or pretentious. A recent article in a prominent journal was entitled "Effects of informational valence and occupational favorability on vocational differentiation: A test of the disconfirmation hypothesis". While we are sympathetic with the authors' attempt to describe their study precisely, and often find ourselves writing in technical jargon, this sort of prose runs the risks of sounding pompous (by using specialised words like valence, favorability or differentiation) and of lulling the readers to sleep (all those "ation" rhythms rock you like a cradle).

George Orwell's much quoted spoof rewrite of a Biblical passage is a paradigmatic example of the contrast between vigorous writing and psychological waffle:

Here is a well-known verse from Ecclesiastes:

I returned and saw under the sun, that the race is not to the swift, nor the battle to the strong, neither yet bread to the wise, nor yet riches to men of understanding, nor yet favour to men of skill; but time and chance happeneth to them all.

Here it is in modern English:

Objective consideration of contemporary phenomena compels the conclusion that success or failure in competitive activities exhibits no tendency to be commensurate with innate capacity, but that a considerable element of the unpredictable must be taken into account.

(Orwell, 1946/1968, p. 156; reproduced by permission of the estate of the late S. M. B. Orwell)

Many style guides are available to help combat the tendency to write like Orwell's second paragraph. We recommend Lanham's (1979) amusing and idiosyncratic *Revising Prose*, which presents a ten-step method for editing one's own writing, and Strunk and White's (1959) miniature gem *The Elements of Style*, which many American readers will have met as undergraduates.

Psychology journals have complicated stylistic requirements of their own, which can deter novice authors. The British Psychological Society and the American Psychological Association have both published helpful style manuals (American Psychological Association, 1983; British Psychological Society, 1989). The APA manual, in particular, is comprehensive and detailed, ranging from general issues about layout and style to minutiae about where to put commas in the reference list. It also includes a helpful section on how to avoid sexist language and ethnic bias. Sternberg's (1988) *Psychologist's Companion* summarises the APA guidelines and provides much useful advise on how to write up a project.

Publication

It is always worth considering publishing your research, even though your primary aim may be to write it up for a course requirement or as part of a local evaluation. The initial research report itself may not be very useful. Dissertations and theses are often long, formalised and indigestible, and evaluation reports are usually geared to a local audience. On the other hand, research reports in professional journals at least aim for brevity and comprehensibility. If the study does not meet the exacting methodological standards of the APA or BPS flagship journals, consider less demanding outlets, often those attached to specific sections, divisions or interest groups of a professional body. You may also want to present your work at conferences, which is often a good stepping-stone to publication.

The process of submitting an article for publication is as follows:

1. Identify the journal that you are aiming for, as different journals have different requirements, both in terms of content and style. The anticipated readership of the journal will partly determine what material to include and how to present it.

2. The front or back cover of the journal will have a section describing the topics and the kinds of articles the journal publishes, and another headed something like "instructions for authors", which gives the journal's stylistic rules and instructions for submitting the typescripts to the editor.

3. Send the original typescript and as many copies as requested, with a short cover letter addressed to the editor. You should receive an acknowledgement of receipt within two or three weeks.

4. If your paper does not meet the broad requirements of the journal, the editor will send it straight back. Otherwise, it will be sent out to reviewers, who ideally are blind to the authors' identity. Reviewers are normally asked to send papers back to the editor within a month, but often take longer. On the basis of the reviews, the editor then makes one of the following decisions: accept the paper immediately, accept it subject to specified amendments, request revisions and resubmission, or reject it. Mainstream journals tend to have high rejection rates: for example, in 1992 the *Journal of Counseling Psychology* and the *Journal of Consulting and Clinical Psychology* both had 73% rejection rates (American Psychological Association, 1993) and the *British Journal of Clinical Psychology* had a 66% rejection rate (British Psychological Society, 1993).

5. The editor will communicate his or her decision to you in a covering letter, with copies of the reviews. You then have to decide how to proceed, based on your perception of the

reviewers' and editor's comments on your work. Bad reviews, both in the sense of negative ones or sloppy ones, can be upsetting. The whole process can be somewhat arbitrary, in that different reviewers do not always agree (Fiske & Fogg, 1990; Griffiths, 1992). Even if you get unfavourable reviews, it is important not to give up. At least try a couple of other journals before concluding that your work is not worth publishing. The potential pleasure and professional recognition that come from getting your work in print repays some investment of effort.

Authorship Issues

If the research has been done as part of a team (or if your supervisor has had a major input), the issue arises of who will be listed as authors and in what order. Authorship issues can often arouse feelings of competition or resentment in the research team and so it is helpful to start discussing them early on in a research project (see Chapter 3), although sometimes everyone's contributions can only be evaluated once the study is completed.

To be listed as an author, an investigator should have made a substantial scientific contribution to the paper, e.g. a major contribution to the formulation or design (American Psychological Association, 1992; Fine & Kurdek, 1993). Minor contributions that do not merit authorship, e.g. help with interviewing or data analysis, or a senior doctor's permission to study patients under his or her care, should be mentioned in the acknowledgements section. The order of authorship should reflect the value of each person's contribution.

Utilisation

Ideally, research should serve a purpose, not be just an empty exercise. You can increase the likelihood of its having an impact if you actively promote your findings. Articles in academic journals are only read by a select few, so it is worth putting effort into disseminating your work more widely (Richardson, Jackson & Sykes, 1990). This can be done informally, by discussing the research with people who might use it to make decisions (e.g. managers, policy makers, government officials). Or it could be done by writing more accessible articles, e.g. in trade journals such as *Nursing Times*, *Psychology Today* or in the popular press.

The process of how research findings get taken up, if at all, is not always clear. Academic research can feel narrow and inward looking, just feeding on itself, but sometimes findings do permeate through to influence practice. Weiss (1972, 1986) has developed models of research utilisation, which Tizard (1990) interestingly illustrates in the educational context. The thrust of Weiss's work is that the relationship between research and policy is non-linear and complex. The naive idea that research has a direct influence on policy is rarely borne out in practice. Often research is ignored, misapplied or used to buttress only one side of an argument.

However, there are cases where, for better or worse, research findings appear to strike a chord and become incorporated into far-reaching policy decisions. The studies carried out in the 1950s and 1960s, demonstrating the dehumanising effects of long-stay institutions, provide an example of research influencing practice. Although this research may have been used simplistically, and possibly only as a cover for cost-cutting by the Government, it also made forceful points that have an enduring resonance.

THE END

By the time you have finished writing up your research—particularly if it is a student project—you are probably thoroughly fed up with it and painfully aware of its flaws. You may even be thinking of giving up research altogether. Although we understand that reaction, having felt it many times ourselves, we hope that you will give yourself a well-earned break and that after you have recovered you will return to do more research. Consider going back to the drawing-board and using your hard-won wisdom to start the cycle again by designing a better study. The field of clinical and counselling psychology needs to strengthen its knowledge base through high-quality research. Psychologists who can draw on both research and clinical skills—whom we would call good scientist–practitioners—are central to this process.

CHAPTER 12 Summary and conclusions

> Thus scientific methodology is seen for what it truly is—a way of preventing me from deceiving myself in regard to my creatively formed hunches which have developed out of the relationship between me and my material.
>
> (Rogers, 1955, p. 275)

We started this book by comparing a research project to telling a story. Our own narrative of how a research project progresses is now drawing to a close. The book has been structured around the four basic stages of the research process, that is, the steps that researchers go through when they are doing a project (although they do not usually go through them in the neatly ordered sequence that we have depicted). These stages are: (1) groundwork, (2) measurement, (3) design and (4) analysis, interpretation and dissemination. Separating out the important issues according to the stage in which they are prominent is helpful both when planning research and also when reading research.

This chapter brings together and summarises some central ideas that run through the book. There are three sections: methodological pluralism (matching the method to the problem), how to appraise a piece of research (either your own or someone else's), and combining research with practice.

Methodological Pluralism

Our central theme has been methodological pluralism: that no single approach to research is best overall, rather what is important is that the methods are appropriate for the questions under investigation. It can also be labelled appropriate methodology, by analogy with the catchphrase "appropriate technology" (although strictly speaking the word methodology should only be used in its precise meaning of the study of methods). No single research method is inherently superior to any other: all methods have their relative advantages and disadvantages.

However, we want to make it clear that methodological pluralism is not equivalent to methodological anarchy. Unlike Feyerabend (1975), we are not saying that "anything goes". Quite the reverse, in that we have tried to outline methodological rules and principles within the context of each method. Some of these principles are common to all approaches, some are relevant only to specific research approaches or genres.

Wherever they are applied, the central purpose of these methodological rules is, as Carl Rogers aptly said in the quotation forming the epigraph to this chapter, to prevent one from deceiving oneself and others by drawing conclusions that are not supported by the data. In terms of the simple model of research that we presented in Chapter 2, the essence of the research attitude is finding ways to test your ideas against your experience of the world.

This book has attempted to integrate traditional and emergent methods. Although the proponents of each approach have often represented warring factions, we believe that the debate has often been too polarised and that it is possible, indeed desirable, to combine multiple methods within a single study or research programme.

Our message is not that knowing about research methods enables you to produce the perfect piece of research. However, we do hope that, having read this book, you will be better able to make informed choices in your own research, or at least informed compromises. As we have said throughout, there are always compromises and trade-offs to be made in psychological research. However, although we are saying that there is no one right way to do research, there definitely are wrong ways. Consideration of how research might be done badly leads in to the next section, on appraising research.

Appraising Research

We have aimed to give readers the conceptual tools needed to become both better producers and better consumers of research. So far, we have not explicitly covered how to evaluate a research report, since for simplicity the book has been written from the standpoint of readers who are carrying out a research project themselves. However, the issues that we have raised in the context of planning and executing research are also the issues to consider when you are reading research papers.

The more you know about research methods, the more you are able to recognise the problems in a piece of research. However, this does not mean that appraisal equals negative criticism. It is easy to criticise research. Psychology training often does a good job of teaching students how to pull studies apart; it is usually less good at giving them a sense of perspective. Our own students are often quick to find numerous flaws (many of which we consider to be trivial) in research papers, but they are less able to take a broader view, and to see things in balance.

Thinking about the different stages of the research process helps you to conceptualise some of the important issues to consider when evaluating a piece of research. We have discussed general criteria that apply to all types of research as well as some that apply to specific approaches. We present these general criteria below, as they apply roughly to each of the stages in the research process. (They are adapted from guidelines that we use to assess student dissertations and theses.) Although we have tried to make them as generally applicable as possible, not all of the criteria will apply to all pieces of work, nor will each criterion have equal weight.

Criteria for Evaluating Research

Groundwork. The first question to ask is, "Who cares?" In other words, is the topic worth researching, has it been done before, does the study add to useful knowledge, do the potential results help the development of theory?

continues

---

continued _____

Is the literature review relevant and up to date? Does it cover empirical, methodological and theoretical issues, and does it place the project in the context of scientific research in the area? Is the rationale for the study clearly articulated (possibly including an indication of the conceptual model linking the variables under investigation)? Are appropriate research questions or hypotheses clearly formulated?

Measurement. How are the main constructs defined and operationalised? Do the measurement methods (used in a broad sense to cover both quantitative and qualitative methods) adequately capture the constructs included in the research questions? If quantitative measures are used, do they have acceptable reliability and validity coefficients?

Design. Are the procedures described in sufficient detail to enable the reader to understand what was done and, if necessary, to be able to replicate the study? Is the design of the study appropriate to the research questions? Will it enable the desired inferences to be drawn? Are the size and composition of the sample appropriate to the research questions and data analysis? Does the study conform to the relevant professional and ethical standards?

Analysis. Do the analyses address each of the research questions? Are the data presented clearly? (Any tables and figures should be both understandable and necessary.) Are data reduction techniques or statistical tests used correctly?

Interpretation. Are the findings interpreted in the context of the research questions and the wider theoretical context in which the work was carried out? Are interpretations grounded in the data? (However, speculations are in order if labelled as such.) Are competing explanations for the findings considered? Are the limits of generalisability of the study

continues

continued _____

> assessed? Are any weaknesses of the study addressed? Are the professional implications of the findings discussed?
>
> *Presentation.* Is the paper readable? (Consider its general prose style, use of jargon and sexist or other offensive language.) Is the paper's length appropriate for its content?

In arriving at an overall evaluation of a research paper, take into account that strengths in some areas may compensate for weaknesses in others. Rather than simply listing the flaws of a study, try to estimate how they distort the conclusions of the research (Sommer & Sommer, 1991). Some technical flaws in the procedure may have a negligible impact on the results. The more important or innovative the topic or methods, the more forgivable should be any shortcomings: it is relatively easy to do methodologically sound but trivial research; it is harder to do innovative research that makes a scientific or professional impact.

Combining Research With Practice

An underlying assumption of the book has been the benefits to be gained from the scientist–practitioner approach. Research helps to advance practice by developing and testing new procedures; practice helps to advance research by providing a source of and testing ground for new methods, and by giving a reminder of the complexity of human behaviour that helps to counterbalance the oversimplifying tendency of much research. Although researchers and practitioners have not always seen eye to eye, we believe that the relationship between the two activities is ultimately mutually enriching (see Elliott, in press).

However, although a scientist–practitioner approach is good for the field as a whole, it does not follow that combining the two activities is right for everyone. We recognise that actually carrying out research may not be everyone's cup of tea. As we discussed in Chapter 2, although there are many positive reasons for becoming involved in research, there are also several reasons why combining research and practice is problematic. Different individuals will weigh up each of these reasons differently and decide to what extent, if at all, they want to be involved in doing research. We do maintain, however, that at a minimum, practitioners need to be sufficiently informed about research methods to be able to understand and appraise research, even if they are not actually doing it themselves.

In the past, the scientist–practitioner role has been identified with a narrow conception of research, which has put many psychologists off attempting to do their own research. It is certainly true that some types of research are prohibitively complicated, costly and time consuming for the individual practitioner: comparative therapy outcome research is the ultimate example. It is also unrealistic to expect that most practitioners would have the resources to conduct the kind of research that meets the exacting requirements of the major scientific journals. However, it is possible to work within a broader conceptualisation of the scientist–practitioner model (Powell & Adams, 1993). We have tried to outline some possible methods that can be adopted by practitioners working on their own (especially the small-N approaches outlined in Chapter 8 and the evaluation methods in Chapter 10).

Another strategy to increase one's involvement in research is to make it a group endeavour. For us, one of the central pleasures of research is the process of working with other colleagues. Teamwork gives stimulation and support: discussing mutually interesting ideas, struggling to work through disagreements or differences in perspectives. We would strongly echo Hodgson and Rollnick's (1989) advice to form a research team if at all possible.

We hope to have conveyed the message that research need not be as forbidding a process as is often imagined. Some of the old rigidities are now dissolving; it is widely recognised that there are many different approaches to research. It is possible to work in a genre of research that suits your own values, abilities and ways of thinking. Research is not to be undertaken lightly, it requires time and effort and it can be an intellectual struggle: rigorous thinking does not usually come easily. But we hope that ultimately the potential enjoyment and stimulation that research gives will encourage at least some of our readers to consider becoming involved in it themselves.

REFERENCES

Addison, R. B. (1989). Grounded interpretive research: An investigation of physician socialization. In M. J. Packer & R. B. Addison (Eds.), *Entering the circle: Hermeneutic investigation in psychology*. Albany, NY: SUNY Press.

Adorno, T. W., Frenkel-Brunswick, E., Levinson, D. J. & Sanford, R. N. (1950). *The authoritarian personality*. New York: Harper.

Ainsworth, M. D. S., Blehar, M. C., Waters, E. & Wall, S. (1978). *Patterns of attachment: A psychological study of the strange situation*. Hillsdale, NJ: Erlbaum.

Albury, D. & Schwartz, J. (1982). *Partial progress: The politics of science and technology*. London: Pluto Press.

Allport, G. W. (1962). The general and the unique in psychological science. *Journal of Personality*, **30**, 405–422.

Altman, J. (1974). Observational study of behaviour: Sampling methods. *Behaviour*, **49**, 227–267.

American Psychological Association (1947). Recommended graduate training in clinical psychology. *American Psychologist*, **2**, 539–558.

American Psychological Association (1952). Recommended standards for training counseling psychologists at the doctoral level. *American Psychologist*, **7**, 175–181.

American Psychological Association (1983). *Publication manual* (3rd edn.). Washington, D.C.: American Psychological Association.

American Psychological Association (1992). Ethical principles of psychologists and code of conduct. *American Psychologist*, **47**, 1597–1611.

American Psychological Association (1993). Summary report of journal operations, 1992. *American Psychologist*, **48**, 829–830.

Anastasi, A. (1982). *Psychological testing* (5th edn.). New York: Macmillan.

Anderson, R. J., Hughes, J. A. & Sharrock, W. W. (1986). *Philosophy and the human sciences*. Totowa, NJ: Barnes & Noble.

Armistead, N. (Ed.) (1974). *Reconstructing social psychology*. Harmondsworth: Penguin Books.

Austin, J. L. (1970). *Philosophical papers* (2nd edn.). New York: Oxford University Press.

Ayer, A. J. (1936). *Language, truth and logic*. London: Gollancz.

Bakan, D. (1966). The test of significance in psychological research. *Psychological Bulletin*, **66**, 423–437.

Bakan, P. (1966). *The duality of existence*. Chicago: Rand McNally.

Bakeman, R. & Gottman, J. M. (1986). *Observing interaction: An introduction to sequential analysis*. New York: Cambridge University Press.

Barker, C., Pistrang, N., Shapiro, D. A. & Shaw, I. (1990). Coping and help-seeking in the UK adult population. *British Journal of Clinical Psychology*, **29**, 271–285.

Barker, C., Pistrang, N., Shapiro, D. A., Davies, S. & Shaw, I. (1993). You in Mind: a preventive mental health television series. *British Journal of Clinical Psychology*, **32**, 281–293.

Barker, R. G., Wright, H. F., Schoggen, M. F. & Barker, L. S. (1978). *Habitats, environments, and human behavior*. San Francisco: Jossey-Bass.

Barlow, D. H., Hayes, S. C. & Nelson. R. O. (1984). *The scientist practitioner: Research and accountability in clinical and educational settings*. Oxford: Pergamon.

Barlow, D. H. & Hersen, M. (1984). *Single case experimental designs: Strategies for studying behaviour change* (2nd edn.). Oxford: Pergamon.

Baron, R. M. & Kenny, D. A. (1986). The moderator–mediator variable distinction in social psychological research: Conceptual, strategic and statistical considerations. *Journal of Personality and Social Psychology*, **51**, 1173–1182.

Battle, C. C., Imber, S. D., Hoehn-Saric, R., Stohe, A. R., Nash, C. & Frank, J. D. (1966). Target complaints as criteria of improvement. *American Journal of Psychotherapy*, **20**, 184–192.

Beck, A. T., Rush, A. J., Shaw, B. F. & Emery, G. (1979). *Cognitive therapy of depression*. New York: Guilford.

Beck, A. T., Steer, R. A. & Garbin, M. G. (1988). Psychometric properties of the Beck Depression Inventory: twenty-five years of evaluation. *Clinical Psychology Review*, **8**, 77–100.

Belenky, M. F., Clinchy, B. M., Goldberger, N. R. & Tarule, J. M. (1986). *Women's ways of knowing: The development of self, voice, and mind*. New York: Basic Books.

Bellack, A. S. & Hersen, M. (1988). *Behavioral assessment: A practical handbook* (3rd edn.). New York: Pergamon.

Bennun, I. & Lucas, R. (1990). Using the partner in the psychosocial treatment of schizophrenia: A multiple single case design. *British Journal of Clinical Psychology*, **29**, 185–192.

Bentler, P. M. (1980). Multivariate analysis with latent variables: causal modelling. *Annual Review of Psychology*, **31**, 419–456.

Berger, P. L. & Luckmann, T. (1966). *The social construction of reality: A treatise in the sociology of knowledge*. New York: Doubleday.

Bergin, A. E. (1971). The evaluation of therapeutic outcomes. In A. E. Bergin & S. L. Garfield (Eds.), *Handbook of psychotherapy and behavior change: An empirical analysis*. New York: Wiley.

Bergin, A. E. & Garfield, S. L. (Eds.) (1994). *Handbook of psychotherapy and behavior change* (4th edn.). New York: Wiley.

Bergin, A. E. & Lambert, M. J. (1978). The evaluation of therapeutic outcomes. In S. L. Garfield and A. E. Bergin (Eds.), *Handbook of psychotherapy and behavior change: An empirical analysis* (2nd edn.). New York: Wiley.

Bergin, A. E. & Strupp, H. H. (1972). *Changing frontiers in the science of psychotherapy*. Chicago: Aldine.

Blythe, R. (1979). *The view in Winter*. Harmondsworth: Penguin Books.

Bogdan, R. & Taylor, S. (1976). The judged, not the judges: An insider's view of mental retardation. *American Psychologist*, **31**, 47–52.

Bornstein, P. H., Hamilton, S. B. & Bornstein, M. T. (1986). Self-monitoring procedures. In A. R. Ciminero, K. S. Calhoun & H. E. Adams (Eds.), *Handbook of behavioral assessment* (2nd edn.). New York: Wiley.

Bradburn (1983). Response effects. In P. H. Rossi, J. D. Wright & A. B. Anderson (Eds.), *Handbook of survey research*. Orlando: Academic Press.

Bradburn, N. M. & Sudman, S. (1979). *Improving interview method and questionnaire design: Response effects to threatening questions in survey research*. San Francisco: Jossey-Bass.

Brenner, B., Brown, J. & Canter, D. (1985). *The research interview: Uses and approaches*. London: Academic Press.

Breuer, J. & Freud, S. (1985/1955). Case histories. In J. Strachey (Ed. and trans.), *The standard edition of the complete works of Sigmund Freud* (Vol. 2). London: Hogarth Press.

Brewin, C. R. & Bradley, C. (1989). Patient preferences and randomised clinical trials. *British Medical Journal*, **299**, 313–315.

Brewin, C. R, Wing, J. K., Mangen, S. P., Brugha, T. S. & MacCarthy, B. (1987). Principles and practice of measuring needs in the long-term mentally ill: the MRC Needs for Care Assessment. *Psychological Medicine*, **17**, 971–981.

British Psychological Society (1989). *Style guide: information and advice to authors*. Leicester: British Psychological Society.

British Psychological Society (1990). Ethical principles for conducting research with human participants. *The Psychologist*, **3**, 269–272.

British Psychological Society (1993). Summary of journal operations 1992. *The Psychologist*, **6**, 372.

Brock, D. & Barker, C. (1990). Group environment and group process in psychiatric assessment meetings. *International Journal of Social Psychiatry*, **36**, 111–120.

Bromley, D. B. (1986). *The case-study method in psychology and related disciplines*. Chichester: Wiley.

Brooks, N. (1989). Writing a grant application. In G. Parry & F. N. Watts (Eds.), *Behavioural and mental health research: A handbook of skills and methods*. Hove: Lawrence Erlbaum Associates.

Brown, G. W. & Harris, T. (1978). *Social origins of depression: A study of psychiatric disorder in women*. London: Tavistock.

Bruce, V. (1990). Ethics committees. *The Psychologist*, **3**, 463–464.

Bruce, V. (1991). Applying for research grants. *The Psychologist*, **4**, 439–441.

Bryant, C. G. A. (1985). *Positivism in social theory and research*. London: Macmillan.

Bryman, A. (1988). *Quantity and quality in social research*. London: Unwin Hyman.

Campbell, D. T. & Fiske, D. W. (1959). Convergent and discriminant validation by the multitrait–multimethod matrix. *Psychological Bulletin*, **56**, 81–105.

Campbell, D. T. & Stanley, J. C. (1966). *Experimental and quasi-experimental designs for research*. Chicago: Rand-McNally.

Cape, J. (1991). Quality assurance methods for clinical psychology services. *The Psychologist*, **4**, 499–503.

Cape, J., Pilling, S. & Barker, C. (1993). The measurement and costing of psychology services. *Clinical Psychology Forum*, **60**, 16–21.

Carlson, R. (1972). Understanding women: implications for personality theory and research. *Journal of Social Issues*, **28**, 17–32.

Ceci, S. J., Peters, D. & Plotkin, J. (1985). Human subjects review, personal values, and the regulation of social science research. *American Psychologist*, **40**, 994–1002.

Chalmers, A. F. (1982). *What is this thing called science?* (2nd edn.). Milton Keynes: Open University Press.

Chalmers, A. F. (1990). *Science and its fabrication*. Milton Keynes: Open University Press.

Chomsky, N. (1965). *Aspects of a theory of syntax*. Cambridge, MA: MIT Press.

Christensen, L. B. (1991). *Experimental methodology* (5th edn.). Boston: Allyn & Bacon.

Ciminero, A. R., Calhoun, K. S. & Adams, H. E. (Eds.) (1986). *Handbook of behavioral assessment* (2nd edn.). New York: Wiley.

Clifford, P., Leiper, R., Lavender, A. & Pilling, S. (1989). *Assuring quality in mental health services: The QUARTZ system*. London: Free Association Books.

Cochran, W. G. (1977). *Sampling techniques* (3rd edn.). New York: Wiley.

Cohen, J. (1960). A coefficient of agreement for nominal scales. *Educational and Psychological Measurement*, **20**, 37–46.

Cohen, J. (1988). *Statistical power analysis for the behavioral sciences* (2nd edn.). Hillsdale, NJ: Erlbaum.

Cohen, J. (1990). Things I have learned (so far). *American Psychologist*, **45**, 1304–1312.

Cohen, J. (1992). A power primer. *Psychological Bulletin*, **112**, 155–159.

Compass Project (1989). *Annual report*. London: Bloomsbury Health Authority (now renamed the Camden & Islington Health Authority).

Comte, A. (1830–1842). *Cours de philosophie positive* (6 vols.). Paris: Bachelier.

Cone, J. D. & Foster, S. L. (1982). Direct observation in clinical psychology. In P. C. Kendall & J. N. Butcher (Eds.), *Handbook of research methods in clinical psychology*. New York: Wiley.

Cook, T. D. & Campbell, D. T. (1979). *Quasi-experimentation: Design and analysis issues for field settings*. Chicago: Rand-McNally.

Cowen, E. L. (1978). Some problems in community program evaluation research. *Journal of Consulting and Clinical Psychology*, **46**, 792–805.

Cowen, E. L. & Gesten, E. (1980). Evaluating community programs. In M. S. Gibbs, J. R. Lachenmeyer & J. Sigal (Eds.), *Community psychology*. New York: Gardner.

Cox, D. R., Fitzpatrick, R., Fletcher, A. E., Gore, S. M., Spiegelhalter, D. J. & Jones, D. R. (1992). Quality of life assessment: Can we keep it simple? *Journal of the Royal Statistical Society* (Series A), **155**, 353–393.

Crombie, I. K., Davies, H. T. O., Abraham, S. C. S. & Florey, C. du V. (1993). *The audit handbook: Improving health care through clinical audit*. Chichester: Wiley.

Cronbach, L. J. (1957). The two disciplines of scientific psychology. *American Psychologist*, **12**, 671–684.

Cronbach, L. J. (1975). Beyond the two disciplines of scientific psychology. *American Psychologist*, **30**, 116–127.

Cronbach, L. J. (1982). *Designing evaluations of educational and social programs*. San Francisco: Jossey-Bass.

Cronbach, L. J., Gleser, G. C., Nanda, H. & Rajaratnam, N. (1972). *The dependability of behavioral measurements: Theory of generalizability of scores and profiles*. New York: Wiley.

Cronbach, L. J. & Meehl, P. E. (1955). Construct validity in psychological tests. *Psychological Bulletin*, **52**, 281–302.

Crowne, D. P. & Marlowe, D. (1960). A new scale of social desirability independent of psychopathology. *Journal of Consulting Psychology*, **24**, 349–354.

Crowne, D. P. & Marlowe, D. (1964). *The approval motive: Studies in evaluative dependency*. New York: Wiley.

Davidson, P. O. & Costello, C. G. (Eds.) (1969). *N = 1: Experimental studies of single cases*. New York: Van Nostrand.

Davison, G. C. & Stuart, R. B. (1975). Behavior therapy and civil liberties. *American Psychologist*, **30**, 755–763.

Dawis, R. V. (1987). Scale construction. *Journal of Counseling Psychology*, **34**, 481–489.

Denzin, N. K. (1989). *Interpretive biography*. Newbury Park, CA: Sage.

Department of Health (1989). Medical audit. *Working paper 6 of working for patients*. London: HMSO.

Derogatis, L. R. (1977). *SCL-90 administration, scoring, and procedures manual*. Baltimore, MD: Johns Hopkins University Press.

Derogatis, L. R. (1983). *SCL-90-R administration, scoring and procedures manual - II*. Towson, MD: Clinical Psychometric Research.

DeRubeis, R. J., Hollon, S. D., Evans, M. D. & Bemis, K. M. (1982). Can psychotherapies for depression be discriminated? A systematic investigation of cognitive therapy and interpersonal therapy. *Journal of Consulting and Clinical Psychology*, **50**, 744–756.

Dey, I. (1993). *Qualitative data analysis: A user-friendly guide for social scientists*. London: Routledge.

Dilke, O. A. W. (1987). *Mathematics and measurement*. London: British Museum Press.

Dillman, D. A. (1978). *Mail and telephone surveys: The total design method*. New York: Wiley.

Dillman, D. A. (1983). Mail and other self-administered questionnaires. In P. H. Rossi, J. D. Wright & A. B. Anderson (Eds.), *Handbook of survey research*. Orlando: Academic Press.

Donabedian, A. (1980). *The definition of quality and approaches to its assessment*. Ann Arbor: Health Administration Press.

Dukes, W. F. (1965). "N=1". *Psychological Bulletin*, **64**, 74–79.

Durlak, J. A. & Lipsey, M. W. (1991). A practitioner's guide to meta-analysis. *American Journal of Community Psychology*, **19**, 291–332.

Eagleton, T. (1983). *Literary theory: An introduction*. Oxford: Basil Blackwell.

Ebel, R. L. (1951). Estimation of the reliability of ratings. *Psychometrika*, **16**, 407–421.

Edwards, A. L. (1953). *Edwards Personal Preference Schedule*. San Antonio, Texas: The Psychological Corporation.

Elliott, R. (1983). Fitting process research to the practising psychotherapist. *Psychotherapy: Theory, Research & Practice*, **20**, 47–55.

Elliott, R. (1984). A discovery-oriented approach to significant change events in psychotherapy: Interpersonal Process Recall and Comprehensive Process Analysis. In L. N. Rice & L. S. Greenberg (Eds.), *Patterns of change: Intensive analysis of psychotherapy process*. New York: Guilford.

Elliott, R. (1989a). Comprehensive Process Analysis: Understanding the change process in significant therapy events. In M. J. Packer &

R. B. Addison (Eds.), *Entering the circle: Hermeneutic investigation in psychology*. Albany, New York: SUNY Press.

Elliott, R. (1989b). Issues in the selection, training and management of raters. Paper presented at Society for Psychotherapy Research, Toronto, Canada.

Elliott, R. (1989c). Statistical considerations for sample size in qualitative research. Unpublished manuscript, Department of Psychology, University of Toledo, USA.

Elliott, R. (1991). Five dimensions of therapy process. *Psychotherapy Research*, **1**, 92–103.

Elliott, R. (in press). Therapy process research and clinical practice: Practical strategies. In M. Aveline & D. A. Shapiro (Eds.), *Research foundations for psychotherapy practice*. Chichester: Wiley.

Elliott, R., Clark, C., Kemeny, V., Wexler, M., Mack, C. & Brinkerhoff, J. (1990). The impact of experiential therapy on depression: The first ten cases. In G. Lietaer, J. Rombauts & R. Van Balen (Eds.), *Client-centered and experiential psychotherapy towards the nineties*. Leuven, Belgium: Leuven University Press.

Elliott, R., Fischer, C. & Rennie, D. (1994). Evolving guidelines for publication of qualitative research studies. Unpublished manuscript, Department of Psychology, University of Toledo, USA.

Elliott, R. & Wexler, M. M. (1994). Measuring the impact of sessions in process-experiential therapy of depression: The Session Impacts Scale. *Journal of Counseling Psychology*, **41**, 166–174.

Endicott, J., Spitzer, R. L., Fleiss, J. L. & Cohen, J. (1976). The Global Assessment Scale: A procedure for measuring overall severity of psychiatric disturbance. *Archives of General Psychiatry*, **33**, 766–771.

Eysenck, H. J. (1952). The effects of psychotherapy: An evaluation. *Journal of Consulting Psychology*, **16**, 319–324.

Eysenck, H. (1975). Who needs a random sample? *Bulletin of the British Psychology Society*, **28**, 195–198.

Eysenck, H. J. & Eysenck, S. B. G. (1975). *The Eysenck Personality Questionnaire (Adult)*. Sevenoaks: Hodder & Stoughton.

Farquhar, J. W., Maccoby, N., Wood, P. D., & Alexander, J. K., Brietrose, H., Brown, B. W., Haskell, W. L., McAlister, A. L., Meyer, A. J., Nash, J. D. & Stern, M. P. (1977). Community education for cardiovascular health. *Lancet*, **1**, 1192–1195.

Fassinger, R. E. (1987). Use of structural equation modeling in counseling psychology research. *Journal of Counseling Psychology*, **34**, 425–436.

Fenton Lewis, A. & Modle, W. J. (1982). Health indicators: what are they? An approach to efficacy in health care. *Health Trends*, **14**, 3–7.

Fetterman, D. M. (1989). *Ethnography: Step by step*. Newbury Park, CA: Sage.

Fewtrell, W. D. & Toms, D. A. (1985). Pattern of discussion in traditional and novel ward round procedures. *British Journal of Medical Psychology*, **58**, 57–62.

Feyerabend, P. (1975). *Against method*. London: Verso.

Feynman, R. P. (1985). *"Surely you're joking, Mr. Feynman!"* London: Vintage Books.

Fine, M. A. & Kurdek, L. A. (1993). Reflections on determining authorship credit and authorship order on faculty–student collaborations. *American Psychologist*, **48**, 1141–1171.

Firth-Cozens, J. (1993). *Audit in mental health services*. Hove: Lawrence Erlbaum Associates.

Fiske, D. W. & Fogg, L. (1990). But the reviewers are making different criticisms of my paper! Diversity and uniqueness in reviewer comments. *American Psychologist*, **45**, 591–598.

Fiske, S. T. & Taylor, S. E. (1991). *Social cognition* (2nd edn.). New York: McGraw-Hill.

Flick, S. N. (1988). Managing attrition in clinical research. *Clinical Psychology Review*, **8**, 499–515.

Fonagy, P. (1982). Integration of psychoanalysis and empirical science: A review. *International Review of Psycho-Analysis*, **9**, 125–145.

Fonagy, P. & Moran. G. (1993). Advances in the systematic study of the individual case. In N. E. Miller, L. Luborsky, J. Barber & J. Docherty (Eds.), *A guide to psychotherapy research and practice*. New York: Basic Books.

Foster, S. L. & Cone, J. D. (1986). Design and use of direct observation. In A. R. Ciminero, K. S. Calhoun & H. E. Adams (Eds.) (1986). *Handbook of behavioral assessment* (2nd edn.). New York: Wiley.

Frank, J. D. (1973). *Persuasion and healing: A comparative study of psychotherapy* (revised edn.). Baltimore: Johns Hopkins University Press.

Fransella, F. (1981). Repertory grid technique. In F. Fransella (Ed.), *Personality: Theory, measurement and research*. London: Methuen.

Freud, S. (1905/1953). Fragments of an analysis of a case of hysteria ("Dora"). In J. Strachey (Ed. and trans.), *The standard edition of the complete works of Sigmund Freud* (Vol. 7). London: Hogarth Press.

Freud, S. (1905/1977). *Case histories* (2 vols.). Harmondsworth: Pelican.

Freud, S. (1909/1955). Analysis of a phobia in a five year old boy ("Little Hans"). In J. Strachey (Ed. and trans.), *The standard edition of the complete works of Sigmund Freud* (Vol. 10). London: Hogarth Press.

Friedrich, J. & Lüdtke, H. (1975). *Participant observation: theory and practice*. Farnborough: Saxon House.

Garfinkel, H. (1967). *Studies in ethnomethodology*. Englewood Cliffs, New Jersey: Prentice Hall.

Gergen, K. J. (1985). The social constructionist movement in modern psychology. *American Psychologist*, **40**, 266–275.

Giorgi, A. (1975). An application of phenomenological method in psychology. In A. Giorgi, C. Fischer & E. Murray (Eds.), *Duquesne studies in phenomenological psychology* (Vol. 2). Pittsburgh, PA: Duquesne University Press.

Giorgi, A. (1985). Sketch of a psychological phenomenological method. In A. Giorgi (Ed.), *Phenomenology and psychological research*. Pittsburgh: Duquesne University Press.

Glaser, B. G. & Strauss, A. L. (1967). *The discovery of grounded theory: Strategies for qualitative research*. Chicago: Aldine.

Goffman, E. (1961). *Asylums: Essays on the social situation of mental patients and other inmates*. Garden City, New York: Doubleday.

Gold, R. L. (1958). Roles in sociological field observations. *Social Forces*, **36**, 217–223.

Goldfried, M. R. & Kent, R. N. (1972). Traditional versus behavioral personality assessment: A comparison of methodological and theoretical assumptions. *Psychological Bulletin*, **77**, 409–420.

Good, D. A. & Watts, F. N. (1989). Qualitative research. In G. Parry & F. N. Watts (Eds.), *Behavioural and mental health research: A handbook of skills and methods*. Hove: Lawrence Erlbaum Associates.

Goodman, G. (1972). *Companionship therapy: Studies in structured intimacy*. San Francisco: Jossey-Bass.

Goodman, G. & Dooley, D. (1976). A framework for help-intended communication. *Psychotherapy: Theory, Research and Practice*, **13**, 106–117.

Gorsuch, R. L. (1974). *Factor analysis*. Philadelphia: W.B. Saunders.

Gottman, J. M. (1981). *Time-series analysis: A comprehensive introduction for social scientists*. New York: Cambridge University Press.

Gottman, J. M. & Roy, A. K. (1990). *Sequential analysis: A guide for behavioral researchers*. New York: Cambridge University Press.

Graham, S. (1992). "Most of the subjects were white and middle class": Trends in published research on African Americans in selected APA journals, 1970–1989. *American Psychologist*, **47**, 629–639.

Green, R. S. & Attkisson, C. C. (1984). Quality assurance and program evaluation: similarities and differences. *American Behavioral Scientist*, **27**, 552–582.

Greenberg, L. S. & Pinsof, W. (Eds.) (1986). *The psychotherapeutic process: A research handbook*. New York: Guilford.

Greenberg, L. S., Rice, L. N. & Elliott, R. (1993). *Facilitating emotional change: The moment-by-moment process*. New York: Guilford Press.

Griffiths, M. (1992). Under (peer) pressure. *The Psychologist*, **5**, 336.

Guba, E. G. & Lincoln, Y. S. (1989). *Fourth generation evaluation*. Newbury Park, CA: Sage.

Guerin, D. & MacKinnon, D. P. (1985). An assessment of the California child passenger restraint requirement. *American Journal of Public Health*, **75**, 142–144.

Gynther, M. D. & Green, S. B. (1982). Methodological problems in research with self-report inventories. In P. C. Kendall & J. N. Butcher (Eds.), *Handbook of research methods in clinical psychology*. New York: Wiley.

Hamlyn, D. W. (1970). *The theory of knowledge*. Garden City, NY: Doubleday Anchor.

Hammen, C. (1992). Life events and depression: The plot thickens. *American Journal of Community Psychology*, **20**, 179–193.

Hand, D. J. (1994). Deconstructing statistical questions. *Journal of the Royal Statistical Society* (Series A), **157**, in press.

Hardy, G. E. (in press). Organisational issues: Making research happen. In M. Aveline & D. A. Shapiro (Eds.), *Research Foundations for Psychotherapy Practice*. Chichester: Wiley.

Harman, B. H. (1976). *Modern factor analysis* (3rd edn.). Chicago: University of Chicago Press.

Harré, R. (1974). Blueprint for a new science. In N. Armistead (Ed.), *Reconstructing social psychology*. Harmondsworth: Penguin Education.

Hartnoll, R., Daviaud, E., Lewis, R. & Mitcheson, M. (1985). *Drug problems: Assessing local needs—A practical manual for assessing the nature and extent of problematic drug use in a community*. London: Drug Indicators Project, Department of Politics and Sociology, Birkbeck College, London University.

Hathaway, S. R. & McKinley, J. C. (1951). *Minnesota Multiphasic Personality Inventory manual*. New York: Psychological Corporation.

Hawks, D. (1981). The dilemma of clinical practice—Surviving as a clinical psychologist. In I. McPherson & A. Sutton (Eds.), *Reconstructing psychological practice*. London: Croom Helm.

Hayes, S. C. (1981). Single case experimental design and empirical clinical practice. *Journal of Consulting and Clinical Psychology*, **49**, 193–211.

Helman, C. G. (1990). *Culture, health and illness: An introduction for health professionals* (2nd edn.). London: Wright.

Henwood, K. L. & Pidgeon, N. (1992). Qualitative research and psychological theorising. *British Journal of Psychology*, **83**, 97–111.

Herman, J. L. (Ed.) (1988). *Program evaluation kit* (9 Vols., various authors) (2nd edn.). Newbury Park, CA: Sage.

Hesse, H. (1943). *Das Glasperlenspiel* (trans. as *The glass bead game*). Zurich: Fretz & Wasmuth.

Hill, C. E. (1991). Almost everything you ever wanted to know about how to do process research on counseling and psychotherapy but didn't know who to ask. In C. E. Watkins & L. J. Schneider (Eds.), *Research in counseling*. Hillsdale, NJ: Erlbaum.

Hinshaw, S. P., Henker, B., Whalen, C. K., Erhart, D. & Dunnington, R. E. (1989). Aggressive, prosocial, and nonsocial behavior in hyperactive boys: Dose effects of methylphenidate in naturalistic settings. *Journal of Consulting and Clinical Psychology*, **57**, 636–643.

Hodgson, R. & Rollnick, S. (1989). More fun, less stress: how to survive in research. In G. Parry & F. N. Watts (Eds.), *Behavioural and mental health research: A handbook of skills and methods*. Hove: Lawrence Erlbaum Associates.

Horowitz, M. J. (1982). Strategic dilemmas and the socialization of psychotherapy researchers. *British Journal of Clinical Psychology*, **21**, 119–127.

Hoshmand, L. T. & Polkinghorne, D. E. (1992). Redefining the science–practice relationship and professional training. *American Psychologist*, **47**, 55–66.

Howard, G. S. (1991). Culture tales: A narrative approach to thinking, cross-cultural psychology, and psychotherapy. *American Psychologist*, **46**, 187–197.

Howard, G. S. (1992). Behold our creation! What counseling psychology has become and might yet become. *Journal of Counseling Psychology*, **39**, 419–442.

Howard, K. I., Kopta, M., Krause, M. S. & Orlinsky, D. E. (1986). The dose–effect relationship in psychotherapy. *American Psychologist*, **41**, 159–164.

Howard, K. I., Krause, M. S. & Orlinsky, D. E. (1986). The attrition dilemma: Towards a new strategy for psychotherapy research. *Journal of Consulting and Clinical Psychology*, **54**, 106–110.

Howell, D. C. (1992). *Statistical methods for psychology* (3rd edn.). Belmont: Duxbury Press.

Hoyle, R. H. (1991). Evaluating measurement models in clinical research: Covariance structure analysis of latent variable models of self-conception. *Journal of Consulting and Clinical Psychology*, **59**, 67–76.

Hsu, L. M. (1989). Random sampling, randomization, and equivalence of contrasted groups in psychotherapy outcome research. *Journal of Consulting and Clinical Psychology*, **57**, 131–137.

Humphries, L. (1970). *Tearoom trade*. Chicago: Aldine.

Husserl, E. (1931). *Ideas: General introduction to pure phenomenology*. London: George Allen & Unwin. (Original German edition, 1913).

Iglehart, J. K. (1992). The American health care system: Managed care. *New England Journal of Medicine*, **327**, 742–747.

Imber, S. D., Glanz, L. M., Elkin, I., Sotsky, S. M., Boyer, J. L. & Leber, W. R. (1986). Ethical issues in psychotherapy research: Problems in a collaborative clinical trials study. *American Psychologist*, **41**, 137–146.

Irvine, J., Miles, I. & Evans, J. (Eds.) (1979). *Demystifying social statistics*. London: Pluto Press.

Jackson, L. & Elliott, R. (June, 1990). Is experiential therapy effective in treating depression?: Initial outcome data. Paper presented at Society for Psychotherapy Research, Wintergreen, VA, USA.

Jackson, P. R. (1989). Analysing data. In G. Parry & F. N. Watts (Eds.), *Behavioural and mental health research: A handbook of skills and methods.* Hove: Lawrence Erlbaum Associates.

Jacobson, N. S., Follette, W. C. & Revenstorf, D. (1984). Psychotherapy outcome research: Methods for reporting variability and evaluating clinical significance. *Behavior Therapy*, **15**, 336–352.

Jacobson, N. S. & Truax, P. (1991). Clinical significance: A statistical approach to defining meaningful change in psychotherapy research. *Journal of Consulting and Clinical Psychology*, **59**, 12–19.

Jahoda, M. (1958). *Current concepts of positive mental health.* New York: Basic Books.

James, W. (1907/1981). *Pragmatism.* Indianapolis: Hackett.

Jennings, J. L. (1986). Husserl revisited: the forgotten distinction between psychology and phenomenology. *American Psychologist*, **41**, 1231–1240.

Jones, E. E., Ghannam, J., Nigg, J. R. & Dyer, J. F. P. (1993). A paradigm for single-case research: The time series study of a long-term psychotherapy for depression. *Journal of Consulting and Clinical Psychology*, **61**, 381–394.

Jones, E. E. & Nisbett, R. E. (1971). The actor and the observer: divergent perceptions of the causes of behaviour. In E. E. Jones, D. E. Kanouse, H. H. Kelley, R. E. Nisbett, S. Valins & B. Weiner (Eds.), *Attribution: Perceiving the causes of behavior.* Morristown, NJ: General Learning Press.

Kazdin, A. E. (1981). Drawing valid inferences from case studies. *Journal of Consulting and Clinical Psychology*, **49**, 183–192.

Kazdin, A. E. (1982). *Single case research designs: Methods for clinical and applied settings.* Oxford: Oxford University Press.

Kazdin, A. E. & Bass, D. (1989). Power to detect differences between alternative treatments in comparative psychotherapy outcome research. *Journal of Consulting and Clinical Psychology*, **57**, 138–147.

Kelly, G. A. (1955). *The psychology of personal constructs.* New York: Norton.

Kelly, J. G (1990). Changing contexts and the field of community psychology. *American Journal of Community Psychology*, **18**, 769–792.

Kennedy, P., Fisher, K. & Pearson, E. (1988). Ecological evaluation of a Rehabilitative Environment for spinal cord injured people: Behavioural mapping and feedback. *British Journal of Clinical Psychology*, **27**, 239–246.

Kenny, D. A. (1979). *Correlation and causality.* New York: Wiley.

Keppel, G. (1991). *Design and analysis: A researcher's handbook* (3rd edn.). Englewood Cliffs, New Jersey: Prentice Hall.

Kerlinger, F. N. (1986). *Foundations of behavioral research* (3rd edn.). New York: Holt, Rinehart & Winston.

Kiesler, D. J. (1966). Some myths of psychotherapy research and the search for a paradigm. *Psychological Bulletin*, **65**, 110–136.

Kimble, G. A. (1984). Psychology's two cultures. *American Psychologist*, **39**, 833–839.

Kirk, R. E. (1982). *Experimental design: Procedures for the behavioral sciences* (2nd edn.). Belmont, CA: Brooks/Cole.

Kirschenbaum, H. (1979). *On becoming Carl Rogers*. New York: Delta.

Koch, S. (1964). Psychology and emerging conceptions of knowledge as unitary. In T.W. Wann (Ed.), *Behaviourism and phenomenology*. Chicago: University of Chicago Press.

Korchin, S. J. (1976). *Modern clinical psychology: Principles of intervention in the clinic and community*. New York: Basic Books.

Korchin, S. J. & Cowan, P. (1982). Ethical perspectives in clinical research. In P. C. Kendall & J. N. Butcher (Eds.), *Handbook of research methods in clinical psychology*. New York: Wiley.

Kraemer, H. C. & Thiemann, S. (1987). *How many subjects? Statistical power analysis in research*. Newbury Park, CA: Sage.

Kraemer, H. C. (1981). Coping strategies in psychiatric clinical research. *Journal of Consulting and Clinical Psychology*, **49**, 309–319.

Krippendorff, K. (1980). *Content analysis: An introduction to its methodology*. London: Sage.

Krupnik, J. L. & Pincus, H. A. (1992). The cost-effectiveness of psychotherapy: A plan for research. *American Journal of Psychiatry*, **149**, 1295–1305.

Kuhn, T. S. (1970). *The structure of scientific revolutions* (2nd edn.). Chicago: University of Chicago Press.

Kurz, D. E. (1983). The use of participant observation in evaluation research. *Evaluation and Program Planning*, **6**, 93–102.

Kvale, S. (1983). The qualitative research interview: A phenomenological and hermeneutical mode of understanding. *Journal of Phenomenological Psychology*, **14**, 171–196.

Labott, S., Elliott, R. & Eason, P. (1992). "If you love someone, you don't hurt them": A comprehensive process analysis of a weeping event in psychotherapy. *Psychiatry*, **55**, 49–62.

Labov, W. & Fanshel, D. (1977). *Therapeutic discourse*. New York: Academic Press.

Laing, R. D. (1959). *The divided self: An existential study in sanity and madness*. London: Tavistock Publications.

Lakatos, I. (1970). Falsification and the methodology of scientific research programmes. In I. Lakatos & A. Musgrave (Eds.), *Criticism and the growth of knowledge*. Cambridge: Cambridge University Press.

Lakatos, I. & Musgrave, A. (Eds.) (1970). *Criticism and the growth of knowledge*. Cambridge: Cambridge University Press.

Lambert, M. J. (1983). Introduction to assessment of psychotherapy outcome: Historical perspective and current issues. In M. J. Lambert, E. R. Christensen & S. S. DeJulio, *The assessment of psychotherapy outcome.* New York: Wiley.

Lambie, J. (1991). The misuse of Kuhn in psychology. *The Psychologist,* **4,** 6–11.

Lanham, R. (1979). *Revising Prose.* New York: Scribners.

Larsen, D. L., Attkisson, C. C., Hargreaves, W. A. & Nguyen, T. D. (1979). Assessment of client/patient satisfaction: development of a general scale. *Evaluation and Program Planning,* **2,** 197–207.

Lather, P. (1991). *Getting smart: feminist research and pedagogy with/in the postmodern.* New York: Routledge.

Lazarus, A. A. & Davison, G. C. (1971). Clinical innovation in research and practice. In A. E. Bergin & S. L. Garfield (Eds.), *Handbook of psychotherapy and behavior change.* New York: Wiley.

Lebow, J. (1982). Consumer satisfaction with mental health treatment. *Psychological Bulletin,* **91,** 244–259.

Lembcke, P. A. (1967). Evolution of the medical audit. *Journal of the American Medical Association,* **199,** 543–550.

Levine, M. & Perkins, D. V. (1987). *Principles of community psychology: Perspectives and applications.* New York: Oxford University Press.

Levi-Strauss, C. (1958/1963). *Structural anthropology.* Garden City, NY: Doubleday Anchor.

Lieberman, I. D., Yalom, I. & Miles, M. B. (1973). *Encounter groups: First facts.* New York: Basic Books.

Lincoln, Y. & Guba, E. G. (1985). *Naturalistic inquiry.* Beverly Hills, CA: Sage.

Lissitz, R. W. & Green, S. B. (1975). Effect of the number of scale points on reliability: a Monte Carlo approach. *Journal of Applied Psychology,* **60,** 10–13.

Llewelyn, S. P. & Hume, W. I. (1979). The patient's view of therapy. *British Journal of Medical Psychology,* **52,** 29–35.

Llewelyn, S. P., Elliott, R., Shapiro, D. A., Firth, J. & Hardy, G. (1988). Client perceptions of significant events in prescriptive and exploratory periods of individual therapy. *British Journal of Clinical Psychology,* **27,** 105–114.

Lovie, A. D. & Lovie, P. (1991). Graphical methods for exploring data. In A.D. Lovie & P. Lovie (Eds.), *New developments in statistics for psychology and the social sciences.* Leicester: British Psychological Society.

Luria, A. R. (1973). *The working brain: An introduction to neuropsychology.* New York: Basic Books.

Lykken, D. T. (1968). Statistical significance in psychological research. *Psychological Bulletin,* **70,** 151–159.

Lyotard, J.-F. (1984). *The post-modern condition: A report on knowledge* (originally published 1979 as *La condition postmoderne: rapport sur la savoir*). Manchester: Manchester University Press.

Mahoney, M. J. (1976). *Scientist as subject: The psychological imperative.* Cambridge, Mass.: Ballinger.

Mahrer, A. R. (1988). Discovery-oriented psychotherapy research: rationale, aims, and methods. *American Psychologist*, **43**, 694–702.

Mair, M. (1989). *Between psychology and psychotherapy: A poetics of experience.* London: Routledge.

Malinowski, B. (1929). *The sexual life of savages in North Western Melanesia.* London: Routledge & Kegan Paul.

Mangen, S. (1988). Assessing cost-effectiveness. In F.N. Watts (Ed.), *New developments in clinical psychology* (Vol. 2). Chichester: Wiley.

Marrow, A. J. (1969). *The practical theorist: The life and work of Kurt Lewin.* New York: Basic Books.

Maxwell, R. J. (1984). Quality assessment in health. *British Medical Journal*, **288**, 1470–1472.

May, R., Angel, E. & Ellenberger, H. F. (1958). *Existence: A new dimension in psychiatry and psychology.* New York: Basic Books.

McCormack, H. M., Horne, D. J. de L. & Sheather, S. (1988). Clinical applications of visual analogue scales: a critical review. *Psychological Medicine*, **18**, 1007–1019.

McCracken, G. (1988). *The long interview.* Newbury Park, CA: Sage.

McGlenn, M. L. (1990). A qualitative study of significant weeping events. Doctoral dissertation, University of Toledo.

McGuire, W. J. (1973). The yin and yang of progress in social psychology: Seven Koan. *Journal of Personality and Social Psychology*, **26**, 446–456.

McKillip, J. (1987). *Need analysis: Tools for the human services and education.* Newbury Park, CA: Sage.

Meehl, P. (1978). Theoretical risks and tabular asterisks: Sir Karl, Sir Ronald, and the slow progress of soft psychology. *Journal of Consulting and Clinical Psychology*, **46**, 806–834.

Merbaum, M. & Lowe, M. R. (1982). Serendipity in research in clinical psychology. In P. C. Kendall & J. N. Butcher (Eds.), *Handbook of research methods in clinical psychology.* New York: Wiley.

Messer, S. B., Sass, L. A. & Woolfolk, R. L. (Eds.) (1988). *Hermeneutics and psychological theory: Interpretive perspectives on personality, psychotherapy and psychopathology.* New Brunswick, New Jersey: Rutgers University Press.

Miles, M. B. & Huberman, A. M. (1984). *Qualitative data analysis: A sourcebook of new methods.* Beverly Hills, CA: Sage.

Milgram, S. (1964). Issues in the study of obedience: A reply to Baumrind. *American Psychologist*, **19**, 848–852.

Milne, D. (1987). *Evaluating mental health practice: methods and applications.* Beckenham: Croom Helm.

Milne, D., Britton, P. & Wilkinson, I. (1990). The scientist–practitioner in practice. *Clinical Psychology Forum,* **30,** 27–30.

Mintz, J. (1981). Tactical problems in research design. Paper presented to the Society for Psychotherapy Research, Aspen, Colorado.

Mintz, J. & Kiesler, D. J. (1982). Individualized measures of psychotherapy outcome. In P. C. Kendall & J. N. Butcher (Eds.), *Handbook of research methods in clinical psychology.* New York: Wiley.

Mischel, W. (1968). *Personality and assessment.* New York: Wiley.

Moondog (1991). Quoted on Kaleidoscope, BBC Radio 4, 20 May 1991.

Moran, G. S. & Fonagy, P. (1987). Psychoanalysis and diabetic control: A single case study. *British Journal of Medical Psychology,* **60,** 357–372.

Moras, K. & Hill, C.E. (1991). Rater selection for psychotherapy process research: An evaluation of the state of the art. *Psychotherapy Research,* **1,** 113–123.

Morley, S. (1989). Single case research. In G. Parry & F. N. Watts (Eds.), *Behavioural and mental health research: A handbook of skills and methods.* London: Lawrence Erlbaum Associates.

Morley, S. & Adams, M. (1989). Some simple statistical tests for exploring single-case time-series data. *British Journal of Clinical Psychology,* **28,** 1–18.

Morley, S. & Adams, M. (1991). Graphical analysis of single-case time-series data. *British Journal of Clinical Psychology,* **30,** 97–115.

Morris, W. (Ed.) (1981). *The American Heritage dictionary of the English language.* Boston: Houghton Mifflin.

Morrow-Bradley, C. & Elliott, R. (1986). Utilization of psychotherapy research by practising psychotherapists. *American Psychologist,* **41,** 188–197.

Moser, C. A. & Kalton, G. (1971). *Survey methods in social investigation.* London: Heinemann.

Mostyn, B. (1985). The content analysis of qualitative research data: A dynamic approach. In M. Brenner, J. Brown & D. Canter (Eds.), *The research interview: Uses and approaches.* London: Academic Press.

Moustakas, C. (1990). *Heuristic research: Design, methodology, and applications.* Newbury Park, CA: Sage.

Murray, H. A. (1938). *Explorations in personality.* New York: Oxford University Press.

National Health Service Management Executive (1991). *Local research ethics committees (Health Service Guidelines HSG(97)5).* London: Department of Health.

Neimeyer, R. A. (1993). An appraisal of constructivist psychotherapies. *Journal of Consulting and Clinical Psychology,* **61,** 221–234.

Nelson, R. O. (1981). Realistic dependent measures for clinical use. *Journal of Consulting and Clinical Psychology,* **49,** 168–182.

Newell, A. (1977). Protocol analysis. In P. Johnson-Laird & P. Wason (Eds.), *Thinking: Readings in cognitive science*. New York: Cambridge University Press.

Nisbett, R. E. & Ross, L. (1980). *Human inference: Strategies and shortcomings of social judgement*. Englewood Cliffs, N.J.: Prentice Hall.

Nisbett, R. E. & Wilson, T. D. (1977). Telling more than we know: Verbal reports on mental processes. *Psychological Review*, **84**, 231–239.

Norusis, M. J./SPSS Inc. (1990). *SPSS/PC+ Manuals*. Chicago: SPSS Inc.

Nunnally, J. C. (1978). *Psychometric theory* (2nd edn.). New York: McGraw-Hill.

Oakes, M. (1986). *Statistical inference: A commentary for the social and behavioural sciences*. Chichester: Wiley.

Oakley, A. (1981). Interviewing women: a contradiction in terms. In H. Roberts (Ed.), *Doing feminist research*. London: Routledge & Kegan Paul.

Oppenheim, A. N. (1966). *Questionnaire design and attitude measurement*. London: Heinemann.

Orford, J. (1992). *Community psychology: Theory and practice*. Chichester: Wiley.

Orwell, G. (1946/1968). Politics and the English language. Originally published in *Horizon*, reprinted in *The collected essays and letters of George Orwell (Vol. 4): In front of your nose, 1945–1950*. Harmondsworth: Penguin Books.

O'Sullivan, K. R. & Dryden, W. (1990). A survey of clinical psychologists in the South East Thames Health Region: Activities, role and theoretical orientation. *Clinical Psychology Forum*, **29**, 21–26.

Overall, J. E. & Gorham, D. R. (1962). The brief psychiatric rating scale. *Psychological Reports*, **10**, 799–812.

Øvretveit, J. (1986). *Organisation of multidisciplinary community teams*. London: Institute of Organisation and Social Studies, Brunel University.

Packer, M. J. & Addison, R. B. (Eds.). (1989). *Entering the circle: Hermeneutic investigation in psychology*. Albany, NY: SUNY Press.

Pantelis, C., Taylor, J. & Campbell, P. (1988). The South Camden survey: an experience of community based research. *Bulletin of the Royal College of Psychiatrists*, **12**, 98–101.

Parloff, M. B. (1986). Placebo controls in psychotherapy research: A *sine qua non* or a placebo for research problems? *Journal of Consulting and Clinical Psychology*, **54**, 79–87.

Parry, G. (1989). Writing a research report. In G. Parry and F. N. Watts (Eds.), *Behavioural and mental health research: A handbook of skills and methods*. Hove: Lawrence Erlbaum Associates.

Parry, G. (1992). Improving psychotherapy services: Applications of research, audit and evaluation. *British Journal of Clinical Psychology*, **31**, 3–19.

Parry, G. & Gowler, D. (1983). Career stresses on psychological therapists. In D. Pilgrim (Ed.), *Psychology and Psychotherapy: Current trends and issues*. London: Routledge.

Parry, G., Shapiro, D. A. & Firth, J. (1986). The case of the anxious executive: A study from the research clinic. *British Journal of Medical Psychology*, **59**, 221–233.

Patton, M. Q. (1990). *Qualitative evaluation and research methods* (2nd edn.). Newbury Park, CA: Sage.

Paul, G. L. (1967). Strategies of outcome research in psychotherapy. *Journal of Consulting Psychology*, **31**, 109–118.

Paulhus, D. L. (1984). Two-component models of socially desirable responding. *Journal of Personality and Social Psychology*, **46**, 598–609.

Payne, S. L. B. (1951). *The art of asking questions* (Studies in Public Opinion number 3). Princeton: Princeton University Press.

Pearce, S. (1983). Pain. In J. Nicholson & B. Foss (Eds.), *Psychology survey No. 4*. Leicester: British Psychological Society.

Peck, D. F. (1985). Small N experimental designs in clinical research. In F. N. Watts (Ed.), *New developments in clinical psychology*. Chichester: Wiley.

Peplau, L. A. & Conrad, E. (1989). Feminist methods in psychology. *Psychology of Women Quarterly*, **13**, 379–400.

Perls, F. S., Hefferline, R. F. & Goodman, P. (1951). *Gestalt therapy*. New York: Julian Press.

Peterson, D. R. (1991). Connection and disconnection of research and practice in the education of professional psychologists. *American Psychologist*, **46**, 422–429.

Phillips, J. P. N. (1986). Shapiro personal questionnaire and generalized personal questionnaire techniques: A repeated measures individualized outcome measurement. In L. S. Greenberg & W. M. Pinsof (Eds.), *The psychotherapeutic process: A research handbook*. New York: Guilford.

Phoenix, A. (1990). Social research in the context of feminist psychology. In E. Burman (Ed.), *Feminists and psychological practice*. London: Sage.

Pilgrim, D. & Treacher, A. (1992). *Clinical psychology observed*. London: Routledge.

Pistrang. N. (1990). Leaping the culture gap. *The Health Service Journal*, **100**(5204), 878–879.

Pistrang, N. & Barker, C. (1992). Disclosure of concerns in breast cancer. *Psycho-Oncology*, **1**, 183–192.

Polkinghorne, D. (1983). *Methodology for the human sciences*. Albany, NY: Human Sciences Press.

Polkinghorne, D. (1989). Phenomenological research methods. In R. S. Valle & S. Halling, *Existential–phenomenological perspectives in psychology: Exploring the breadth of human experience* New York: Plenum.

Pollio, H. R. (1982). *Behavior and existence*. Monterey, CA: Brooks/Cole.

Popper, K. R. (1959). *The logic of scientific discovery*. New York: Basic Books. (Original German edition, 1934.)

Popper, K. R. (1963). *Conjectures and refutations: The growth of scientific knowledge*. London: Routledge & Kegan Paul.

Potter, J. & Wetherell, M. (1987). *Discourse and social psychology*. London: Sage.

Powell, G. E. & Adams, M. (1993). Introduction to research on placement. *Clinical Psychology Forum*, **53**, 12–17.

Reason, P. & Rowan, J. (Eds.) (1981). *Human enquiry: A sourcebook of new paradigm research*. Chichester: Wiley.

Regier, D. A., Boyd, J. H., Burke, J. D., Rae, D. S., Myers, J. K., Kramer, M., Robins, L. N., George, L. K., Karno, M. & Locke, B. Z. (1988). One-month prevalence of mental disorders in the United States based on five Epidemiologic Catchment Area Sites. *Archives of General Psychiatry*, **45**, 977–986.

Reichenbach, H. (1938). *Experience and prediction: An analysis of the foundations and the structure of knowledge*. Chicago: University of Chicago Press.

Rennie, D. L. (1990). Toward a representation of the client's experience of the psychotherapy hour. In G. Lietaer, J. Rombauts, & R. Van Balen (Eds.), *Client-centered and experiential psychotherapy towards the nineties*. Leuven, Belgium: Leuven University Press.

Rennie, D. L. (1993). Client deference in the psychotherapy relationship. Department of Psychology, York University, Toronto. Paper submitted for publication.

Rennie, D. L., Phillips, J. R. & Quartaro, G. K. (1988). Grounded theory: a promising approach to conceptualization in psychology. *Canadian Psychology*, **29**, 139–150.

Rice, L. N. & Greenberg, L. S. (Eds.) (1984). *Patterns of change*. New York: Guilford Press.

Rice, L. N. & Sapiera, E. P. (1984). Task analysis and the resolution of problematic reactions. In L. N. Rice & L. S. Greenberg (Eds.), *Patterns of change*. New York: Guilford Press.

Richardson, A., Jackson, C. & Sykes, W. (1990). *Taking research seriously: Means of improving and assessing the use and dissemination of research*. London: HMSO.

Riger, S. (1992). Epistemological debates, feminist voices: Science, social values, and the study of women. *American Psychologist*, **47**, 730–740.

Robins, L. N., Helzer, J. E., Croughan, J. & Ratcliff, K. S. (1981). National Institute of Mental Health Diagnostic Interview Schedule. *Archives of General Psychiatry*, **38**, 381–389.

Roethlisberger, F. S. & Dickson, W. J. (1939). *Management and the worker*. Cambridge, Mass.: Harvard University Press.

Rogers, C. R. (1955). Persons or science? A philosophical question. *American Psychologist*, **10**, 267–278.

Rogers, C. R. (1957). The necessary and sufficient conditions of therapeutic personality change. *Journal of Consulting Psychology*, **21**, 95–103.

Rogers, C. R. (1967). A silent young man. In C. R. Rogers, E. T. Gendlin, D. J. Kiesler & C. Truax, *The therapeutic relationship and its impact: A study of psychotherapy with schizophrenics*. Madison, Wisconsin: University of Wisconsin Press.

Rogers, C. R. (1975). Empathic: An unappreciated way of being. *Counseling Psychologist*, **5**, 2–10.

Rogers, C. R. (1985). Towards a more human science of the person. *Journal of Humanistic Psychology*, **25**, 7–24.

Rorer, L. (1965). The great response style myth. *Psychological Bulletin*, **63**, 129–156.

Rose, S., Kamin, S. J. & Lewontin, R. C. (1984). *Not in our genes: Biology, ideology and human nature*. Harmondsworth, Penguin Books.

Rosenhan, D. L. (1973). On being sane in insane places. *Science*, **179**, 250–258.

Rosenhead, J. (Ed.) (1989). *Rational analysis for a problematic world: Problem structuring methods for complexity, uncertainty and conflict*. Chichester: Wiley.

Rosenthal, R. (1978). How often are our numbers wrong? *American Psychologist*, **33**, 1005–1008.

Rosenthal, R. (1991). *Meta-analytic procedures for social research* (revised edn.). Newbury Park: Sage.

Rossi, P. H. & Freeman, H. E. (1993). *Evaluation: A systematic approach* (5th edn.). Newbury Park: Sage.

Rossi, P. H., Wright, J. D. & Anderson, A. B. (Eds.) (1983). *Handbook of survey research*. Orlando: Academic Press.

Rudestam, K. E. & Newton, R. R. (1992) *Surviving your dissertation: A comprehensive guide to content and process*. Newbury Park: Sage.

Runyan, W. M. (1982). *Life histories and psychobiography*. New York: Oxford University Press.

Russell, B. (1961). *History of Western philosophy*. London: George Allen & Unwin.

Sacks, H., Schegloff, E. A. & Jefferson, G. (1974). The simplest systematics for the organization of turn-taking in conversation. *Language*, **50**, 696–735.

Sacks, O. (1985). *The man who mistook his wife for a hat*. London: Duckworth.

Sarbin, T. R. (Ed.) (1986). *Narrative psychology: The storied nature of human conduct*. New York: Praeger.

Scarr, S. (1988). Race and gender as psychological variables: Social and ethical issues. *American Psychologist*, **43**, 56–59.

Schlesselman, J. J. (1982). *Case-control studies: Design, conduct, analysis*. New York: Oxford University Press.

Schwartz, D., Flamant, R. & Lellouch, J. (1980). *Clinical trials*. London: Academic Press. (Original French edition, 1970.)

Schwartz, J. (1992). *The creative moment: How science made itself alien to modern culture*. London: Jonathan Cape.

Scriven, M. (1972). The methodology of evaluation. In C. H. Weiss (Ed.), *Evaluating action programs*. Boston, Mass.: Allyn & Bacon.

Searle, J. R. (1969). *Speech acts: An essay in the philosophy of language*. Cambridge: Cambridge University Press.

Shallice, T. (1979). Case study approach in neuropsychological research. *Journal of Clinical Neuropsychology*, **1**, 183–211.

Shallice, T. (1988). *From neuropsychology to mental structure*. Cambridge: Cambridge University Press.

Shallice, T., Burgess, P. W. & Frith, C. D. (1991). Can the neuropsychological case-study approach be applied to schizophrenia? *Psychological Medicine*, **21**, 661–673.

Shapiro, D. A. (1989). Outcome research. In G. Parry & F. Watts (Eds.), *Behavioural and mental health research: A handbook of skills and methods*. Hove: Lawrence Erlbaum Associates.

Shapiro, D. A., Barkham, M., Hardy, G. E. & Morrison, L. A. (1990). The second Sheffield Psychotherapy Project: Rationale, design and preliminary outcome data. *British Journal of Medical Psychology*, **63**, 97–108.

Shapiro, D. A., Barkham, M., Rees, A. Hardy, G. E., Reynolds, S., & Startup (1994). Effects of treatment duration and severity of depression on the effectiveness of cognitive-behavioral and psychodynamic-interpersonal psychotherapy. *Journal of Consulting and Clinical Psychology*, **62**, 522–534.

Shapiro, D. A. & Shapiro, D. (1977). The "double standard" in the evaluation of psychotherapies. *Bulletin of the British Psychological Society*, **30**, 209–210.

Shapiro, D. A. & Shapiro, D. (1983). Comparative therapy outcome research: Methodological implications of meta-analysis. *Journal of Consulting and Clinical Psychology*, **51**, 42–53.

Shapiro, M. B. (1961a). A method of measuring psychological changes specific to the individual psychiatric patient. *British Journal of Medical Psychology*, **34**, 151–155.

Shapiro, M. B. (1961b). The single case in fundamental clinical psychological research. *British Journal of Medical Psychology*, **34**, 255–262.

Shapiro, M. B. (1967). Clinical psychology as an applied science. *British Journal of Psychiatry*, **113**, 1039–1042.

Shapiro, M. B. (1985). A reassessment of clinical psychology as an applied science. *British Journal of Clinical Psychology*, **24**, 1–11.

Shavelson, R. J., Webb, N. M. & Rowley, G. L. (1989). Generalizability theory. *American Psychologist*, **44**, 922–932.

Sheatsley, P. B. (1983). Questionnaire construction and item writing. In P. H. Rossi, J. D. Wright & A. B. Anderson (Eds.), *Handbook of survey research*. Orlando: Academic Press.

Shlien, J. (1970). Phenomenology and personality. In J. T. Hart & T. M. Tomlinson (Eds.), *New directions in client-centered therapy*. Boston: Houghton Mifflin.

Shoham-Salomon, V. & Hannah, M. T. (1991). Client–treatment interaction in the study of differential change processes. *Journal of Consulting and Clinical Psychology*, **59**, 217–225.

Sidman, M. (1960). *Tactics of scientific research*. New York: Basic Books.

Sieber, J. E. & Stanley, B. (1988). Ethical and professional dimensions of socially sensitive research. *American Psychologist*, **43**, 49–55.

Siegel, S. & Castellan, N. J. (1988). *Nonparametric statistics for the behavioral sciences* (2nd edn.). New York: McGraw-Hill.

Singer, B. R., Lovie, A. D. & Lovie, P. (1986). Sample size and power. In P. Lovie & A. D. Lovie (Eds.), *New developments in statistics for psychology and the social sciences*. Leicester: British Psychological Society.

Skinner, B. F. (1953). *Science and human behavior*. New York: Macmillan.

Skinner, C. J. (1991). Time series. In P. Lovie & A. D. Lovie (Eds.), *New developments in statistics for psychology and the social sciences* (Vol. 2). Leicester: British Psychological Society.

Sloane, R. B, Staples, F. R., Cristol, A. H., Yorkston, N. J. & Whipple, K. (1975). *Psychotherapy versus behavior therapy*. Cambridge, Mass.: Harvard University Press.

Smith, J. K. & Heshusius, L. (1986). Closing down the conversation: The end of the quantitative–qualitative debate among educational inquirers. *Educational Researcher*, **15**, 4–12.

Smith, M. L. & Glass, D. V. (1977). Meta-analysis of psychotherapy outcome studies. *American Psychologist*, **32**, 752–760.

Snow, R. E. (1991). Aptitude–treatment interaction as a framework for research on individual differences in psychotherapy. *Journal of Consulting and Clinical Psychology*, **59**, 205–216.

Snyder, C. R. & Forsyth, D. R. (Eds.) (1991). *Handbook of social and clinical psychology: The health perspective*. New York: Pergamon.

Sommer, B. & Sommer, R. (1991). *A practical guide to behavioral research: Tools and techniques* (3rd edn.). Oxford: Oxford University Press.

Spence, D. P. (1986). Narrative smoothing and clinical wisdom. In T. R. Sarbin (Ed.), *Narrative psychology: The storied nature of human conduct*. New York: Praeger.

Spinelli, E. (1989). *The interpreted world: An introduction to phenomenological psychology*. London: Sage.

Sternberg, J. C. (1988). *The psychologist's companion: A guide to scientific writing for students and researchers*. Cambridge: Cambridge University Press.

Stevens, A. & Gabbay, J. (1991). Needs assessment needs assessment. *Health Trends*, **23**, 20–23.

Stevens, S. S. (1935). The operational definition of psychological concepts. *Psychological Review*, **42**, 517–527.

Stevens, S. S. (1946). On the theory of scales of measurement. *Science*, **103**, 677–680.

Stewart, I. (1989). *Does God play dice? The new mathematics of chaos*. London: Penguin Books.

Stiles, W. B. (1980). Measurement of the impact of psychotherapy sessions. *Journal of Consulting and Clinical Psychology*, **48**, 176–185.

Stiles, W. B. (1993). Quality control in qualitative research. *Clinical Psychology Review*, **13**, 593–618.

Stiles, W. B., Shapiro, D. A. and Elliott, R. (1986). Are all psychotherapies equivalent? *American Psychologist*, **41**, 165–180.

Strain, P. S. & Kerr, M. M. (1984). Writing grant applications: some general guidelines. In A. S. Bellack & M. Hersen (Eds.), *Research methods in clinical psychology*. Oxford: Pergamon.

Strauss, A. & Corbin, J. (1990). *Basics of qualitative research: Grounded theory procedures and techniques*. Beverly Hills, CA: Sage.

Strauss, J. S., Harding, C. M., Hafez, H. & Lieberman, P. (1987). The role of the patient in recovery from psychosis. In J. S. Strauss, W. Boker & H. Brenner (Eds.), *Psychosocial treatment of schizophrenia*. New York: Hans Huber.

Strunk, W. & White, E. B. (1959). *The elements of style*. New York: Macmillan.

Strupp, H.H. 1980. Success and failure in time-limited psychotherapy. *Archives of General Psychiatry*, **37**, 595–603; 708–717; 831–841; 947–954.

Sudman, S. (1976). *Applied sampling*. New York: Academic Press.

Sudman, S. & Bradburn, N. M. (1982). *Asking questions: A practical guide to questionnaire design*. San Francisco: Jossey-Bass.

Sudnow, D. (Ed.) (1972). *Studies in social interaction*. New York: The Free Press.

Sue, S., Fujino, D. C., Hu, L., Takeuchi, D. T. & Zane, N. W. S. (1991). Community mental health services for ethnic minority groups: A test of the cultural responsiveness hypothesis. *Journal of Consulting and Clinical Psychology*, **59**, 533–540.

Taylor, S. J. & Bogdan, R. (1984). *Introduction to qualitative research methods: The search for meanings* (2nd edn.). New York: Wiley.

Terkel, S. (1972). *Working*. New York: Pantheon.

Terwee, S. J. S. (1990). *Hermeneutics in psychology and psychoanalysis*. Berlin: Springer-Verlag.

Thornton, H. M. (1992). Breast cancer trials: a patient's viewpoint. *The Lancet*, **339**, 44–45.

Tinsley, H. E. A. & Tinsley, D. J. (1987). Uses of factor analysis in counseling psychology research. *Journal of Counseling Psychology*, **34**, 414–424.

Tinsley, H. E. A. & Weiss, D. J. (1975). Interrater reliability and agreement of subjective judgements. *Journal of Counseling Psychology*, **22**, 358–376.

Tizard, B. (1990). Research and policy: Is there a link? *The Psychologist*, **13**, 435–440.

Tukey, J. W. (1977). *Exploratory data analysis*. Reading, Mass.: Addison-Wesley.

Veroff, J., Kulka, R. A. & Douvan, E. (1981). *Mental health in America: Patterns of help-seeking from 1957 to 1976*. New York: Basic Books.

Watson, J. B. (1919). *Psychology from the standpoint of a behaviorist*. Philadelphia: Lippincott.

Watson, J. B. (1931). *Behaviourism*. London: Kegan Paul.

Watson, J. B. & Rayner, R. (1920). Conditioned emotional reactions. *Journal of Experimental Psychology*, **3**, 1–14.

Watts, F. N. (1984). Applicable research in the NHS. *Bulletin of the British Psychological Society*, **37**, 41–42.

Webb, E. J., Campbell, D. T., Schwartz, R. D. & Sechrest, L. (1966). *Unobtrusive measures: Nonreactive research in the social sciences*. Chicago: Rand McNally.

Weick, K. D. (1985). Systematic observational methods. In G. Lindzey & E. Aronson (Eds.), *Handbook of social psychology* (3rd edn.). Vol. 1: Theory and method. New York: Random House.

Weiner, D. N. (1948). Subtle and obvious keys for the MMPI. *Journal of Consulting Psychology*, **12**, 164–170.

Weiss, C. H. (1972). *Evaluation research*. Englewood Cliffs, N.J.: Prentice Hall.

Weiss, C. H. (1986). Research and policy making: a limited partnership. In F. Heller (Ed.), *The use and abuse of social science*. London: Sage.

Weissman, M. M. (1987). Advances in psychiatric epidemiology: Rates and risks for major depression. *American Journal of Public Health*, **77**, 445–451.

Wertz, F. J. (1983). From everyday to psychological description: Analyzing the moments of a qualitative data analysis. *Journal of Phenomenological Psychology*, **14**, 197–241.

Wertz, F. J. (1985). Methods and findings in the study of a complex life event: being criminally victimized. In A. Giorgi (Ed.), *Phenomenology and psychological research*. Pittsburgh: Duquesne University Press.

White, P. A. (1990). Ideas about causation in philosophy and psychology. *Psychological Bulletin*, **108**, 3–18.

Whyte, W. F. (1943). *Street corner society: The social structure of an Italian slum*. Chicago: University of Chicago Press.

Whyte, W. H. (1959). *The organisation man*. New York: Simon & Shuster.

Wiggins, J. S. (1973). *Personality and prediction: Principles of personality assessment*. Reading, MA: Addison-Wesley.

Wilkinson, S. (Ed.) (1986). *Feminist social psychology: Developing theory and practice*. Milton Keynes: Open University Press.

Wilson, B. (1987). Single case experimental designs in neuropsychological rehabilitation. *Journal of Clinical and Experimental Neuropsychology*, **9**, 527–544.

Wilson, S. (1990). *Tate Gallery: An illustrated companion*. London: Tate Gallery.

Winer, B. J. (1971). *Statistical principles in experimental design* (2nd edn.). New York: McGraw-Hill.

Winter, D. A. (1992). *Personal construct psychology in clinical practice*. London: Routledge.

Wittgenstein, L. (1921/1961). *Tractatus logico-philosophicus*. London: Routledge.

Yalom, I. D. (1980). *Existential psychotherapy*. New York: Basic Books.

Yalom, I. D. & Elkin, G. (1974). *Everyday gets a little closer: A twice told therapy*. New York: Basic Books.

Yin, R. K. (1989). *Case study research: Design and methods* (revised edn.). Newbury Park, CA: Sage.

Young, H. H. (1982). A brief history of quality assurance and peer review. *Professional Psychology*, **13**, 9–13.

Young, M. & Willmott, P. (1957). *Family and kinship in East London*. London: Routledge & Kegan Paul.

Young, R. M. (1979). Why are figures so significant? The role and critique of quantification. In J. Irvine, I. Miles & J. Evans (Eds.), *Demystifying social statistics*. London: Pluto Press.

Zimbardo, P. G. (1973). On the ethics of interventions in human psychological research: With special reference to the Stanford prison experiment. *Cognition*, **2**, 243–256.

Zimet, C. N. (1989). The mental health care revolution: Will psychology survive? *American Psychologist*, **44**, 703–708.

INDEX

THE WILEY SERIES IN CLINICAL PSYCHOLOGY

Series Editor

Fraser N. Watts   *MRC Applied Psychology Unit,*
Cambridge, UK

J. Mark G. Williams   *Department of Psychology, University College*
of North Wales, Bangor, UK

continued from page ii

Wiley Books of Related Interest

PSYCHOLOGICAL MANAGEMENT OF SCHIZOPHRENIA
Edited by Max Birchwood *and* Nicholas Tarrier

A practical guide for mental health professionals wanting to develop and
enhance their skills in new treatment approaches. Includes coverage of:
family interventions and network support; early warning systems to
anticipate and control relapse; strategies to control distressing
symptoms; and improving recovery from acute psychosis.

0-471-95056-4 paper 176pp 1994

QUALITY AND EXCELLENCE IN HUMAN SERVICES
Paul Dickens

A comprehensive introductory volume on the important and topical
issue of quality assurance. The book covers current issues, including
BS5750/ISO9000, and suggests practical ways of implementing a TQM
approach within human services.

0-471-94054-2 paper 204pp 1994

EXPLORING STATISTICS WITH MINITAB
A WORKBOOK FOR THE BEHAVIOURAL SCIENCES
Andrew Monk

Provides students with the background and practical skills needed to
take advantage of the statistical packages now available for mainframes
and microcomputers.

0-471-92391-5 paper 266pp 1991

STRESS AND HEALTH
ISSUES IN RESEARCH METHODOLOGY
Edited by Stanislav Kasl *and* Cary L. Cooper

Provides researchers and practitioners in health psychology, medicine,
and human resources with background for a critical appreciation of
published research as well as with bases for action research in practice
settings.

0-471-95493-4 paper 334pp 1987

Wine-Books of Related Interest

by Eddington's expedition to observe a solar eclipse in Africa, in order to test a deduction from Einstein's theory of relativity that light will bend in the presence of a gravitational field.

In psychology, such unequivocal falsifications of theoretically derived predictions are less common. One area where they can be found is in neuropsychological case studies of patients with acquired brain damage. The presence of certain patterns of dysfunction in a single case can be used to refute theories of mental structure (Shallice, 1988).

As an example of a non-falsifiable theory, consider this statement, by the painter Mondrian: "The positive and the negative break up oneness, they are the cause of all unhappiness. The union of the positive and negative is happiness" (quoted by Wilson, 1990, p. 144). This certainly appears to be some sort of psychological theory, but it is not clear to what extent it could generate falsifiable propositions, and thus what could be done to test its validity. According to Popper, a statement that cannot be falsified is unscientific (although it is not necessarily meaningless). Religion and poetry may have meaning, but they are not falsifiable.

For Popper, good science is characterised by a series of bold conjectures, which will be ultimately falsified. This approach is encapsulated in the title of one his books, *Conjectures and Refutations* (1963). A good theory is one that makes a large number of falsifiable propositions. A bad theory, or an unscientific one, is one that is incapable of falsification. However, all theories must be considered to be tentative; it is impossible to know the world exactly. Every theory in its time will be falsified and replaced by another (as Newtonian mechanics was supplanted by Einstein's theory of relativity).

The falsifiability criterion places those fields which rely on *post hoc* explanatory methods outside the boundaries of science. In particular, it rules out psychoanalysis and Marxism, fashionable theories in Popper's Vienna of the 1920s, which he explicitly says were his main targets (Popper, 1963). On the other hand, behavioural approaches, with their philosophy of "prediction and control" (Skinner, 1953), would be included.

This version of falsificationism has a number of problems. The main one is that no theory ever completely accounts for all the known data. Inconsistencies always exist, but the theory may well be retained in spite of them, as they could be explained in other ways than the falsification of the theory, e.g. measurement error or unexplained extra variables. Refutation is never cut and dried: there is always scope to deny that it has occurred. One example is in the extended debate in the psychotherapy outcome literature over the effectiveness of psychodynamically oriented therapy. Comparative outcome studies have now demonstrated beyond reasonable doubt that psychodynamically oriented therapy, as well as other forms of therapy, have, on average, beneficial effects (Stiles, Shapiro & Elliott, 1986). However, some critics fought a long rearguard action against this conclusion, which was possible to do if the evidence was appraised in a partisan way (Shapiro & Shapiro, 1977).

Paradigms and scientific revolutions

It therefore becomes a central problem to explain how one theory is replaced by another. Since there are always unexplained or contradictory observations within a scientific field, what determines when one theory is rejected and replaced by another? This issue is the point of departure for the work of Thomas Kuhn, one of the central figures of twentieth-century philosophy of science. In *The Structure of Scientific Revolutions* (1970), he applies the tools of historical analysis to address these questions.

Kuhn proposed the concept of a "paradigm", that is, the central body of ideas within which a body of scientists are working at any given time. The paradigm determines which phenomena scientists consider important and the methods that they use to make their observations. Scientists working within a paradigm are said to be doing "normal science": they are elaborating theories rather than attempting to refute them. Eventually, the accumulated deficiencies of a paradigm lead to its overthrow and replacement by another paradigm, in what Kuhn labels a "scientific revolution". For example, the replacement of Aristotelian cosmology (that the earth was at the centre of the universe) by Copernican theory (that the earth moved around the sun) was a scientific revolution.

The concept of a paradigm is central to Kuhn's work. It fits well with the physical sciences, but there is much debate about how well it can be applied in the social sciences (Lambie, 1991). What is the guiding paradigm of psychology, or are there multiple paradigms—or is it still in a pre-paradigmatic state? Arguably, cognitive behaviourism and Freudian psychoanalysis may be considered as concurrent paradigms, although this is perhaps ducking awkward questions of which theory better accounts for the available evidence (Lambie, 1991).

Kuhn's views and their relationship to those of Popper were hotly debated when they first appeared (Lakatos & Musgrave, 1970). Lakatos accused Kuhn of propounding a "mob psychology" of scientific revolutions (Lakatos, 1970, p. 178).

The problem in Kuhn's work is that it proposes no criteria for considering one theory as better than another, and thus no sense in which scientific understanding could be said to be progressing. Feyerabend's (1975) anarchistic view takes this to an extreme. Under a slogan of "anything goes", Feyerabend appears to be claiming that different theories are "incommensurable" and that there are therefore no rational grounds for preferring one to another. For example, psychoanalysis and experimental psychology may be incommensurable since they have different criteria for which evidence is acceptable: psychoanalysis derives its evidence from the consulting room, experimental psychology from the laboratory (Fonagy, 1982). So the anarchistic view would accord astrology, voodoo and Babylonian astronomy the same scientific status as quantum mechanics or relativity (Chalmers, 1982). The viewpoint is pithily summed up by the composer and poet Moondog (1991):

> "What I say of science here, I say without condition
> That science is the latest and the greatest superstition."
> (Louis Hardin, Managarm; reproduced by permission)

It seems as though the views of Popper and of Kuhn are "incommensurable": they are using different concepts to discuss somewhat different phenomena. Popper takes a logical approach, Kuhn a historical one. While trying to avoid the danger of falling into a relativist, "anything goes" position ourselves, we would contend that much of value can be taken from both sets of writings.

From Popper, researchers can take the central admonition of making bold theories that lead to clear and risky predictions, and being ready to give these theories up in the face of contradictory evidence.

Popper also urges researchers to put their thoughts into clear and precise language. As an example, Rogers' (1957) seminal paper on the necessary and sufficient conditions of therapeutic personality change is written with admirable clarity and makes bold hypotheses about the central mechanisms of therapeutic change.

Kuhn also encourages the taking of intellectual risks, although from a different standpoint. By clearly delineating the constrictions of "normal science", he urges researchers to question the assumptions of the paradigm that they are implicitly or explicitly working within, and to ask whether that paradigm is worth challenging. His work also suggests that scientists look ahead to the next paradigm revolution and ask whether their work will have any enduring value.

The methodological pluralist stance that informs this book owes something to the spirit that animates Feyerabend's writing. We agree with his stress on the value of diversity and the dangers of scientific conformity. We do, however, strongly disagree with his rejection of the canons of scientific method. As we hope to show, it is possible to articulate criteria to evaluate work conducted within the various different scientific traditions in clinical and counselling psychology. For the remainder of this book we will be adopting a broad working definition of science, as a body of knowledge founded upon systematic conceptual and empirical research.

Social and Political Issues

As Kuhn (1970) illustrates, science is not conducted in a cultural and political vacuum. It is done by scientists working within a particular scientific, professional and cultural community at a specific moment in history. Sociologists of knowledge (e.g. Berger & Luckmann, 1966) and social constructionists (e.g. Gergen, 1985) look at how social factors influence the development of thought. For example, what is seen as "real" may vary from culture to culture.

Sociological and historical methods can be applied to examine science itself, to look at how socioeconomic and political forces shape the kind of science that is practised within a given culture (Chalmers, 1990; Schwartz, 1992): how one set of ideas gains prominence over another. These analyses are often carried out